The San Francisco
SURVIVAL
GUIDE

by
Molly Dick

A Complete Resource Guide for Living in the City

For information regarding sales of this book,
please contact:

CrossRoads Publications
314 Woodland Road
Kentfield, CA 94904
(415) 461-8422

ISBN 0-9635622-0-7

The San Francisco
SURVIVAL GUIDE

" If you're alive, you can't be bored in San Francisco. If you're not alive, San Francisco will bring you to life. "

—William Saroyan

Introduction

Even in San Francisco, sometimes just dealing with everyday life can get you down. It could be worse. You could be going through this in Des Moines. Or Missoula. Or Saginaw. If you have to survive somewhere, the Bay Area is just about the perfect place to be singularly solitary, on the search or sublimely satisfied.

The variety of locales and climates throughout the Bay Area can lead you on endless searches for the ultimate bike trip, the perfect family hike, the most romantic inn along Highway 1 or on the Silverado Trail. You may be seeking solitary walks along Pt. Reyes Beach, literary lectures at Herbst Theatre or Tuesday Tennis in Golden Gate Park, followed by a stroll through the Arboretum or a free taste of Shakespeare in the Park. You may want to plug into environmental organizations like the Sierra Club, attend a political forum at the Commonwealth Club or drop off your youngster while you work out in one of the City's top fitness centers. It's all there to sample and experience and enjoy.

The San Francisco Survival Guide will provide you with many of the sources and resources I have accumulated over the years. Information was also contributed by friends, acquaintances and business associates from a broad cross-section of the community whose opinion I not only trust, but would highly recommend.

The recommendations on the following pages are not guarantees nor are they paid solicitations. I've tried to offer several choices in each category. It will be up to you to decide who and what suits you best, and along the way, I hope you will come up with special finds of your own.

I hope this guide helps you to "hit the ground running". Perhaps you've just arrived in town and you're alone and it's kind of daunting. You might be single and are wondering where other unattached individuals are hanging out. Or you could be a new parent who is feeling a little overwhelmed with the choices for day care or pre-school. Maybe you are just lucky enough to be one of those fifth-generation San Franciscans we all envy, but you find that you are living life by rote, automatically going through the motions.

Whatever the reason, I hope you use **The San Francisco Survival Guide**, enjoy it and tell your friends about it. But don't tell the ones who live in Saginaw. Unless you want them to move here.

Molly Dick

City Map

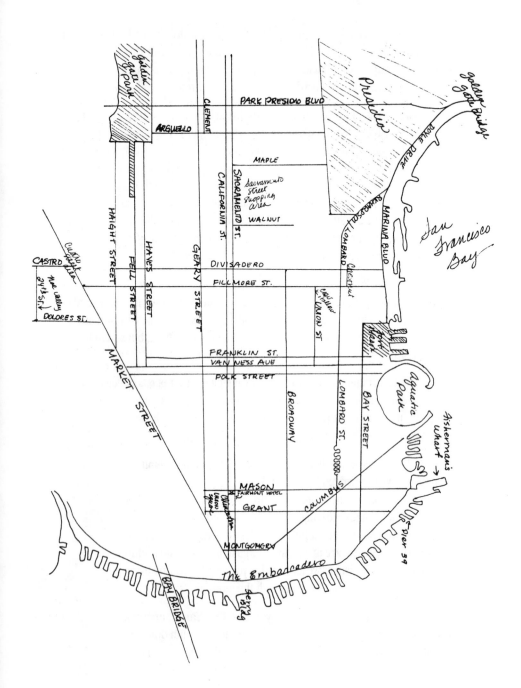

Don't Call It Frisco.

As an invaluable aid, I have compiled some of the clichés that will keep even the most recent arrival from saying the wrong thing at the wrong time. The following catch-words are essential to the vocabulary of any would-be San Franciscan.

HOW TO BE AN INSTANT SAN FRANCISCAN

The City
San Francisco (Never refer to Oakland as "The City".)

The Lake
Lake Tahoe

The Bay
San Francisco Bay

The Bridge
Golden Gate

The Rock
Alcatraz

The Beach
Stinson Beach

The Wharf
Fisherman's Wharf

The Pyramid
The TransAmerica building

The Mark
Mark Hopkins Hotel

The Ocean
The Pacific, of course. Woody Allen once said he could never get used to the ocean being on his left side!

The Niners
Those beloved former Super Bowl Champs, the "San Francisco Forty-Niners".

The Stick
Candlestick Park

The Grove
Bohemian Grove

The Big Game
Cal/Stanford (Don't even think Harvard/Yale or Michigan/Ohio State!)

BART
Bay Area Rapid Transit

"CAL-OQUIALISMS"

CAL

Now this is very important. CAL refers to the University of California at Berkeley. It should never be confused with any other "Cal" school like Southern Cal or Cal State or UC San Diego or UC Santa Barbara. This is The CAL where it seems everyone in the Bay Area went to college. The CAL fan 1) is intensely loyal 2) would never miss "The Big Game" and 3) would cheerfully slit your throat should you be rooting for that Other School (read my lips, Stanford) at said Game.

DIRECTIONS

A key question to ask when requesting directions to anywhere in the City is "AND WHAT IS THE CROSS-STREET?" Not only will it be extremely helpful in ascertaining where you are going, but it also immediately labels you as a knowledgeable, street-wise San Franciscan. Some San Franciscans claim you can drive almost anywhere in the City and get there in under three turns. See if it works!

> *"It's an odd thing, but anyone who disappears is said to be seen in San Francisco."*
>
> *–Oscar Wilde*

THE FOG

San Francisco has very little in the way of cloud formation. What to a non-San Franciscan may appear to be clouds, is actually The Fog. The fog is an endless source of conversation. It is the one topic that can be mindlessly discussed anywhere and everywhere and never fails to fascinate even the most blase of San Franciscans. But remember, it is only truly relevant in the summer months. September through October are San Francisco's finest months weather-wise. November through January it often rains. But June, July and August are glorious months to dwell on the fog. Be sure to use phrases like "Looks like the fog is rolling in!", or "The fog is finally burning off!" You can usually count on 3 1/2 "fog days" followed by 3 1/2 clear days (sort of).

THE HILLS OF SAN FRANCISCO

One phrase sums up the hills of San Francisco: "Go climb a street." Believe it or not, your car will survive the hills, although you will discover brake relining is a thriving business in the City. Whenever you get tired of walking, just lean against a street. When planning to walk, drag out the Reeboks and bid farewell to those Charles Jourdans. Always beam lovingly every time you see a cable car trundling by. But remember, never, never drive up a hill behind one!

DRESS CODE IN SAN FRANCISCO

San Francisco is the city that knows no seasons, which is why the dress code is very simple. It never alters! There is no such ritual as putting away the winter clothes and airing out the summer clothes. You will not need summer clothes in San Francisco because the weather does not vary enough to warrant the expense (the average yearly temperature is 60 degrees). And to thoroughly confuse you, the weather can fluctuate greatly from one area in the City to the next, even block to block.

Take the money you would have spent on a summer wardrobe and reinforce your stock of sweaters, jackets and light wool suits. LAYER is the key when dressing in San Francisco. Always be prepared to peel down (as the fog burns off) or add on (as the fog rolls in). Never leave your home without some sort of layered effect. And always look smugly bemused when you spot the goose-pimpled, seer-suckered, camera-crested tourists huddling in line for a cable car at the corner of Powell on a "mild" summer afternoon.

FIFTH GENERATION SAN FRANCISCANS

A word must be mentioned about this prodigious group of San Franciscans! I remember being gently amused the first time a friendly local took me by the arm at a crowded cocktail party and murmured earnestly in my ear, "Al Wooley here, 5th-generation San Franciscan." I could hardly reply in kind, "Molly Dick here, 1st-generation Miamian". Most people have trouble believing there are those who are even *born* in Miami. They usually think it's the place you go to die.

I was impressed with Mr. Wooley's statement until I began to meet 3rd, 4th and 5th-generation San Franciscans everywhere – on street corners, in dressing rooms, even at child observation class. My toddler, JJ, was introduced to another little boy by his mother who announced proudly, "And this is Tyler Randolph Ridgley – *6th* -generation" (you know what!). I looked appropriately awed. JJ beaned him with a block. The entire Bay Area began to seem composed of nothing but multi-generation San Franciscans who informed you of this fascinating fact at any opportunity.

Funny, I don't remember coming across this phenomenon in Trenton...

"Cities are like gentlemen. They are born, not made. You are either a city or you are not. Size has nothing to do with it. I bet San Francisco was a city from the very first time it had a dozen settlers."

–Will Rogers

SAN FRANCISCO DO'S

DO order a California wine with dinner, after all the Napa Valley is your backyard.

DO curb your wheels when parking on a street with a 31.5 per cent grade. Beyond safety, it's the law. And with San Francisco's hills, it's a necessity.

DO remember that it is customary, when journeying beyond San Francisco, to say you are going "down the Peninsula" when referring to those towns including Burlingame, Hillsborough, Atherton, Menlo Park, Palo Alto, etc. Be sure and say "across the Bay", if you ever have need to travel to Berkeley or Oakland, and don't forget it is "up to Marin" when you seek the sunny locales of Sausalito, Mill Valley, Tiburon, Larkspur or San Rafael.

DO get up early, take a cable car to the wharf and watch the fishermen go out for the catch.

"If it pleases Providence to make a car run up and down a slit in the ground for many miles and if for two pence half penny I can ride in that car, why shall I ask the reason for the miracle?"
–Rudyard Kipling

DO walk across the Golden Gate Bridge. But be prepared, it can be quite windy and surprisingly noisy.

DO order your tickets to Alcatraz Island in advance *(especially in the summer)*. And wear comfortable shoes — it's a lot of walking.

DO go inside Coit Tower to view the fresco murals. They were painted by 25 artists in 1933. And don't miss the 360° views outside!

DO wait for pedestrians in the crosswalk. In California, they have the right-of-way, and the S.F.P.D. will not hesitate to ticket you.

DO take a walk along the recently "deconstructed" Embarcadero Freeway. The waterfront is magnificently "unfettered"!

DO remember that when you mention you are "going back east" to a San Franciscan, they usually think Chicago. If you say you are travelling to Washington, you must remember to add "DC". A San Franciscan will think Seattle. And never confuse Novato with Nevada when talking to a Marinite. The natives don't like it...

DO check out the very best airport art in America in the United terminal the next time you are walking the endless corridors of SFO. The exhibits tend to be fascinating, whimsical and delightful.

SAN FRANCISCO DON'TS

DON'T waste water. Even with the recent big rains, seven years of drought tend to keep San Franciscans in a permanent mind-set of drought preparedness.

DON'T drive through the majestic Presidio without your eyes and ears wide open. It is filled with one hundred year old Eucalyptus trees whose life span doesn't far exceed that. One sixth-generation native who is a descendant of the Levi Strauss family, steadfastly refuses to even enter the Presidio, for fear of toppling limbs from those giant wonders.

DON'T wear your summer clothes in the summer. Mark Twain allegedly said, "The coldest winter I ever spent was a summer in San Francisco."

DON'T call them trolleys. The hum you hear beneath the street is a steel cable.

DON'T pronounce Ghirardelli with a soft G. "Say Gear-ar-delly". And for that matter, don't pronounce it "Gary" Blvd., it's "Gear-y"! And of course, it's "Keer-ny", not Kearny St. and "Goff", not Gough (go) St. Now is that clear?

DON'T wear an L.A. Dodger's cap - especially to Candlestick Park and don't forget to bundle up even in May.

DON'T wear your bathing suit to North Beach. Instead, bring your appetite for Italian food.

DON'T look for fresh sourdough bread on Sundays.

DON'T reside in San Francisco without accessorizing your wardrobe in colors of red and gold. This is "49er" country.

But Above All, Don't Call It Frisco!

"You imagine purgatory is something like this except not such good parking. It's always, 'How am I doing? Where am I on the food chain? Let's make a deal.' I just feel safer in San Francisco. Here, it's like being a hemophiliac in a razor factory."
–Robin Williams, on life in Los Angeles

"NOW YOU ARE AN OFFICIAL SAN FRANCISCAN"

The following quiz will help determine whether you are now truly a San Franciscan at heart. This means you really do like sourdough bread, you find the fog fascinating and you tremble with unconcealed delight over the prospect of the Big Game.

A score of 100 points or more . . . **You've Arrived.**

A score of 50 points or less . . . **Back to the drawing boards.**

A score of 25 points or less . . . **Welcome to San Francisco. Now go home.**

---

1. You have participated in the annual running of the Bay To Breakers Race in May. **10 points**

You have walked, jogged or run this famous race ridiculously attired. **20 points**

You have at least gotten up at an indecently early hour on a Sunday morning to gain the best vantage point for observing this extraordinary event. **5 points**

"Those who settle for less, have never been to San Francisco."
–Anonymous

2. You were standing at the Bridge (Golden Gate, of course) suitably garbed in windbreaker or down vest in April to observe Opening Day On The Bay, the official start of the sailing and yachting season. **10 points**

You participated in Opening Day in a small or large boating vessel. **20 points**

At that point in time, or at any other time, you successfully walked the Bridge (both ways). **10 points**

3. You have attended at least one service at Glide Memorial United Methodist Church presided over by the illustrious Reverend Cecil Williams at 330 Ellis Street. This is a uniquely San Francisco experience, regardless of your religious denomination! **10 points**

Take an extra 10 points for attending Easter Sunrise Services. **10 points**

4. You have attended the elegant Black and White Ball benefiting the San Francisco Symphony, which takes place throughout the entire Civic Center in May. **15 points**

Take an extra 5 points if you dressed warmly enough and your feet didn't hurt. **5 points**

5. You have ventured, gingerly or otherwise, onto Castro Street on Halloween Night for the outrageous Halloween Parade. **5 points**

Take an extra 15 points for wearing a costume yourself! **15 points**

6. You have found yourself huddled on Crissy Field, surrounded by a cast of thousands, to observe the 4th of July Fireworks Celebration. This event is usually obliterated by a fog-shrouded sky. **10 points**

7. You have enjoyed, in black tie, either the Opening of the Opera or the Opening of the Symphony, events near and dear to the hearts of every stylish (and wealthy) San Franciscan. **Opera 25 points; Symphony 20 points**

8. You have attended at least one performance of San Francisco's own **Beach Blanket Babylon**, the City's longest running musical comedy review. But, of course, to be an official San Franciscan, attendance of a minimum of five performances is required. **10 points for each performance**

"San Francisco is Beautiful People wearing a bracelet of bridges."

–Hal Lipset,
Private Detective

9. You have consumed, over the course of six months, exclusively California wines and can naturally speak with quiet authority on the relative merits of Cabernets, Pinot Noirs, Sauvignon Blancs, Zinfandels and the like. **10 points**

Take an extra 10 points if you have officially tasted these wines at the appropriate wineries in Napa or Sonoma (never refer to this area as "the Valley" or "the Wine Country"). **10 points**

10. And finally, when returning from even the most exciting or romantic or memorable vacation, you find that you are not saddened at the thought of coming home, not when home means San Francisco. **10 points**

Welcome To The Neighborhood

San Francisco could truly be said to be a series of small inter-connecting villages, each with its own distinctive style and flavor. You can wander from the Italian section of North Beach, to the heart of Chinatown, to the sophisticated and glamorous shopping streets of Union Square, all within a five minute walk of each other. To fall in love with San Francisco is to explore and experience her neighborhoods. Listed below are a few of the many colorful, historical and sometimes inexplicable locales in the City.

ALAMO SQUARE

The views from Alamo Square are famous round the world. A popular site to film movies, it has been dubbed "postcard row" because of the row of perfectly preserved Victorians backdropped by dramatic downtown skyscrapers. Designated a historic district by the City Planning Commission, Alamo Square is also filled with cozy bed and breakfast inns. It was even once a haven for White Russians in the thirties who gathered at 1198 Fulton Street, known as "The Tsar's Embassy".

THE AVENUES AND "NORTH OF LAKE"

Refers to the streets running numerically east and west, starting at Arguello Blvd and dead-ending at the ocean. Some people feel the fog officially starts here. Many of these homes were built from the rubble of the Great Quake. "North of Lake" refers to the area north of Lake Street and borders Mountain Lake Park (where there is no mountain, but it does have a great children's playground).

Also located in the Avenues is the bustling and ethnically diverse Clement Street shopping area. Parking is impossible, but keep trying because you'll find the street brimming with greek delis, kosher meat markets and some of the finest chinese restaurants around.

BAGHDAD BY THE BAY

A romanticized 19th-century reference to San Francisco.

THE BARBARY COAST

The name given to San Francisco during the Gold Rush days.

THE CASTRO

Located on Upper Market near Castro Street, this is the hub of San Francisco's gay community. Gay entrepreneurs have truly transformed this once derelict area of shabby Victorians and run-down shops into something creative and revitalized, including the sparkling "Path of Gold" lamp posts which illuminate Lower Market. There are now imaginative boutiques, gay bookstores, bars and cafes.

▶ *Of historical interest in the Castro is the Names Project at 2362 Market, home of the AIDS memorial quilt and the historic Castro Theater at 429 Castro, one of the last grand movie palaces. If the mood in the Castro is a somber one these days, it still reflects a pride that is an integral part of San Francisco's uniqueness and diversity.*

CHINATOWN

The Gateway to Chinatown is at Grant and Bush and welcomes you to a 24-block labyrinth of authentic shops, renowned restaurants, temples, museums and teeming humanity in every direction. Said to contain the world's largest Chinese population outside of China.

COW HOLLOW

Refers to the one-time dairy land west of Van Ness Avenue between Russian Hill and the Presidio, the Marina and Pacific Heights. Located within this upscale neighborhood of charming Victorian homes is Union Street, one of the most popular shopping and restaurant areas in the City. Not a cow in sight however.

THE FARALLONES

A chain of islands 32 miles from San Francisco's shore and visible from the City only on the clearest of days. Populated by sea lions and sea birds, this is a well-known marker for sailors.

THE FINANCIAL DISTRICT

Bordered by Clay and Market, Kearney and the Embarcadero, this is the financial and business heartbeat of the City. It is often called the Gateway to the Far East because of its proximity to major cities in the Orient, with whom San Francsico enjoys a flourishing trade and commercial relationship.

HAIGHT-ASHBURY ("THE HAIGHT")

Along the panhandle of Golden Gate Park lies the former haven for peace and flower power which came into being more than a quarter of a century ago in the Summer of Love. Now this somewhat more gentrified area still has a dash of punk with its funky stores filled with antiques, second hand clothes and tourist-type kitsch.

JACKSON SQUARE

A six-block historic district which was saved from total destruction during the '06 Quake by the superhuman efforts of firefighters, local citizens and even the US Navy. A mile-long hose was stretched all the way from Fisherman's Wharf over Telegraph Hill to the intersection of Montgomery and Broadway to save what remains of what was once called the Barbary Coast. Today it is a charming collection of sophisticated restaurants, decorator showrooms and expensive antique shops.

JAPANTOWN

For the city's 12,000+ residents of Japanese descent, Japantown offers a taste of Tokyo, minus two or three million people. At the heart of things is Japan Center at Post and Buchanan, a huge complex of restaurants, cinemas, hotels, shops, theatres, sushi bars, baths and even a five-tiered pagoda. Look for Cherry Blossom Festival every April with its exciting calendar of events.

LANDS END

A wild and forbidding tangle of wind-torn vegetation, this remote stretch of seacoast lies at the edge of Lincoln Park.

TIPS TO CONSIDER

Best place to catch the views and ogle the manses of the super rich?

On Broadway, between Lyon and Webster. *And if you're a fitness freak, jog up and down the Lyon Street steps.*

THE MARINA

Developed on landfill on the site of the 1915 Panama-Pacific Exposition (of which the beautiful Palace of Fine Arts is the one remaining edifice), the Marina is one of the sunniest, flattest and most treeless parts of the City. Hard-hit by the '89 quake, it nevertheless remains an extremely popular place to live for the younger, professional set with its many flats for rent, its proximity to the Marina Green for jogging and Chestnut Street for browsing, eating and people-watching.

THE MISSION

Mission Street, the main "paseo" of the district, once linked Mission Dolores, the oldest building in San Francisco, to the Presidio. Boasting the best weather in the City, this district has always been a bustling center for the predominantly hispanic population. It is well-known for its wonderful open air markets, taquerias and Mexican bakeries.

"I love San Francisco because for me it is full of memories... Every block is a short story, every hill a novel. Every home is a poem. Every dweller within immortal. That is the whole truth."

–William Saroyan, writer

NOB HILL

In the 19th-century, this was home to the nouveau riche gold, silver and railroad barons, or "nabobs" from which it derived its name. Today it is synonymous with "old" wealth as well as being the site of many of the City's finest restaurants and hotels, the magnificently gothic Grace Cathedral and the exclusive Pacific Union Club.

▷ *Savor the appeal of the Italian Renaissance when viewing the famed Ghiberti doors of Grace Cathedral which were cast in Florence. Midnight Mass is memorable here. A must-attend.*

NORTH BEACH

Which isn't a beach at all, and in the center of which is Washington Square, which isn't a square at all and which doesn't contain a statue of Washington, but of Benjamin Franklin. Now that should clear things up. Cradled by Telegraph Hill on the east and Russian Hill on the west, where Grant crosses Columbus & Broadway, is one of the most fascinating areas of the City with its proud Italian heritage.

TIPS TO CONSIDER

*Try and catch the **Columbus Day Parade** in October as you sip an espresso at any number of outdoor cafes or coffee houses. With its jazz clubs, art galleries, inns, and first rate Italian restaurants, **North Beach** is a perfect place to linger, day or night.*

NOE VALLEY

One of the few neighborhoods to be spared any destruction from the Big Quake, this charming collection of rainbow-colored Victorians nestles beneath Twin Peaks and often enjoys sunny weather when the rest of the City is blanketed in fog. Once a village of farms and streams, today it has retained this delightful quality with colorful shops and restaurants. Dolores Street winds prominently throughout the valley and is flanked by stately palms, more typical of a Southern California locale.

PACIFIC & PRESIDIO HEIGHTS

Virtually indestinguishable neighboring enclaves (although it is argued that the weather is better in the more venerable Pacific Heights). Encompassing stately homes, the wooded parklands of the Presidio and views out over the Bay, the common denominator here is Money, old or new. And a great deal of it is required to buy a piece of the action. House prices can vary dramatically for the north or "view" side of the the street.

RUSSIAN HILL

Deriving its name from Russian soldiers purportedly buried here, Russian Hill offers sweeping views of the Bay from many of its winding streets and terraces. The famous Lombard Street curves down the steep hill in nine hairpin turns and is deservedly called The Crookedest Street. World class views from the Hyde Street hill.

SEA CLIFF

A short drive west down the Avenues or Lake Street and you will find you have arrived in Paradise. Elegant, Mediterranean-style homes sit on lush, oversized lots with drop-dead views of the Golden Gate Bridge and the distant hills of Marin. The only problem? Some of the worst weather in the City can be found in beautiful, almost-perennially foggy Sea Cliff.

SOUTH OF MARKET (SOMA)

Dubbed SoMa by those anxious to equate this trendy area to its counterpart, New York's SoHo. Nevertheless, this two square mile area south of Market Street does indeed attract the younger, offbeat, artistic and avant-garde population. With its loft living spaces, hot night spots and restaurants, thriving art gallery scene and bargain-hunting factory outlets, SoMa is more than a state of mind. The heart of the interior design world is located here, as well as the flower mart and dozens of exhibition halls, including Moscone Center at Third and Howard, which host a multitude of special events.

THE SUNSET

The western-most residential section of the City, bordering the Pacific. With its almost constant blanket of fog, one rarely, if ever, sees the sunset. Hence, the logical choice of names.

STERN GROVE

Located on the "other side of the Park", this lush, wooded area composed of twelve acres, was donated to the City by Rosalie Stern with the stipulation that free outdoor concerts would be held on that site. That request has been granted to this day.

▶ *Visitors and music lovers take heed! Stern Grove can be a cold and foggy spot for many of its outdoor summer events. Garb yourself in typical San Francisco apparel-layers!*

TELEGRAPH HILL

Located at the northeast corner of the City and offering sweeping views out over the Bay Bridge and the East Bay, Telegraph Hill is named for the early telegraph system (semaphores) located here and used to signal ships as they entered the Golden Gate.

MOST FAMOUS LOCALE ON TELEGRAPH HILL?

*It would have to be **Coit Tower**, the legacy of Lilly Coit who left a bequest to San Francisco "for the purpose of adding beauty to the city I have always loved". Designed to resemble a fire hose, it was built to honor the brave San Francisco firemen who gave their lives fighting the infernos from the aftermath of the '06 Quake.*

THE TENDERLOIN

The word was originally coined in the 1800s to describe the teeming wards contained within this twenty square block district west of fashionable Union Square. In recent years, thousands of immigrants from southeast Asia have made this area home, and the shops and restaurants reflect their presence.

▶ *The Tenderloin is very much a heads-up kind of neighborhood, especially at night, and streetwise San Franciscans manoeuver through here with care after-hours.*

TREASURE ISLAND

This substantial island which has its own exit off the Bay Bridge is located between Oakland and San Francisco and was the site of the 1939 Golden Gate Exposition. It now functions as a Naval base, but parts of it are open to the public. The views of the City are worth the drive, especially if you make it in non-rush hour traffic. Robert Louis Stevenson did *not* base his book on this locale.

TWIN PEAKS

This 910-degree summit features panoramic views in all directions as far as the eye can see. A residential area whose most prominent feature is Sutro Tower, a tall radio/tv tower which dominates the landscape.

The Streets of San Francisco

It was on Montgomery Street in May of 1848 that Sam Brannan ran stumbling through the muddy potholes brandishing a bottle glistening with golden fragments, screaming "Gold! Gold from the American River!"

Van Ness Avenue today may look woefully like Auto Row or Sofa Bed City but in its heyday, it was one of the most elegant streets in San Francisco, filled with the mansions of the newly rich. In April of 1906 it became forevermore "the street that saved the City". It was here that firefighters were finally able to check the spread of the conflagration ignited by the earthquake.

At 140 Maiden Lane is the Frank Lloyd Wright Building, the prototype for the famed Guggenheim Museum in New York.

LITERARY LANDSCAPES

In 1978, the San Francisco Board of Supervisors passed an ordinance to name twelve streets after authors and artists who lived and worked in the City. Tracking them down is a full day's excursion which should ultimately end in a fine meal of Dungeness crab, a bottle of dry white Chardonnay, a hunk of sourdough bread and a long hot bath...Go for it!

JACK LONDON STREET

South of Market, it runs between Brannan and Townsend, Second and Third. A plaque at 615 Market marks the spot where London was supposedly born, although he grew up in Oakland and spent the final years of his life in Glen Ellen.

AMBROSE BIERCE STREET

Just a few blocks from Jack London Street is Ambrose Bierce Street between Market and Mission. A newspaper columnist who wielded a scathing pen, he never felt comfortable in San Francisco although he resided here for more than thirty years.

ISADORA DUNCAN LANE

A plaque at the entrance of 501 Taylor, a few feet north of Geary, marks the spot where this legendary dancer and muse was born in 1877.

DASHIELL HAMMETT STREET

One of San Francisco's favorite literary lions is honored west of Stockton off Post. Many of his stories used the City as a backdrop, particularly "The Maltese Falcon".

MARK TWAIN PLAZA

After you have tracked down Dashiell Hammett Street, take a walk through Chinatown, across Washington, past the "Pyramid" to Montgomery. That area between Washington and Clay was part of the famous "Montgomery Block", built in 1853, where the young Twain worked as a reporter, under the tutelage of Bret Harte.

JACK KEROUAC STREET

North Beach of course. Retrace your steps back to Columbus and head north to the beloved City Lights Bookstore. Right next door, in what was once called Adler Alley, is the spot which now honors the Father of the Beat Generation.

WILLIAM SAROYAN PLACE

Cross Columbus to 848 Pacific to the area where author Saroyan spent many formative years in the late thirties. He based many of the characters in his plays and stories on friends and acquaintances in his favorite hangout, Izzy Gomez Saloon.

BOB KAUFMAN STREET

A bit east, within sight of Coit Tower, you will find a street named after angry young poet of the Beat Generation and beloved figure in North Beach, Bob Kaufman. Known as the "Black Rimbaud" even though he was half-Jewish!

KENNETH REXROTH PLACE

Who? Rexroth was among the City's first literary lions who produced twenty volumes of poetry. In the sixties, in his flat on Scott, he held a series of literary soirees which attracted leading writers, poets and artists of his time. Go back across Columbus, at Vallejo.

VIA BUFANO

Beloved local sculptor, Benny Bufano, is honored at Grover Place, between Greenwich and Filbert. His works are found in public places all over San Francisco as well as in New York's Metropolitan Museum and in museums throughout Europe. But he always held a very special love for the City and considered it home.

RICHARD HENRY DANA PLACE

Where Leavenworth ends at Beach, at Fisherman's Wharf, it becomes Richard Henry Dana Place. Author of "Two Years Before the Mast", he discovered San Francisco when he sailed into the Golden Gate in 1835 and fell in love with its incredible natural beauty.

FRANK NORRIS STREET

You're almost through! One last jaunt completes your tour. On the east side of Polk, between Pine and Bush, is the spot which memorializes the short but brilliant life of Frank Norris. Author of "McTeague" and several other novels of the naturalist school, he often used San Francisco as a backdrop for his work. He died at the age of 32.

STREET-WISE

Oldest:	Grant Avenue
Longest:	Mission Street (7.29 miles)
Widest:	Van Ness Avenue (125 ft.)
Narrowest:	De Forest Way (4 1/2 ft.)
Crookedest:	Lombard Street
Steepest:	Filbert, from Leavenworth to Hyde (31.5% grade)

WALKING TOURS

You don't have to be a tourist to be interested in a more in-depth study of your hometown, especially when that town is San Francisco. So whether you have friends in for a first-time visit or it's one of those crisp, sparkling October days in the City and you're yearning for something different, try one of these tours. You may fall in love with San Francisco all over again!

Antique Amblings
Bella Passeggiata–
Beautiful Walks in SF
648-8159

Delight in the charms of city streets with this tour which offers a number of delightful three to four-hour walks. These include a tour of Victorian architecture, Art in the Park, North Beach and many other places of interest.

Chinatown Adventure Tours with the Wok Wiz
750 Kearny
355-9657

A unique and educational stroll through a Chinatown you may never have seen before with chef, cookbook author and food critic, Shirley Fong-Torres. The fun-filled tour includes a fascinating array of activities within the alleys and passageways of Chinatown.

Friends of Recreation and Parks
Golden Gate Park
221-1311

Free guided walking tours by docents who point out the many wonders of Golden Gate Park as well as its history and horticulture. May through October.

City Guides
Friends of the
SF Library
557-4266

Free tours available weekdays offer a lively and anecdotal look at San Francisco's history, architecture and culture from the Gold Rush Days to its Beaux Art Splendor. No reservation required. Schedules available throughout the City or call for information.

Shopper Stopper
Discount Shopping Tours
(707) 829-1597

This 6+ hour tour covers just about all the bases of discount, hassle-free shopping including some closed-to-the public warehouses. Full day of door-to-door bargain hunting delights.

SHOPPING TIP

Be sure and check out "Bargain Shopping in the Bay Area" on page 137.

Sports & Fitness

Whether you are a super jock or couch potato, the following sports and fitness resources are highly recommended and user-friendly!

Note: *Organizations such as Park & Recreation Departments, Jewish Community Centers and YMCAs offer a wide range of*

activities in adult sports, ranging from pick-up basketball and volleyball games to organized outings for skiing or biking. Membership fees are nominal compared to private clubs, and there is a constant flow of activity to pick and choose from on a year-round basis.

HEALTH & FITNESS CENTERS

Embarcadero YMCA
169 Steuart Street
957-9622

This unusual up-scale YMCA is located in the heart of San Francisco with drop-dead views to boot. It's membership is young and professional with a large and active singles crowd. This "Y" offers a first class fitness center, basketball court, racketball courts, a 34-meter pool and a roof-top running track. It also features a series of trips and events offered on a regular basis. The membership is moderate.

San Francisco Jewish Community Center
3200 California Street
346-6040

The JCC offers a huge program of both athletic and non-athletic events which will be listed throughout the book in the corresponding sections. Many of the programs are offered to non-members as well, and are extremely reasonably priced. (Ask for Danny Schwager.) Personal Training with Nancy Morano is available to both members and non-members by appointment only. She'll help develop specific goals in weight training, endurance, posture awareness, etc. Coed exercise is available to members only on Thursday evenings.

The San Francisco Bay Club
150 Greenwich
433-2200

This private club is surely one of the most popular exercise facilities in San Francisco. Activities include 2 rooftop tennis courts, racketball, squash, basketball, a pool, aerobic clinics, health and beauty services and a wide range of classes, seminars and parties throughout the year.

The Telegraph Hill Club
1850 Kearny (at Chestnut)
982-4700

Owned by the same corporation which owns the Bay Club, this club also offers an extensive workout facility as well as basketball, racketball and volleyball. Call for more information regarding league play. This facility is smaller and less expensive than the Bay Club and prides itself on being a warm and very friendly environment. Majority of members are in the 25-35 year old range.

Pacific Club
200 Redwood Shores Pkwy.
Redwood City
593-9100

This fabulous new facility is located just off 101 South at the Holly Avenue exit. It's worth the short trip from the City. The drop-dead setting includes 3 outdoor heated pools, 5 outdoor tennis courts, extensive grounds, full workout and spa facilities, squash, racketball, basketball, etc. The elegant dining room and grill are the sites for endless social events and parties throughout the year. This private club is pricey, but worth it.

In Shape
2328 Fillmore (in Pacific Heights)
346-5660
3214 Fillmore (in the Marina)
922-3700

No membership required in either of the two locations. You can drop in and pay for one aerobic class or sign up for a series. Various levels and types of classes offered.

Santé West Fitness
3727 Buchanan
563-6222

Another well-run facility for a wide variety of aerobic, step and fitness classes primarily for women in the Marina. Easy access for parking and right across the street from the Marina Safeway.

Physis Downtown Fitness Center
1 Post Street
989-7310

In the heart of the Financial District, Physis offers a 40' indoor pool, full workout facility, 45 aerobic classes a week, full medical lab and nutritional counselling. Call for more information.

Golden Gate Fitness Center
358 Golden Gate Ave.
776-7113

This is a full service fitness and work-out facility specializing in personal fitness training. Very convenient for those living or working in the Civic Center. Reasonable membership fees.

SOFTBALL

San Francisco Rec. & Park Dept.
753-7023

Co-ed Softball leagues begin play in the spring. There are ten leagues with approximately nine teams in each league, depending on ability (each team has 5 men and 5 woman). Here's the catch. If you are not aware of an existing team to join, you must put together your own . Contact the department in early January for sign-up, with team rosters due in February. Play begins in March. Summer league play is also available. Co-ed softball seems to be a thriving and popular activity in the City. It just requires some investigation and/or the willingness to field your own team.

HELPFUL HINT

Don't panic if you have impetuously signed up to play coed softball and you have zero ability with a throwing arm to match! Just get assigned to the outfield. Rarely will a ball come your way!

VOLLEYBALL

Volleyball is a great way to meet people, and depending on your level of interest and ability, there are a variety of opportunities to join a local pick-up game or play in a league.

San Francisco Rec. & Park Dept.
753-7027

The action here is on Monday nights at Kezar Pavilion, between Stanyan and Beulah Streets, from 7-9:30 PM. These pickup games are year-round depending on weather. Summer schedule switches to Tuesdays. Games tend to attract the 20-30 year olds. For more information, call Jim Jackson.

SF Volleyball Association
931-6385

Leagues play in three-month seasons in a number of indoor gyms around town, and teams are organized according to ability level. Between seasons, there is open play. For applications and information, call Director Roger Underhill.

Co-ed Volleyball at the JCC

League play is available for beginners to intermediate level every Wednesday night in the gym of the Jewish Community Center. Membership not required.

TENNIS ANYONE?

In the temperate climate of the City you can play tennis year-round on the 130 public courts nestled in parks, playgrounds and recreation centers throughout the City. There are also some wonderful mixed doubles tennis groups to join depending upon your ability level. Private clubs are also available, but can be expensive and/or have a long waiting list.

"After Work Tennis"
899-2565

Takes place on Wednesday evenings on the courts in Golden Gate Park, starting in May and ending in September. Ability level is carefully evaluated and teams are chosen accordingly. This worthwhile group sponsors the Youth Tennis program as well. For more information, call Dave Freitas.

Golden Gateway
370 Drumm
(between Jackson & Washington)
433-2936

In the heart of the Financial District, Golden Gateway is perfect for lunchtime or after-work tennis. There are 9 lighted outdoor courts as well as a newly renovated, completely updated spa, lap pool and workout facility. Small, friendly atmosphere. More reasonably priced than the SF Tennis Club and there is no charge for court time.

The San Francisco Tennis Club
645 Fifth Street (at Brannan)
777-9000

This private club is considered the place to play tennis if you're serious about the game. For the singles crowd there is also a wide variety of activities above and beyond all the tennis action. There are 12 indoor courts and 16 rooftop courts (which presents a challenge to the return of a lob on a typically foggy San Francisco day!). Besides tennis, there is a complete fitness center, personal weight trainers, steam, sauna and jacuzzi, a brand new dining room as well as the more casual bar and grill. To complete this perfect set-up, the Club is part of a worldwide affiliate of dining, golf and resort clubs which is included with membership.

▶▶ *There is a newly instituted **Junior Executive membership** for under 35 year olds which makes the club extremely appealing to younger members as well.*

BICYCLING

There are some wonderful scenic bike routes which wind through San Francisco. One tour is through Golden Gate Park. The best route to follow is South Drive. It connects with both the Great Highway at the Pacific Ocean, and Sunset Blvd. which leads south towards Lake Merced. The other runs north of San Francisco and across The Golden Gate Bridge into Marin County.

Start to Finish
633 Townsend (South of Market)
861-4004
1619 Fourth St., San Rafael
459-3990

Offers one of the largest selections of bikes and accessories to rent or buy in the Bay Area. Locations in SF and Marin.

▶ *Any good bike shop can give you more details on great places to bike.*

The Fogtown Frenzy
(415) 731-3644 (The Fog Line)

The principle activity of this chartered multi-sport and social organization is cycling, and its 22 members are exuberant and serious bikers. Prospective members must participate in at least two events to be considered for membership. Cycling events are scenic and challenging. Mountain biking/hiking weekends, cross country skiing and even an occasional evening of dancing.

BRIGHT IDEA!

Suggest a biking expedition to a friend! If you can ride a bike, you can look and feel like you're ready for the Tour de France. Pack a light picnic lunch and stop someplace romantic along the way.

ANNUAL BIKING EVENTS

Both these events are sponsored by Rhody Co. Productions. For more details, call 668-2243.

Software Publisher's Biathlon

This annual event held every October is not for the faint-hearted. It includes a 12-mile hike and a 5-mile run, with nearly 2000 people participating.

American Youth Hostel Great San Francisco Bike Adventure

Now this is more like it. That is, if you like to cycle alongside 15,000 other recreational bikers! Held every October and benefitting the Youth Hostel Association, this popular event starts and finishes in the Marina and loops around the City for 15 leisurely miles.

WANT MORE?

For a challenging bike ride in Sonoma see page 169, Biking in Sonoma, in Great Bay Area Getaways.

GOLF

San Francisco offers golfers five public courses designed to accommodate every ability level. Private clubs tend to be expensive and often have long waiting lists to join. With a number of excellent public courses to play throughout the Bay Area, why not tee off on the ones listed below.

Harding Park Golf Course
Harding Road
(by Skyline Blvd in Lake Merced)
664-4690

There are two courses available. Reservations are preferred, and single golfers will be matched with golfing partners.

Lincoln Park Golf Course
34th and Clement
221-9911

This is one of the only public courses in the heart of San Francisco with drop-dead views of the Golden Gate Bridge and Bay. It is located in lush greenery right next to Lake Merced. Ideal for golfers who like a challenge on every hole! The management is extremely helpful in putting together twosomes or foursomes. Single golfers are encouraged to drop in and feel assured of a game.

18 holes 6,637 yards
Men's par 72 Women's par 73

AFTER A ROUND OF GOLF

Continue on up the hill at Lincoln Park to view the stunning Holocaust Memorial by George Segal as well the architecturally magnificent Palace of the Legion of Honor, currently closed indefinitely for earthquake-proofing.

Golden Gate Park Golf Course
Golden Gate Park, 47th & Fulton
751-8987

This small, but challenging, 9-hole course has a tight, tricky lay. It is fairly hilly and often foggy with brisk sea breezes. There are no reservations. Walk-in only.

McClaren Park Golf Course
Sunnyvale Ave.
(between Brookdale & Persia)
587-2425

Local pros say that if you can shoot an 85 on this course twice around, you can play any course in the country. Very challenging and hilly terrain with some stunning views on a clear day.

Sharp Park Golf Course
California Highway 1, three miles south of Pacifica
359-3380

A fairly flat course of championship calibre alongside the ocean. Plenty of traps to challenge the most competent of golfers.

18 holes 6,398 yards
Men's par 72 Women's par 74

SWIMMING

Swimming is a challenge in the City. The temperate climate which is so ideal for other outdoor sporting activities can be daunting for swimmers. It is often too cold to swim outdoors, especially in the summer! You might want to consider the many workout clubs and centers already listed which have indoor pools.

PUBLIC POOLS

Rossi Pool
Arguello at Anza
(Richmond District)
751-9411

YMCA Stonestown
333 Eucalyptus
759-9622

Sava Pool
19th & Vincente (Sunset District)
753-7000

SWIM CLUBS

The Dolphin Club
502 Jefferson (& Hyde)
441-9329

For the serious swimmer, there is the renowned Dolphin Club, a beloved San Francisco swimming club in existence since 1877. There are over 800 members who at various times throughout the year meet to swim the San Francisco Bay. Meetings are held the third Wednesday of every month at 6:30 PM. There is a membership fee and monthly dues. Call for complete information.

Olympic Club
524 Post
775-4400

This prestigious private downtown club has recently opened its doors, albeit reluctantly, to women in the last year. Membership must be sponsored and there is a waiting list. Club membership fees are high, but here's the good news. It offers an excellent locale for swimming and includes combined membership in its golf and tennis club. The country club is still in SF. There is a reduced fee for younger members and the club appears to be quite social.

Metropolitan Club
640 Sutter
673-0600

"This is a distinctly private club for women", firmly claimed the membership director. No additional information was forthcoming without benefit of sponsoring member. If you would like to make additional enquiries, do find an accommodating sponsor.

MORE INDOOR POOLS

The SF Bay Club, The Embarcadero YMCA, The SF JCC, or Golden Gateway. See page 24 in Fitness Centers.

RUNNING, JOGGING, WALKING, HIKING

No matter what sports medicine experts claim, Americans love to run, anywhere and anyway they can. It truly is the great American passion in all of its manifestations. San Francisco offers enough splendid natural scenery to satisfy even the most jaded native. You can puff up impossible-looking hills, jog in fog-shrouded parks and stroll urban streets. So whether you are an Iron Man triathlete or recreational speedwalker, marathon runner or leisurely stroller, I hope the following resources are helpful.

FAVORITE RUNS AROUND THE CITY

Marina Green

(one mile, grassy flat)
Probably the most popular running area in the City. There are the stupendous views with every step you take, the constant sense of people all around you having a good time, the smell of the salt air, the sight of giant freighters and fragile sailboats floating by. It's all there to savor and enjoy as you feel those endorphins kicking in.

The Financial District

If you don't mind concrete, cars and buses, this is a popular noontime area for a quick jog. Definitely work your way over to the recently de-constructed Embarcadero for a scenically delightful run away from crowds and traffic. And it's flat, flat, flat. A rarity in the City!

Golden Gate Park

This is another very popular place to take a run or jog. Do call the Rec and Park Department to find out about the many trails and paths that wind through the park and are especially tailored for joggers. For runners who want to time their runs, there are four measured tracks just off Middle Drive in the center of the Park. And at Stowe Lake, there is a short scenic one-mile course circling the lake. For more challenging dirt trails, and a steep climb culminating in a stunning view of the entire park, cross one of the bridges leading over to Strawberry Hill. It does pay to be careful, however, and have a sense of where you are going. Street-wise is street-safe and that goes for parks as well. For more park information call **753-7023**.

The Presidio

This has always been a wonderful and often challenging place to run, but now that the Presidio has become a part of the Golden Gate National Recreation Area, it will be part of an exciting new development of preserved parkland in the middle of San Francisco.

RUNNING CLUBS

The Tamalpa Runners, a Marin-based running club, has over a thousand members and welcomes runners of all ability levels. There is a broad range of activities which include interval workouts, track meets, fun runs and frequent parties. And, it's a wonderful excuse to get out of the City on a foggy July afternoon, savor Marin's sunshine and run with fellow enthusiasts.
P.O. Box 701, Corte Madera, CA 94976

CALENDAR OF EVENTS

For an excellent schedule of competitive runs and walks, pick up a complimentary copy of The Northern California Schedule at any athletic supply or shoe store or health club. Or call 472-7223 for more information.

BACK-PACKING & HIKING

City Rock
1250 Doyle Street
Emeryville
(510) 654-2510

This indoor rock-climbing facility is available to climbing enthusiasts on a drop-in basis. Lessons available.

Sierra Club
923-5660

The Sierra Club offers some pretty wonderful backpacking and hiking experiences as well as river rafting and cycling for all ability levels. There is an excellent lecture series and meetings year-round regarding the many outdoor activities offered. Membership includes a subscription to the award-winning Sierra Magazine.

Cal Adventures
UC Berkeley
(510) 642-4000

Some great back-packing weekends can be found through Cal Adventures. These reasonably-priced excursions include transportation and group camping gear. BYOF, or bring your own food, which includes pot-luck dinners for treks to such blissful places as Yosemite, Big Sur, Death Valley. This is a group-oriented experience which has great appeal to the 30 to 40's age range, many of whom are single and all of whom share a love of adventure!

SAILING

Cass' Charters and Sailing
Bridgeway & Napa Street
Sausalito
332-7245

Cass' offers just about the best instruction and charters around. Well-located in Sausalito, just across the Bay from the City with easy parking, this delightful sailing school naturally seems to draw wanna-be sailors of all levels of expertise. Whether you're looking to be part of a crew, interested in hiring a charter or just want to be a competent sailor yourself, this no-nonsense well-organized school is for you.

GO FOR IT!

It's always better when the activity is one which truly interests you and in which you can shine. But any sporting endeavor will accommodate various levels of achievement and you should never feel daunted or intimidated with your lack of prowess in say, softball or sailing! Take along a friend and go for it. Having a sense of adventure, a sense of humor and a willingness to take advantage of the wealth of athletic activities in the Bay Area is all you truly need.

Modern Sailing Academy
2310 Marinship Blvd.
Sausalito
331-6266

Also located in Sausalito, this private sailing club does not require membership to participate in its many sailing activities, but the cost for non-members is significantly higher. Sailing instruction and boat charters are available and once a month there is a social barbeque and a sunset sail on the Hawaiian Chieftain.

Cal Sailing and Windsurfing Club
University Ave.
(across from the Berkeley Marina)
(510) 527-7245

This is the best deal going if you want to learn how to sail the Bay. For a nominal cost, a three-month membership permits you to take advantage of unlimited sailing instruction and equipment use. For thirty years, the Cal Sailing Club has been offering excellent low-cost sailing lessons. Take advantage of the monthly Open Houses which offer free introductory classes. Call for more information.

SKIING

With the accessibility of Lake Tahoe a mere 4 hours or less from the City, there is no excuse not to head up to the mountains at least once to give this sport a try. Granted, it involves a financial commitment even if you lease everything in sight: four-wheel drive to get up there, lift tickets, lessons, lodgings and food-whew! And let's not forget the unexpected delays in getting up or down Route 80 or Highway 50. But what a "high" when you finally make it happen and you are actually whizzing down the slopes in a, hopefully, competent and fluid style!

SKI CLUBS

Cal Adventures
UC Berkeley
(510) 642-4000

You didn't have to go to Cal to take advantage of some wonderful group-oriented cross-country or back country ski trips at reasonable prices. Call for additional info.

SKI TRIPS

Recommended resorts for skiing, places to stay and things to do in Lake Tahoe can be found in the Great Getaways Section on page 192.

HORSEBACK RIDING

Golden Gate Park Stables
JFK Drive opposite 35th Ave.
668-7360

Riding in the City is pretty much limited to basic trail rides throughout the Park in groups of six. Lessons are available.

EXOTIC TRAIL RIDES

*How about mounting up for a two-hour horseback ride through local redwood forests or vineyards with spectacular views of the Sonoma Valley to boot? Take your pick from a number of exotic trail rides by moonlight, a stopover for lunch or a barbeque dinner. Sound intriguing? Call the **Sonoma Cattle Company** at (707) 996-8566 in Glen Ellen for more information.*

SPORTING EVENTS

For those who like to watch as well as participate in athletics, listed below are all the sporting events you can take advantage of in the San Francisco Bay Area on a seasonal basis.

BASEBALL

San Francisco Giants
Candlestick Park
Giants Dr. & Gilman Ave.
Ticket sales and information:
467-8000

Oakland Athletics
Oakland Coliseum
Nimitz Freeway
Oakland
Ticket sales and information:
638-0500

FOOTBALL

San Francisco 49ers
Candlestick Park
Giants Dr. & Gilman Ave.
Ticket sales and information:
468-2249

BASKETBALL

Golden State Warriors
Oakland Coliseum Arena
Nimitz Fwy.
Oakland
Ticket sales and information:
638-6000

HORSE RACING

Bay Meadows
2600 S. Delaware St.
at 25th Street
San Mateo
573-7223

Golden Gate Fields
Gilman Street off I-80
Albany
526-3020

SOCCER

San Francisco Bay Blackhawks
39375 Cedar Blvd.
Newark
736-6801

COLLEGE TEAMS

California Golden Bears Football
U.C. Berkeley
Berkeley
Tickets: **(510) 642-5150**

Stanford Cardinal Football
Stanford University
Palo Alto
Tickets: **723-1021**

Looking Good, Feeling Good

The search for a top hairdresser, facialist or masseuse is an on-going, perennial one. Here is a crop of current favorites!

PERSONAL NEEDS

HAIR CARE
FOR MEN AND WOMEN

Rumours
3665 Sacramento
346-3333

Owner Dennis will do a fine job cutting hair for men or women in this lovely salon on Sacramento Street. Manicures are also available with Jana or Tanya, delightful Russian sisters!

Benvenuto Miller Salon
166 Grant
433-7174

This salon is featured as a hair spa and color specialist. Make-up, facials and manicures are also available at this new spot on Grant and Maiden Lane. Owner Antonio Benvenuto has been offering top-quality hair care for years in Marin. This is his San Francisco debut.

di Pietro Todd Salon
177 Post
397-0177

Located in the heart of Union Square, this is one of the hottest places for hair care in the City. This busy, full-service salon also offers in-house massages and facials as well as manicures, pedicures and a make-up department. Top cutters include owner John di Pietro, Joseph or Peter. For great natural-looking tints and highlights, Sandy runs an extremely well-organized show in the color department and is highly recommended. There is even a wonderful lunch and cappucino bar!

Roy's Salon
3384 Sacramento
563-9999

Gray and Pam are great for color and owner Roy does wonderful cuts.

St Tropez
1980 Union Street
563-3514

This salon, located on bustling Union Street, offers top-quality hair care, and a manicurist and facialist on site. Maurice is highly recommended, and there are four other top cutters as well.

77 Maiden Lane
391-7777

Another great, full-service salon on Maiden Lane. For cuts, consider Jean Michel or Michael. There is a full color department headed by Tim Brannon, as well as two make-up artists, three manicurists and a mother/daughter facialist team. Massage is not available.

The Exchange Barbershop
435 Pine Street & Montgomery
781-9658

In business since 1966, this is the financial district barbershop. There are seven hair-cutters, a manicurist and a shoe shine operator. Walk in or by appt.

BEST AND LEAST EXPENSIVE FITNESS/BEAUTY PROGRAM

- *Walk the hills of San Francisco.*
- *Moisturize your face with unbottled, absolutely pure natural fog (available in large quantities).*
- *Revitalize your sore muscles with fresh Bay breezes.*
- *Purchase, at no cost whatsoever, a total sunblock available on any average summer day in the City. Not offered in the fall.*

FACIALS AND SKIN CARE

Besides the salons indicated which feature in-house facialists, the following are also recommended.

Lana's
3061 Sacramento
346-6420

This small salon on Sacramento offers fine European facials.

Visage
329 Primrose Road, Suite 109
Burlingame
347-0465

Besides being a professional skin care and make-up studio in Burlingame, owner-aesthetician Denise Spanek will come to you, by appointment, for consultation on skin care, facial treatments, application for special events and one-on-one make-up lessons. She also offers an excellent line of cosmetics. Evening appointments available.

La Belle Skin & Body Care Salon
233 Grant
433-7644

This large, professionally-run salon on Grant has been offering a wide range of health and beauty services for fifteen years. These include European facials, waxing, make-up consultation and massage therapy. There are a number of half-day or full-day "packages", (including lunch), to which you may treat yourself. Or give a gift of a "package" to someone special. The perfect urban spa!

Billie O'Neil
1922 Lombard Street
775-SKIN

By appointment only on Mon., Tues. and Sat. Fine skin-care consultation and professional facials offered.

Coreen Cordova Make-Up Salon
177 Post
434-0957

Located in the di Pietro Todd Salon, renowned make-up artist Coreen Cordova and her staff, reside over an excellent make-up department. Lessons, applications and make-overs are offered and a wide range of make-up and cosmetics are also available for sale.

MASSAGE

Besides being offered in many of the salons above, you may also want to consider a massage at the following:

Veronica Laboure
221-1111

Veronica Laboure is a professional, licensed massage therapist who will come to your home, by appointment only. A luxury indeed.

Kabuki Hot Springs
1750 Geary
922-6000

In the heart of Japantown is a San Francisco tradition imported directly from Japan. The Kabuki offers authentic Shiatsu massage as well as a full spa facility. State licensed and certified. Located just below the best movie theater in the City, the Kabuki 8 Theatres!

BEAUTY RESOURCES

Beautyland Beauty Supply, Inc.
180 O'Farrell
989-1818

Cosmetics, skin-care and nail care products are sold at discounted prices with assistance from qualified and trained cosmetologists.

The Face Place
2117 Fillmore
567-1173

With locations all over the City, including the Financial District at 339 Kearny, The Face Place offers a "cosmetic" experience" and carries hundreds of colors for eyes, lips and nails. Also available, by appointment, are treatments in massage, aromatherapy and waxing. None of the cosmetics are tested on animals nor do they contain animal products.

MEDICAL RESOURCES AND HEALTH SERVICES

The Bay Area is home to some of the finest physicians, hospitals, medical schools and research facilities in the world. Choosing a doctor may be the most important decision you ever make. With more than 17,000 doctors in dozens of different specialties and sub-specialties practicing throughout the Bay Area, finding the one who is best for you, and the needs of your family, can be a daunting prospect indeed.

This chapter will not address the issue of who is *best* in terms of physicians, medical care or health services. What it will offer are guidelines to consider when you are ready to make decisions. It will also offer resources, hotlines and programs to contact for verification or advice. In the end, after you have researched and interviewed and verified your choices for medical care, it should all boil down to how you *feel* about the physician. Trust your reactions and make sure the chemistry is there for a successful doctor/patient relationship.

"All doctors look good on paper," claims Dr. George D. LeMaitre, author of 'How to Choose a Good Doctor'. "The really good physicians have heart, and the patients can sense it."

–Anonymous

GUIDELINES FOR CHOOSING A PHYSICIAN

Start looking while you are healthy, not when you are sick, anxious, rushed or worried. This is particularly important if you belong to an HMO (health maintenance organization), where your primary-care physician will be controlling, to a greater or lesser degree, your access to specialists. Be able to make your decisions with a clear head, allowing yourself to think calmly and logically.

Get referrals. The first thing you need to do is to find a good primary-care physician you can trust and respect. He will handle the bulk of your medical needs and will be your best source for finding a specialist.

Nurses are a great source for referrals, particularly those who work in hospitals. On a daily basis, they witness not only how skilled doctors are, but how they treat their patients. Nurses in top neonatology depts. of hospitals are excellent resources for recommending skilled and caring pediatricians.

A wonderful resource. For all kinds of consumer-related medical information consider the Planetree Health Resource Center at California Pacific Medical Center. There is a free library owned by this non-profit group to help people access to, and an understanding of, the health-care system. This includes a directory of doctors by specialty, newsletters from support groups and articles on current research from medical journals.

Where a doctor practices. Where he has admitting privileges may be as important as the choice of the doctor. Three Bay Area hospitals–Stanford, UCSF and San Francisco General–made this year's list of forty-three top quality hospitals in a nationwide survey.

Check credentials. Is the doctor board-certified in his or her specialty? It doesn't necessarily mean this doctor is more competent than a non-certified colleague, but it does mean that he or she took several years of advanced training and passed a rigorous exam. You can verify this by calling the American Board of Medical Specialties at 1-800-776-CERT.

Practical considerations. Cost, insurance acceptability or even location can affect your choices. When my own children were younger, I always felt that proximity was a major factor in choosing a pediatrician. When a child has a hundred and four degree temperature or complains of severe neck pain, you don't want to be battling rush-hour traffic to get to your pediatrician.

When to interview? Once you are reasonably confident of a doctor's medical qualifications, it is time to interview the doctor to see if his or her style, personality and philosophy match your own.

- Do you have to wait an unreasonable amount of time to see the doctor?

- Is the staff understanding and sympathetic to your needs?

- Do you get the doctor's undivided attention, or is he or she watching the clock?

- Does he answer your questions in language you can understand or is he abrupt and condescending?

Lastly, how much emphasis does the doctor put on patient education? Does he or she make available brochures or articles which may interest you? Are his staff members trained to help answer your questions and involve you in your own care? A doctor who does is indicating to you that you are an active partner in the overwhelming process of finding good medicine.

HOSPITALS AND MEDICAL CENTERS

UCSF at Mt Zion Medical Center
1600 Divisadero at Sutter
Main number, **567-6600**
24-hour emergency, **885-7520**

Mt. Zion, now part of the giant UC medical system, is one of the oldest hospitals in the City and specializes in geriatrics and cancer care.

California Pacific Medical Center
3700 California
Main number, **387-8700**
24-hour emergency, **750-6031**

2333 Buchanan
Main number, **563-4321**
24-hour emergency, **923-3333**

With the merger of Children's Hospital and Pacific Presbyterian Hospital, there now exists a comprehensive and highly-regarded medical center specializing in neonatology, oncology, transplants and maternal/child health. Special programs of interest include:

- A free resource library run by Planetree Health Resource Center.

- A "birthing suite" – a luxurious one-stop shop where women labor, deliver and recover all in the same room with a soothing, un-hospital-like atmosphere.

- A first-class neonatology division with the state's lowest infant mortality rate, despite the fact that it is a state-designated intensive care nursery. There is an elaborate parent education program, intensive monitoring for women at risk and high nurse-to-patient ratio.

San Francisco General Hospital
1001 Potrero
Main number, **206-8000**
24-hour emergency, **206-8111**

Specialties here are the Trauma Center, AIDS treatment and Infection Control. In case of a terrible automobile accident, this is the place to go.

The Medical Center at UCSF
505 Parnassus
Main number, **885-7277**
24-hour emergency, **476-1037**

Specialties include cancer diagnosis and treatment, transplants, obstetrics/pediatrics. The very sickest babies are brought here and receive near-miraculous care at this world-renowned teaching hospital. Special programs include:

"Great Expectations", a designated parent education and information center. It includes a lending library, parenting classes on a wide range of topics, practical workshops for single parents and a hospital hotline for information.

Seton Hall Medical Center
1900 Sullivan Avenue
Daly City
992-4000

Special departments here include the SF Heart Institute and SF Wound Care. There is also an orthopedics and spine care department.

Davies Medical Center
Castro and Duboce
565-6000

Specialties include acute rehabilitation, micro-surgery and limb salvage, HIV research and treatment.

Saint Francis Memorial Hospital
900 Hyde
Main number, **775-4321**
24-hour emergency, **353-6300**
This is the premier burn center in the Bay Area. It also specializes in rehabilitation services (sports/spine/work ready) and has a cancer care unit.

Kaiser Permanente
Medical Center
2425 Geary
202-2000

Kaiser specializes in health education, chemical dependency, high-risk obstetrics and newborn intensive care.

Saint Mary's Hospital and
Medical Center
450 Stanyan
668-1000
24-hour emergency, **750-5700**
Specializes in cardiac and cardiovascular care, orthopedics and spine care. Special programs include:

"Health Connection", an in-house referral service. It has a sophisticated computer data bank which can match you up with a doctor by specialty, background, board certification, foreign languages spoken or insurance plan.

USEFUL MEDICAL RESOURCES

EMERGENCY

Fire, Police or Medical Emergencies
911

Direct line for Police
553-1234

Direct line for Fire
861-8020

Ambulance
431-2800

Poison Control, (24 hours)
(800) 523-2222

MEDICAL

SF Medical Society
561-0853

SF Dental Referral
421-1435

Cancer Information Service
(800) 422-6237

Medi-Cal Information
558-1000

AMBULANCE SERVICE

Emergency, paramedic and routine ambulance transportation serving the Bay Area. Also offers emergency medical consulting and education classes. Available 24 hours-a-day.
2829 California Street
931-3900

MEDICAL

Medical Board of California
(800) 633-2322

SF Smokers Quitline
554-9999

DISASTER SERVICES

American Red Cross (24 hours)
202-0600

SF Office of Emergency Services
554-6556

COUNSELING

California Self-Help Center
(800) 222-5465

State-wide referrals to support groups for abuse, addiction, aging, bereavement, emotional problems, parenting and other concerns.

Catholic Charities of SF
864-7400

Jewish Family and Childrens Services
567-8860

CRISIS

AIDS hotline (24 hours)
(800) 367-2437

Alcoholics Anonymous
661-1828

Drug Abuse
(800)444-9999

Rape Crisis (24hours)
647-7273

Suicide Prevention
(800) 231-6946

ALL-NIGHT PHARMACIES

Walgreen's (24-hour prescriptions)
3201 Divisadero
931-6417
498 Castro
861-3136

SENIOR SERVICES

Seniors Center
775-1866

Seniors Information
621-1033

CHILD SERVICES

Runaway Hotline (24 hours)
(800) 231-6946

Children's Protective Services (24 hours)
665-0757

Food Glorious Food

Where are people eating these days? They're eating anywhere the food is good, the service tops, the atmosphere lively and the price is reasonable. Are you grabbing a quick bite on the way home from work or en route to a movie? Is this to be a leisurely, romantic meal by candlelight when money is no object? Or do you want the makings for the ultimate picnic, that solitary evening at home alone or the best Chinese food going?

THE RESTAURANT SCENE

RISE AND SHINE!

Ella's
500 Presidio
441-5669

One of the best breakfast spots around (and do try lunch here as well). Focusing on "neoclassical American cooking", which simply translates as great food, Ella's specialty is her incredible homemade breads and pastries. Open every day for breakfast and lunch. Wed-Friday for dinner.

San Francisco is a Restaurant Town, no doubt about it. It is not, however, a Deli Town. Head for New York, L.A. or Chicago when you yearn for corned beef or pastrami. We always bring back sandwiches on the plane coming home from Manhattan. There is nothing like munching on a pastrami on rye from Carnegie Deli while the rest of the passengers stare in envy!

Il Fornaio
1265 Battery
986-0100

Breakfast is served in this delightful downtown eatery from 7-10 AM. The perfect Financial District breakfast meeting spot.

Doidge's Kitchen
2217 Union St.
921-2149

And now for something completely different! Doidge's is homey, relaxed and unpretentious. A popular spot for the Marina and Union Street crowd.

Sears Fine Foods
439 Powell
986-1160

A must-visit at least once. Located in the heart of Union Square, this is a tourist's delight, but the locals seem to frequent it just as often.

Campton Place Restaurant
340 Stockton
781-5155

The spot for the ultimate Power Breakfast, brunch on the weekend with prospective in-laws or just because you're feeling extravagant!

> *"If I were King, I would close all cafes, for those who frequent them become dangerous hot-heads."*
> *–Charles de Montesquieu*

LUNCH ON THE RUN

Fast food takes on a whole new flavor as downtown eateries have popped up with the philosophy that a quick bite can still be a great eating experience.

Kelly's on Trinity
333 Bush St.
362-4454

An airy, Ninety's style cafeteria with an enticing display case full of nifty sandwiches like Mom never imagined, mouth-watering salads and a few hot entrees.

Emporio Armani
Express Restaurant
1 Grant Avenue
677-9010

Located on the mezzanine of the gleaming new Armani boutique in a neoclassic, 1910 bank building. One of four Armani cafes worldwide, you will discover superbly presented Italian fare in a casually elegant setting. A much needed place to lunch in the Union Square area.

Rustico
300 De Haro Street at 16th
252-0180

It's worth a trek to SoMa (South of Market) to experience still another Italian eatery set in a whimsical loft in the designer showcase district. Pizzas, salads and sandwiches are all great.

Caffe Trinity
1145 Market at Grove
864-3333

This is an exquisite jewel of a cafe with a no holds barred ambience. It is simply enchanting with a divine Italian menu of light fare to match. Sandwiches made to order with a perfect espresso is heaven.

RESTAURANTS WHICH FOREVER CHANGED THE WAY WE EAT

Chez Panisse
1517 Shattuck Ave
Berkeley
(510) 548-5525

It's hard to believe this landmark restaurant is twenty years old. Wasn't it yesterday that it revolutionized American cooking and we all stood in line for a chance to savor history in the making? Still a must for those who have never been and for those who have been too rarely.

▶ *For a lighter and less expensive taste of Chez Panisse, try the Grill upstairs. It attracts a younger crowd and has a fun, upbeat, far less serious air about it!*

TIP

Check out the Browsing in Berkeley section on page 176 for a wealth of things to do in this fascinating part of the Bay Area.

CHARMING BELDEN PLACE

This tiny side street between Bush & Pine, Kearny & Montgomery, in the heart of the Financial District, is a treasure of marvelous restaurants, coffee houses and bistros. One side of the street feels distinctly Italian and the other side is decidedly French! Be sure and dine al fresco at any number of outdoor tables which dot the street. And try to sample any of the following:

Cafe Tiramisu
28 Belden
421-7044

A delightful Italian street cafe with an emphasis on natural ingredients and superb pasta dishes.

Cafe Bastille
22 Belden
986-5673

This original french bistro serves lunch and dinner as well as the best live jazz going on the weekends. A must!

Sam's Grill
374 Bush
421-0594

One of the oldest continuing restaurants in the City, where the standards of fine cooking and renowned seafood have remained high.

Stars Restaurant
150 Redwood Alley
861-7827

If there is one eating scene which captures San Francisco's sense of style, it's this masterpiece from Chef Jeremiah Tower. There is a "buzz" at Stars, a constant high in which every woman there feels beautiful and sexy and every man feels powerful and amusing. Whether you are catching a drink and a bite from the bar menu, or ending an evening dining after the opera, Stars is the ultimate kick.

▶▶ *The younger crowd can often be found at the popular Star's Cafe. And it can be the perfect place to catch a quick meal before the symphony, opera or a movie at the Opera Plaza across the street. Like Chez Panisse Grill, it offers a lively atmosphere, lower prices and lighter fare.*
555 Golden Gate
861-4344

Square One
190 Pacific
788-1110

Chef/owner Joyce Goldstein has deeply influenced the look and taste of California Cuisine with her innovative and eclectic restaurant, Square One. The ambitious, Mediterranean-influenced menu changes daily and Square One today is nationally recognized.

"Don't let love interfere with your appetite. It never does with mine."
—Anthony Trollope

Greens Restaurant
Building A, Fort Mason
off Marina Blvd.
771-6222

Before Greens, vegetarian food meant munchy, crunchy health food which may have been good for you, but didn't exactly offer a gastronomic thrill. Like Cranks Restaurant in London in the seventies, Greens has changed forever the way we view vegetarian fare. And speaking of the views, they are absolutely breathtaking.

FABULOUS FORT MASON

*If you stop in at Greens for lunch, plan on spending some time in the extraordinary Fort Mason complex. This former Army command post was the main debarkation point for US troops fighting in the Pacific in World War II. Today it houses an eclectic collection of thriving cultural & arts organizations including the San Francisco Museum of Modern Art Rental Gallery, The Mexican Museum, Make A Circus, Performing Arts Workshop, The African American Historical Society and 50 other resident organizations. Call General Information, **441-5706**, for a monthly calendar of over a thousand activities.*

GOLDEN OLDIES

Every would-be San Franciscan, young or old, should try the following eating houses, many of which date back to the 19th century and all of which are worth trying.

Tadich Grill
240 California St.
391-2373

One of the most famous fish houses in the City, dating back to 1849. Tadich's is so popular among locals and tourists alike that there are no reservations. So plan on eating early or waiting at the busy bar-not a bad alternative if you are on your own.

Jack's
615 Sacramento
986-9854

Jack's is well-known for its fresh cracked crab and political and business deal-making dinners upstairs. The simple, no-frills dining room has been turning out first class meals since 1864.

Ernie's
847 Montgomery St.
397-5969

If you're an old movie buff, you may recognize the Ambrosia Room in Ernie's which was where Jimmy Stewart fell in love with Kim Novak in Hitchcock's "Vertigo".

PS. The food is still better than ever.

Trader Vic's
20 Cosmo Place
776-2232

This is still The venerable Polynesian-style society hangout. Food may not always be up to par, but the appetizer platter at the beginning of the meal and the coconut ice cream roll at the end are always worth the price of admission!

HOT NEW RESTAURANTS

The sheer number of new restaurants to hit the San Francisco dining scene is staggering. It seems as if almost daily, a new eating spot is being touted as hot, hot, hot. Listed below are just a few noteworthy newcomers who seem to have that Special Something.

One Market
One Market Plaza
Market and Steuart St.
777-5577

Super Chef Brad Ogden is back in the City, after putting the Campton Place Restaurant on the map, with a very uptown downtown winner of a restaurant. Located in the heart of the financial district, this spacious new eating place, with views of the Bay and the Ferry Building, offers up farm-fresh American cooking featuring a wood-burning oven and a spit roast. Whether you are seeking a spot for the ultimate Power Breakfast, a leisurely lunch or an elegant dinner, head for Market One. Or if you just want to sit back, sip a glass of wine and enjoy the scene in the bar area, this is The Place to be.

Fringale
570 Fourth Street
543-0573

A french classic combined with the best of California cuisine, offered up by renowned Basque chef Gerald Hirigoyen.

Restaurant LuLu
816 Folsom
495-5775

A sophisticated, eye-catching restaurant with wonderful cuisine right out of the Riviera.

Elka
1611 Post Street
922-7788

This is a remarkable new restaurant located in the Miyako Hotel in Japantown. Named after its talented owner/chef, Elka, it offers a Japanese/California cuisine in a dramatic setting which complements the exotic fare.

Moose's
1652 Stockton
between Union & Filbert
989-7800

"Once again, there's a moose on the loose in North Beach". Ed Moose's latest restaurant venture seems to be a roaring success. This upscale Italian restaurant/bar is noisy, social, modern and always bustling with action. The cooking and the clientele often seem to be on the cutting edge and yet the ambience is classic and comfortable. Lunch and dinner served daily and live music in the evening.

Geordy's
One Tillman Place, off Grant Ave.
between Sutter and Post
362-3175

Stunning new restaurant which food critic Patricia Unterman gives rave reviews. "Geordy's comes closest to being a New York restaurant...which has absorbed the Northern California lessons of freshness and seasonality. You are drawn back by the delicious, classic modern food...This one is a keeper."

OTHER HOT SPOTS AROUND TOWN

Caribbean Zone
55 Natoma
541-9465

Casual, Caribbean fare with an active bar scene in this bustling restaurant in an alley off Howard and Mission.

Fog City Diner
1300 Battery
982-2000

Located in a renovated old diner which was once a hangout for the longshoremen who worked on Fishermen's Wharf, Fog City is now a favorite hangout of the Levi Plaza/Embarcadero Center crowd. Always busy, always good.

L'Avenue
3854 Geary
386-1555

This perfect French restaurant may be "out in the Avenues" but it is undeniably one of the finest french bistros.

Zuni Cafe
1658 Market St.
552-2522

This is still the place to be seen even with its Market Street locale, the near impossible parking and its dense and noisy atmosphere. However, the food remains innovative and creative and here's a big plus. This restaurant is open until 12:30 AM. Not your typical closing time for San Francisco restaurants.

Johnny Love's
1500 Broadway
931-6053

While highly touted as one of the hot spots on the single scene, it is well worth a visit. The food is quite remarkable. There is a separate entrance to the restaurant area, somewhat removed from the bustling bar scene.

Postrio
545 Post
776-7825

Granted, even though Postrio's is hard to get into, expensive, noisy and not always as perfect as it should be, it is an exciting place to try at least once! The food is mouth-watering in a truly drop-dead setting.

▶ *At the very least, arrive early at Postrio, grab a table in the bar area for a beer or a glass of wine and Postrio's famous smoked salmon pizza.*

ELEGANT AND EXPENSIVE

Masa's
648 Bush
989-7154

The height of sophisticated dining with beautifully prepared dishes. The eternal unsolved mystery is who killed Masa? No one knows.

Fleur De Lys
777 Sutter
673-7779

If I could get engaged here, so could you! One of the most romantic restaurants in the City.

The Blue Fox
659 Merchant St.
981-1177

This award-winning Northern Italian restaurant offers a feeling of old San Francisco classics adapted to contemporary "new" dishes.

The Sherman House
2160 Green Street
563-3600

Available for "Special Celebrations" only, whether it is for two or twenty, The Sherman House is a perfectly elegant choice. The restaurant is in a charming inn of the same name. Valet parking.

▶ *For the ultimate celebration, why not make a reservation to check into this charmer, recommended in Relais and Chateau. The Sherman House offers six beautifully appointed suites and eight rooms, all with feather beds and fireplaces!*

CIVIC CENTER DINING UPDATE

Some incredible restaurants can be found around the Civic Center and are well worth investigating, whether you work in the area, attend the symphony or opera, linger at the Museum of Modern Art or just enjoy eating well.

Kimball's
300 Grove Street at Franklin
861-5555

This popular jazz supper club is one of the finest places around to hear first class jazz, matched only by its counterpart in Emeryville. A popular singles hangout as well, this local jazz hall of fame has safe, accessible parking in the area and is pure heaven for jazz lovers.

Hayes Street Grill
324 Hayes St.
863-5545

The grande dame of Civic Center Dining and a personal favorite, this busy restaurant has the freshest of fish and is always crowded. There is invariably a lively bar scene as people wait cheerfully for a much sought-after table. This place only gets better.

CHECK IT OUT!

Hayes Street, between Laguna and Franklin, has become a mini-SoHo. In this three-block area, you will find everything from thriving art galleries to jazz clubs, from top-rated gyms to vintage clothiers.

Max's Opera Deli
601 Van Ness in Opera Plaza
771-7300

It ain't the Stage Deli, but you could never convince the constant crowds of loyal enthusiasts of that. "Bigger is better" is the philosophy at Max's and the deli sandwiches defy imagination!

Miss Pearl's Jam House
601 Eddy at Larkin
775-5267

Ready to party? It's a perennial jam session and everyone's invited to this hopping South of Market eatery with its exotic Caribbean-California dishes. Miss Pearl's is a bit off the beaten track in the heart of SoMa.

The Most Unusual Cafe in the City

Here's one of my favorites and surely one of the most offbeat places around!

*Check out **Cafe Laundry** in North Beach. With its laundromat on one side and a delightful french bistro on the other, you can arrive with a bag of laundry and an appetite for cappuccino and croissants at eight in the morning or save it for 2 AM and a late night supper. Music is playing day or night in this lively little laundry bistro with its art-filled walls and friendly ambience. Stop by. What a way to make friends and deal with dirty laundry!*
570 Green Street
989-6745

THE SOMA SCENE

South of Market is truly where it's happening these days. SoMa has some of the best restaurants, clubs and singles action in the City.

The Fly Trap
606 Folsom
243-0580

Always bustling, this popular Folsom Street restaurant serves traditional San Francisco fare to a non-traditional crowd!

Embarko
100 Brannan St.
495-2021

Great fun in this lively and moderately priced restaurant with its American ethnic cooking and lively atmosphere.

Eddie Rickenbackers
133 Second Street
543-3498

From the WWI artwork, complete with fighter plane, to the best burgers and down to earth American fare, Eddie R's is the place to have fun.

"Isn't it nice that the people who prefer L.A. to San Francisco live there?"

–Herb Caen

Up and Down Club Bar
1151 Folsom
626-2388

Live music, offered Wed-Saturday, adds sparkle to this SoMa night spot, down the street from Julie's Supper Club. The food is first-rate.

Hamburger Mary's
1582 Folsom
626-1985

Early American clutter with pop, rock and blues in the background. Great burgers, sandwiches and salads at inexpensive prices.

FRESH FROM THE SEA

Aqua
252 California St.
956-9662

This visually beautiful restaurant, just footsteps from Tadich Grill in the heart of the Financial District, is about as far removed from a typical San Francisco seafood restaurant as one can imagine. Sophisticated fare in a seductive setting.

Tadich Grill
240 California
391-2373

What a wonderful contrast to its next door neighbor, Aqua. Both restaurants equally wonderful, but in vastly different ways. Tadich's is old San Francisco, noisy, simple and an enduring favorite.

Scoma's
Pier 47, Jones & Jefferson
771-4383

Well-known seafood restaurant in the heart of the Fisherman's Wharf area.

Swan Oyster Bar
1517 Polk Street
673-1101

Enough cannot be said about the high quality of Swan's seafood. My favorite is to order fresh cracked crab take-out and serve up the world's easiest dinner party with cold crab, salad, a quick pasta dish, and, of course, sourdough bread from Acme's.

Home-made Sauce for Cracked Crab

Actually this recipe originated at Joe's Stone Crab in Miami Beach, as the perfect dipping sauce for perhaps the best crab in the world. It tastes great with the Bay Area's Dungeness variety as well.

4 T Best Foods Mayonnaise (known as "Hellmans" to us Easterners!)
4 t Dijon mustard
A couple dashes of worcestshire sauce
Freshly ground pepper

Mix all ingredients together in small bowl. Add more Dijon if needed.
2 portions.

A TREASURE TROVE OF CHINESE RESTAURANTS

The Bay Area is lucky to have the depth and quality it does in its overwhelming collection of fine Chinese restaurants. I've attempted to list just a few favorites.

Flower Lounge
5322 Geary
692-6666

This restaurant is the current guru of what is considered the best in Chinese cooking today. Everything is fresh, succulent and delicious. It truly is hard to pick a losing dish here. An emphasis on natural flavors and the finest of seafoods characterizes the Flower Lounge.

Harbor Village
4 Embarcadero Center
398-8883

Conveniently located in the Financial District, this restaurant is straight from Hong Kong, and its creative and award-winning specialities provide the perfect Chinese feast.

Wu Kong Restaurant
Rincon Center, 101 Spear Street
957-9300

Some of the finest Northern Chinese food can be found in this lovely restaurant in the atrium of the historic Rincon Center. And highly acclaimed by food critics.

China Moon Cafe
639 Post
775-4789

Chef/owner Barbara Tropp was one of the first to take traditional Chinese cooking into a contemporary and exciting new direction. Located in the Union Square, this is still one of the most innovative Chinese restaurants around. And delicious!

Tommy Toys Cuisine Chinois
655 Montgomery
397-4888

Expensive and sophisticated Chinese fare in a drop-dead setting.

China House Bistro
6th & Balboa
752-2802

Look who has returned to the Richmond! One of the finest Chinese restaurants in the city is back in business. Open nightly for dinner.

JUST ASK!

Ask twenty San Franciscans what their favorite Chinese restaurant is and you will get twenty responses! Everyone knows The Best Chinese Restaurant, and that doesn't include their favorite place for dim sum.

DIM SUM DELIGHTS

Yank Sing
427 Battery
781-1111

One of the most famous spots for dim sum in the City.

Harbor Village
4 Embarcadero Center
398-8883

Hong Kong-style dim sum.

Pearl City
641 Jackson
398-8383

Large, fresh portions in a rustic setting located in Jackson Square.

Wu Kong
Rincon Center, 101 Spear Street
957-9300

Specializes in Shanghai style dim sum.

Canton
655 Folsom
495-3064

Potstickers and foil wrapped chicken a specialty.

Golden Dragon
816 Washington (in Chinatown)
398-3920

Superb dim sum at inexpensive prices.

RISTORANTE ITALIANO DELIZIO!

Italian restaurants abound in San Francisco. The heart of fine eating can always be found in North Beach, the historic center of Italian life in the City. But there is also great Italian dining to be found all over the City as well.

Etrusca
101 Spear St. (Rincon Tower)
777-0330

Elegant and expensive in a visually stunning setting, Etrusca is one of the finest going for sophisticated Northern Italian fare. Bar menu is available at its magnificent horseshoe-shaped bar.

Buca Giovanni
800 Greenwich
776-7766

Wonderful cave-like setting. Serves some of the finest pastas in North Beach.

Ciao
230 Jackson
982-9500

Lively trattoria in historic Jackson Square features fresh grilled meats, fish & pasta.

"The trouble with eating Italian food is that five or six days later you're hungry again."
–George Miller

Roti
155 Steuart St.
495-6500

Another popular downtown eatery located in the Prescott Hotel and filled with a lively Financial District crowd.

Il Fornaio
1265 Battery
986-0100

Always in, always delicious. Robust Italian fare in a beautiful Tuscan setting for breakfast, lunch or dinner.

La Fiammetta
1701 Octavia
474-5077

Tucked away in this Pacific Heights area, this local favorite features classic and innovative Roman cuisine.

Jackson Fillmore Trattoria
2506 Fillmore
346-5288

Small, bustling & lively, this Italian trattoria, favored by a younger, enthusiastic crowd, can be tough to get into on a moment's notice. Reservations only accepted for three or more.

La Pergola
2060 Chestnut
563-4500

Look who's back! This old San Francisco favorite has returned and it's better than ever.

North Beach Restaurant
1512 Stockton
392-1700

A most famous Northern Italian restaurant in North Beach with classic Italian cuisine and a world class wine list.

BEST PIZZA IN THE CITY

Tommaso's
1042 Kearny
398-9696
Old-style pizza in the heart of North Beach.

Postrio
545 Post
776-7825
The world's most elegant & expensive pizza!

Pizzeria Uno
2200 Lombard
563-3144
Chicago-style pizza is a favorite.

Olive's Pizza
3249 Scott at Lombard
567-4488
This pizza gives nearby Uno's a run for its money!

California Pizza Kitchen
438 Geary
563-8911
Fabulous gourmet pizzas in the Theatre district. (And check out their thick, gooey hot fudge sundaes!)

Have any other wonderful pizza favorites? Let me know!

BEST CHEAP EATS IN THE CITY

Anyone can spend a lot of money and dine well in San Francisco. But it is an art to dining well on a budget.

The Slow Club
2501 Miraposa
241-9390
Creative soups, generous sandwiches and eclectic specials.

Zazie
941 Cole
564-5332
Delicious bistro fare in a comfortable ambience.

Des Alpes
732 Broadway
391-4249
Generous family-style meals at this popular Basque eatery.

Mandalay
4344 California
386-3895
Wonderful Thai food at bargain prices

Gira Polli
659 Union
434-4472
Famous for spit-roasted chicken, moist and delish.

Il Pollaio
555 Columbus
362-7727
Great grilled chicken at bargain prices.

BEST SPOTS FOR COFFEE

The latest place to hang-out, re-group, wake up, take a break and sometimes even meet someone interesting, is still over the proverbial cup of coffee. But how times have changed! Today there are a wide range of places to sip a cup of latte, from coffee bars to coffee houses to Financial District quick coffee and muffin stops. The following are recommended favorites.

Caffe Roma
414 Columbus
398-8584

An old North Beach hangout with steaming aromatic coffee (and a pretty fabulous pizza too!) Open during the day. A popular Saturday morning place to linger over a latte and the NY Times!

OLDEST COFFEE ROASTERS IN TOWN?

Freed Teller & Freed's. The most venerable coffee establishment west of New York, this hundred-year-old company cares about coffee. The stand-up bar is a popular Financial District stop. Embarcadero Center West Tower
986-8851

NEWEST COFFEE KID ON THE BLOCK?

Starbucks Coffee Company. This Seattle-based company has hit the coffee world with a bang. Walk-up counter, coffee to go, high-quality beans.
1899 Union at Laguna
921-4049

Bohemian Cigar Store
566 Columbus
362-0536

One of the best coffee houses in North Beach.

Peets Coffee
2156 Chestnut
931-8302

With locations literally all over the City, Peets has pretty much dominated the coffee scene, although the competition is keen.

Has Beans
2411 California at Fillmore
563-0226

This relaxed neighborhood spot for lattes and cappuccino has been around for ten years and is perfect for a weekend morning coffee.

Caffe Puccini
411 Columbus
989-7033

Another North Beach coffee haunt with accompanying opera.

Pasqua
388 Market
329-9491

High volume walk-up espresso bars located all over the City.

South Park Cafe
108 South Park
495-7275

Wonderful coffee bar at lunch bar. Restaurant is highly regarded and, as a coffee hangout, it is also one of the best.

BEST OF THE REST

BEST BAR-B-Q RIBS

MacArthur Park
607 Front Street
398-5700

BEST BURGERS

Hamburger Mary's
1582 Folsom
626-5767

Mo's
1322 Grant Avenue
788-3779
Juicy grilled hamburgers, excellent fries and shakes and even homemade mayo!

Original Joe's
144 Taylor
775-4877

BEST OYSTER BAR

Zuni Cafe
1658 Market
552-2522

BEST MARTINI

BIX
56 Gold Street
433-6300

BEST STEAKS

Harris' Restaurant
2100 Van Ness
673-1888

BEST BAGELS

Holey Bagel
3218 Fillmore
922-1955

BEST AFTERNOON TEA

Ritz Carlton Hotel
600 Stockton
296-7465
Tea served daily in the lounge from 2:30 to 5 PM. Reservations recommended.

Sheraton Palace Hotel
2 New Montgomery St.
392-8600
Afternoon tea and pastries are served in the elegant Garden Court from 2:30 to 5 PM. Reservations are suggested.

BEST ICE CREAM

Double Rainbow
407 Castro
621-2350
Several locations throughout the city.

Rory's Twisted Scoop
2015 Fillmore
346-3692

BEST CHOCOLATE CAKE

Just Desserts
3735 Buchanan St.
922-8675

DIAL A DINNER!

What's the latest trend in eating out? Ordering in!! There are two ways to go with this time-saving, labor-saving, sanity-saving approach to eating. One offers home-cooked meals delivered to your doorstep and the other delivers courses you order from designated restaurant menus. For Bay Area residents, living life in the fast lane and often juggling careers and families, this is the greatest invention since cellophane.

"When my mother had to get dinner for eight, she'd just make enough for sixteen and only serve half."
–Gracie Allen

Delectable Delights
753-2944

Prepared to order dishes, all organic and garden fresh, and delivered directly to your door. Perfect for small dinner parties as well.

Jessie et Laurent
485-1122

Weekly menus of eight or nine dishes including several entrees, one soup and a child's meal. There is a minimum order for these delicious home-cooked meals, but no delivery charge.

Waiters on Wheels
252-1470

Choose from about sixty restaurant menus with delivery daily. Nominal delivery charge and $10 minimum order per restaurant.

WHEN ORDERING

A good rule of thumb when dialing a dinner is to try and order items which will "travel well" or which taste good re-heated. Experts claim simple foods travel best- meat loaf, stews or casseroles, hearty soups and sturdy pastas.

FOOD EMPORIUMS

There is wonderful food shopping to be done in the San Francisco Bay Area. With our temperate climate, our proximity to the agriculturally rich Sacramento Valley and our fresh-from-the-Bay seafood, we can enjoy a year-round bounty of the choicest and most succulent meat, fish and produce. Combine that with an amazing culinary community who insists upon the very best of ingredients from its vendors and suppliers, and you have "Foodie Heaven" for professional cooks and the rest of us hackers!

I grew up thinking that vegetables came in little sealed cartons or else they were frozen. My children take stalks of baby carrots, seedless satsumas, fresh basil and buffalo mozzarella for granted. They may not like it, but they know about it!

MEAT FISH AND POULTRY MARKETS

La Rocca Oyster Bar & Fresh Fish
3519 California (Laurel Village)
387-4100

La Rocca's fish couldn't be fresher and there is a bustling restaurant facility too. Prices are high, but so is the quality.

Swan Oyster Depot
1517 Polk
673-2757 or 673-1101

One of the oldest fish stores in the City. Stop by and shop or enjoy a crab cocktail or a platter of oysters in its busy restaurant on Polk.

Antonelli Meat and Poultry
Cal Mart-3585 California
752-7413

Antonelli's has expanded its space at Cal Mart and will also feature fresh meats as well as fish and fowl.

Bryan's Meats
3473 California
752-3430

Bryan's has moved out of Cal Mart and opened a new shop in Laurel Village, specializing in the same friendly service, top-grade cuts of meat, cooked entrees to go, take-out salads and pasta, and Graffeo coffee.

"I have often noticed that when chickens quit quarreling over their food they often find that there is enough for all of them. I wonder if it might not be the same with the human race."

–Don Marquis

BARGAIN GOURMET FOODS

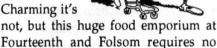

Food 4 Less
1880 Folsom
558-9137

Charming it's not, but this huge food emporium at Fourteenth and Folsom requires no membership, is open 24-hours a day. The savings are outrageous!

Lucca Ravioli
1100 Valencia
647-5581

For sixty-seven years, Lucca has been making quality ravioli. All preparation and distribution is done by the family and in their storefront can be found wonderful values in ravioli and other Italian delicacies.

LOVELY LAUREL VILLAGE

*While you check out **Cal Mart**, don't disregard its arch-competitor at the other end of the street, **Laurel Market**, which has its own loyal following and certainly gives Cal Mart a run for its money. There are some pretty wonderful shops in Laurel Village as well including: **Young Man's Fancy**, the consummate little boys and mens shop for the last few decades at 3527 California, **Judith Ets Hokin**, the complete kitchen shop and cooking school at 3525 California, **Kids Gap** and **Gap Baby** for outfitting your active youngster, and **Standard Five and Dime**, one of the last great five and dime stores around at 3545 California.*

Country Cheese
415 Divisadero
621-8130

Would you believe this popular cheese emporium sells more than three tons of cheese every month? Because they sell in bulk, tremendous savings can be passed on to its customers.

SUPERMARKETS

Marina Safeway
15 Marina Blvd.
563-4946

With some of the best views in the City, this Safeway offers a wide variety of foodstuffs including a bakery, deli, fish and meat department and floral and wine section. Easy parking and open 24 hours a day, seven days a week.

Cal Mart
3585 California
751-3516

This has always been a personal favorite. Not your typical supermarket. You'll find the produce is always fresh and gleaming, the meat and poultry counters conveniently located nearby, the cut flowers colorful and moderately-priced, and best of all, Cal Mart delivers!

Grand Central Grocery
2435 California
567-4902

Good all-round grocery store with well-run produce, meat and fish departments. Opens on Sunday morning at 8 AM.

CHEESE STORES

24th Street Cheese Store
3893 24th Street
821-6658

One of the oldest and most highly-regarded cheese stores in the City, this retail shop specializes in offering a wide variety of cheeses and also sells pate, wine and gourmet food.

> *"Cheese: Milk's leap towards immortality."*
> *–Anonymous*

Creighton's Fine Foods
673 Portola
753-0750

With over 130 varieties of cheese, Creighton's is worth getting over to Portola to investigate. There are also wonderful cheese classes offered on every type of cheese known.

HEALTH FOOD

Real Foods
1234 Sutter (and other locations)
474-8488

Offers fresh fish, meat and deli counter, wide range of organic produce, health food and a full-service grocery store which emphasizes healthy organic fare.

Real Food Deli
2164 Polk   1023 Stanyan
775-2805   **564-1117**

This popular health food store has a full deli, take-out service as well as a place to sit and eat on the premises. Party platters can be ordered.

Rainbow Grocery
1899 Mission at 15th Street
863-0620

All-natural foods, vitamins and cruelty-free skincare products are offered in this collectively-run store on Mission. Customers are encouraged to bring their own containers for purchases, so as to be environmentally-friendly. No meats or liquor sold here.

FRUIT AND PRODUCE

The best way to buy fruit and produce, although granted it's not the quickest or easiest, is to shop the local markets of Chinatown or 22nd and Irving on "the other side of the Park". Not only will prices be cheaper and the produce fresher, it's an experience to savor when your fast-track existence permits.

MARIN FARMER'S MARKET

For the ultimate produce-buying experience, head up to Marin County on a Thursday morning to sample the extraordinary **Farmers Market!** *It is filled with local growers who are selling everything from fruit and produce to flowers and fresh breads. The Farmer's Market is located in the Marin Civic Center, another must-see. Designed by Frank Lloyd Wright, who never lived to see the project completed, the Civic Center is an amazing complex of blue-domed buildings rising out of the surrounding Marin hillside. Civic Center Drive off San Pablo Rd.*
456-3276

GOURMET DELIS AND PREPARED FOODS TO GO

Molinari's
373 Columbus
421-2337

An old-time North Beach Italian deli with a full line of home-made sausages (Rainbow Grocery would shudder!), cheeses generous deli sandwiches to go. They also sell pasta, sauces, wines and vinegars. Take out only.

Vivande
2125 Fillmore
346-4430

Up-scale Italian gourmet take-out (or eat there) deli, with fabulous pastas and a full-service catering department. You can purchase gift baskets filled with delicacies, purchase Italian wines or sample a wide variety of cheeses. The space is also available for private parties in the evening.

Lucca Delicatessen
2120 Chestnut
921-7873

Another great old Italian deli, this one a favorite of the Chestnut Street crowd, with its fresh pasta, as well as prepared pastas and sauces, fresh roasted chickens and turkeys.

Shenson's
5120 Geary
751-4699

Out in the Avenues, Shenson's is the deli of choice for kosher-style deli meats, sandwiches, home-cured dill pickles, home-made latkes and soups. There is space to eat there or take out. Party trays are also available.

Sweet Max's
Deli & Bakery
1 California Street
781-6297
235 Montgomery St.
398-6297

Max's has pretty much saturated the Bay Area (check out Max's in the Stanford Shopping Center!) and the above locations cover the Financial District. Specializing in deli sandwiches, salads and baked goods to eat there or take out.

Haig's Delicatessen
642 Clement
752-6283

A prime example of the diversity of delis in the City. This delightful little shop on Clement Street makes you feel you have stepped into an Arab bazaar which offers you a tantalizing variety of Middle Eastern delicacies. There are small tables at which you can sit and sample humus, techina, dolmas and fresh pastries in crisp phyllo dough.

The Marketplace
at Macy's Cellar
Macy's Union Square
396-4767

The entire bottom floor of Macy's is one vast, beautifully presented gourmet extravaganza of foodstuffs. You can indulge your every food fantasy. There is an espresso/cappuccino bar and a cafe to rest in after a frantic day of shopping.

> *Sample a bowl of delicious French onion soup and sourdough bread across the street at* **The Plum Express**, *downstairs in the Macy's Mens Store. This soup, salad and sandwich bar is the perfect answer to a quick eat in Union Square.*

WINE SHOPS

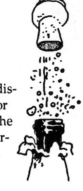

Mr. Liquor
250 Taraval
731-6222

Offers wide variety of discounted wine and liquor with free deliveries in the City with minimum purchase. Closed Sundays.

John Walker & Co.
175 Sutter
986-2707

Located in the heart of the Financial District, John Walker offers world-wide shipping facility (and gift wraps!). Will do wine cellar appraisals. Has wine storage, charge accounts and delivery service for customers.

The Wine Shop
2175 Chestnut
567-4725

A local favorite of the Marina and Chestnut Street crowd for 25 years, this shop offers wine consultation, party planning, a variety of fine champagnes and are even caviar specialists. Just your average everyday wine shop!

"Chardonnay is a red wine masquerading as a white, and Pinot Noir is a white wine masquerading as a red."

—Andre Tchelistcheff

"Burgundy makes you think of silly things: Bordeaux makes you talk about them and Champagne makes you do them."

—Brillat-Savarin

D & M Wine and Liquor Co.
Sacramento & Fillmore
346-1325

This highly-recommended wine shop in the Presidio Heights area sells estate bottled wine and has a large selection of specially discounted champagnes. Also serve as wine consultants.

Cost Plus Wine Shop
2598 Taylor
928-2030

In the Fisherman's Wharf area can be found some of the best bargains in wine, as well as one of the most comprehensive selections of California's premium wine. Low prices and excellent service.

Pacific Wine Company
124 Spear Street
896-5200

This 6000 square foot brick building houses a large selection of boutique California and European wines. There is a tasting bar and world-wide shipping. Closed Sundays.

BAKERIES

Fantasia
3465 California
752-0825

An old-time San Francisco favorite with mouth-watering pastries.

Viennese Cake Box
255 Winston
731-2500
1200 Irving
664-4101

Famous for creating wonderful birthday cakes for kids.

Just Desserts
3735 Buchanan
922-8675

Not only a scrumptious bakery, but also the perfect place for a cup of coffee and a huge slice of carrot cake after a movie!

Tassajara Bread Bakery
1000 Cole St.
664-8947
also in **Greens Restaurant**
Fort Mason, Bldg. A
771-6330

Some of the best homemade bread in the City.

"How long does getting thin take?" Pooh asked anxiously."
–Winnie the Pooh
A.A. Milne

Il Fornaio
1265 Battery, Levi Plaza
986-0646
2298 Union
563-0746

Wonderful Italian pastries and breads available at the take-out counter of this beautiful restaurant.

Bittersweet
23 Alta, SF
921-8728

A delicious work of art individually designed and hand-crafted to the client's wishes. They concentrate on special-order wedding cakes and special celebration cakes. Bittersweet creations not only look terrific... they taste terrific!

WORLD'S GREATEST NEW YORK CHEESECAKE

Once upon a time there was an Armani-clad, Park Avenue with-a-second-home-in-the-Hamptons socialite who had a recipe for perhaps the world's best cheesecake. She took great delight in not sharing this recipe with anyone. Friends begged for it and total strangers offered riches beyond her wildest dreams, in hopes of securing the source of this amazing cheesecake. But she smugly kept it to herself. One day she committed a tiny little indiscretion at the Carlyle Hotel. Which happened to catch the attention of one of the legion of scorned cheesecake-maker wannabe's. She was caught "en flagrante" and a deal was struck—a vow of silence (although it hurt, it hurt) for the treasured recipe, which quickly spread through Manhattan, into the borough of Queens, out to Long Island and eventually worked its way to San Francisco. True story.

World's Greatest New York Cheesecake

18 oz. good quality cream cheese
3/4 cup sugar
3 eggs
1 tsp vanilla
1 Tbsp. lemon juice
1 pint sour cream
pinch of salt

- Beat cream cheese in electric mixmaster for half hour.
- Add sugar, eggs (one at a time, lightly beaten first), salt, vanilla, lemon juice and sour cream. Not necessary to stop mixmaster.
- Pour ingredients into 9" springform pan lined with graham cracker crust.
- Bake 350 degrees for 35 minutes. When done, turn off oven with door open for an hour.
- Decorate top with halved fresh strawberries and refrigerate.
- Share this recipe with a friend. You just never know...

Graham Cracker Crust for W.G.N.Y.C

2 Cups ground graham crackers
(or ground chocolate wafers as an alternative)
1/4 Cup softened butter
3-4 Tbsp. brown sugar
2 Tbsp cinnamon

- Combine graham cracker or chocolate wafer crumbs with sugar and cinnamon in springform pan.
- Add butter and mash with hands so that ingredients become "packed" against sides and bottom of pan. Mold evenly all over pan.

That's Entertainment!

From Special Events to San Francisco night life; from the Performing Arts to the thriving Fine Arts scene, this chapter only begins to scratch the surface of exciting entertainment in the City.

A SPECIAL EVENT

The following sources should help make entertaining a less daunting and far more enjoyable undertaking.

CATERERS

Betty Zlatchen Catering
641-8599

An excellent catering service which prides itself on a thorough and professional approach to parties and special events. Highly imaginative and carefully rendered menus.

By Design
453-2250

This enthusiastic young group creates beautifully prepared meals for cocktail parties, small dinners or large events. The price is reasonable and the final effect is dynamic.

Delicious!
453-3710

Jan Goldberg oversees some wonderful catered events assisted by an enthusiastic and well-organized staff. Her menus are bountiful and beautifully prepared. Jan is a pleasure to work with.

Delectible Delights
753-2944

And now for something completely different. The charming couple who run this delicious catering service offer a menu of international cuisine specializing in all fresh, all organic ingredients. Prepared foods to order and delivered to your door, this is the answer to making a small dinner party a piece of cake!

Paula Le Duc
(510) 547-7825

This is the hottest high-end caterer going. Paula and her staff prepare hot food on site and are well-known for fabulous presentation. There is an emphasis on California cuisine with an ethnic influence, presented in an unbelievably creative style. Food fits the event and the presentation matches the decor of the location. Whether it is a contemporary setting in the City or a rustic ranch in Napa, the food will replicate the decor.

➤ *"Paula Le Duc Allez" provides food to go in architectural designed boxes for corporate or social events, meetings or spontaneous outdoor luncheons. Again, presentation is paramount.*

"The hostess must be like the duck – calm and unruffled on the surface, and paddling like hell underneath."

–Anonymous

Celebrations
340 Presidio
885-2117

For one-stop party shopping, consider Celebrations on Presidio, off Sacramento. Wonderful "instant" printed invitations, balloons, party accessories. A perfect resource for unique party bags and favors. Parking around here is tough, but what else is new?

PARTY PLANNERS

Cheryl Simons Presents...
461-5575

From concept to invitation to spectacular end result, Cheryl Simons is a wonderful event coordinator, with a particular expertise in creating dramatic and imaginative centerpieces. Her "Table Toppers" can be designed for your own theme or you can rent existing centerpieces. Very dynamic and creative.

RSVP
854-6399

Owner Susie Somers will meet with you for a personalized consultation on how you can plan and implement your event from soup to nuts. Under her direction, you will be guided to all the sources which will make the party unique to your special needs. She also creates imaginative invitations designed to your specifications.

Folio
1104 Magnolia
Larkspur
461-0120

Folio is not only the name of one of the hottest event-planning teams in the area, but is also the elegant new site for their shop as well. Filled with unique gifts, personalized invitations and on-site calligraphy, you can also make an appointment for event planning. Owners Judy Sobel and Marcia Rubenstein offer a creative and professional approach to orchestrating that Perfect Event.

PARTY SITES

Spectrum Gallery, A Space for Art & Events
511 Harrison at First
495-1111

Spectrum is a truly unique facility. Designed and built by an event professional, this spacious fine art gallery provides spectacular city views and a state-of-the-art lighting and sound system. There is a stage and dance floor as well as a 1,200' caterer's area. The museum-quality paintings and sculpture produce an elegant and dramatic environment for your event.

Delancey Street
600 Embarcadero
512-5179

Believe it or not, Delancey Street is one of the most popular spots for parties these days. Located in a new complex on the Embarcadero, the Town Hall offers the perfect space for parties for up to four hundred people, with hardwood floors, fireplace, high ceilings and plenty of room to dance. Bring in your own caterer or work with the in-house staff.

Yank Sing
425 Battery
362-4799

Create your own Dim Sum feast in your home, at the site of your choice or take over Yank Sing. It's your call. And you can count on the food being plentiful and delicious, right down to the last fortune cookie.

The Hamlin Mansion
2120 Broadway
331-0544

Event planners called "Parties, Parties, Parties" is the management company for the Hamlin Mansion and all arrangements must be handled through this organization which specializes in all kinds of events. The Italian Baroque mansion was constructed in 1901 by James Flood and is a stately three-story structure with dramatic panoramic views out over the Bay. For intimate dinners or sit-down events up to 250 people, this is one of the most beautiful sites in the City.

Chevy's
432-8060

Now let's head to South of the Border for a Mexican fiesta. Special areas for parties or order in fajitas and all the trimmings for your own celebration!

Hornblower Yachts
788-8866

How about a shipboard fete? Plan a party with all of San Francisco as a backdrop. Be advised, however, that those with queasy stomachs might not agree this is the perfect site for dining and dancing.

MUSIC

Derek Walters Productions
(510) 676-1448

An accomplished, versatile entertainer / DJ who uses an integrated format of sound and big-screen monitors placed throughout the site to create some pretty amazing special effects. Reasonably priced.

Star Tracks
592-5952

Miguel Guitos and his group are the premier interactive entertainers of the Nineties. Using the best of a big band sound as well as the best of the DJ-programmable music, Star Tracks offers "karaoke" as one of its highlights. Directly involving the guests who find themselves singing and performing like stars, Miguel strives to create an event where everyone is involved and having a great time, and he manages to always succeed!

STUDENT MUSICIANS

For wonderful background music, chamber music and small jazz ensembles at prices that can't be beaten, you may want to look into the job placement department of the San Francisco Conservatory of Music. The student musicians are often wonderfully talented and appreciative of work. Call 759-3458 for more information.

San Francisco Saxophone Quartet
587-3478

If you've ever lingered in front of Shreve's on Post Street to listen to this talented group, than you know you are in for something special if you book the Quartet for your party or event.

Royal Society Jazz Orchestra
(800) 371-7756

There are two ways to go with this marvelous group of authentic jazz musicians. There is the smaller group, The Royal Society Sextet, featuring six pieces and the full orchestra of ten pieces. A moderately priced group of professionals who pride themselves on playing the real thing – Swing and jazz from the twenties the way it would have sounded back then. Highly recommended.

VIDEO PHOTOGRAPHERS

Steve Johnson's VTI Video Productions
589-9729

This very talented team produces some extraordinarily memorable video productions for special events. With twelve years experience, VTI was one of the first to create a photographic montage of an event using professional broadcast cameras to tell a personalized story of the honoree. Prices are competitive.

Creative Video
(510) 790-0258

Another first class and well-regarded video photographer who specializes in parties, ceremonies and events.

PHOTOGRAPHERS

Bill Stockwell
491-4575

With thirty years experience, Bill Stockwell still manages to bring to each client a unique, fresh approach. He specializes in event photography and enjoys shooting in a spontaneous, fast-moving style to capture natural genuine emotions.

Elliot Holtzman
457-5447

One of the most accomplished and sought-after photographers in the Bay Area, but you pay handsomely. Specializes in both formal portraiture as well as shoots in more informal settings.

Suki Hill
388-9145

For a spontaneous style of photography often in black and white, Suki Hill is able to capture the essence of her subject. A delightful and talented photographer.

FLORISTS

Main Street Floral Gardens
485-2996

Although based in Marin, this top-rate florist is highly regarded all over the Bay Area for unique and utterly beautiful floral arrangements. Main Street is tailored for special arrangements to be delivered or will work with you on planning the flowers for events.

Flowers Claire Marie
771-5118

Working by appointment, Claire Marie will create wonderful floral arrangements in a loose country style for events. Also provides arrangements for the home and will deliver.

Bloomers
2975 Washington
563-3266

Ask for Patric, the owner, who will assist you in coordinating all of your floral arrangements. Bloomers is consistently high in quality and design and also has a loyal walk-in trade in its shop of marvelous flowers and plants.

Hastings & Hastings
27 Miller Avenue, Mill Valley
381-1272

One of the loveliest shops in Mill Valley, offering a store-front filled with table-top designs, french linens and hand painted dinnerware. Floral arrangements have a signature gardeny-wildflower style. Will assist you with special events and weddings.

FRESH FLOWERS & PLANTS

For the best cut flowers going, San Franciscans head for Paul's Tunnel Flowers on 2139 Polk Street 755-6533. On some days you can see a line of Mercedes and Jags double-parked while the locals scurry into Paul's for a quick hit!

Another favorite? Cal Mart in Laurel Village, 751-3516, has some of the best buys going. The flowers and plants are always fresh. There is free delivery and the parking is decent.

USEFUL PARTY RESOURCES

BALLOONS

The Balloon Lady
1263 Howard
864-3737

One of the best and biggest sources for balloons in the City. Pick up a single balloon or order them by the thousand, as was the case for the Queen of England's visit! Arches, sculptures, tubes and twinkly lights, The Balloon Lady does it all!

CALLIGRAPHY

Sharon Silver
924-5179

Sharon Silver has a fabulous style of calligraphy which is out of the ordinary and well worth considering.

PARTY SUPPLIES

Fantastico
559 6th and Brannan
982-0680

Party supplies for all occasions. Will also do invitations, flower arrangements, bulk paper goods and offer an in-house consulting service.

THE FLOWER MART

Right next door to Fantastico is the wonderful San Francisco Flower Mart, a must-see. Only problem? You have to be in the trade to get in or make a purchase at most shops.

SERVING HELP

Monique & Michel
898-6901

The answer to your dinner party prayers! Extremely professional and charming, Monique not only helps serve, but would be delighted to bring in her own catered creations. Michel is the perfect bartender.

PARTY LINEN RENTALS

Party Prints
259-9707

A wonderful resource for a wide assortment of lovely table linens, when you are looking for something beyond the usual assortment of bland colors and fabrics found in most rental places.

VALET PARKING

Soiree
863-7385

This hot new valet parking group is young, enthusiastic, scrupulously careful and reasonable in price.

CAKES AND CANDY

Cake Work
863-4444

For that special one of a kind wedding cake or for any special event.

The Candy Jar
210 Grant
391-5508

For special events, owner Carla Stacho will go all out to help you create specially designed candy or truffles. For the ultimate chocolate treats, this is tops.

NIGHT LIFE

There __are__ pockets of bustling night life throughout the City. SoMa is always hopping, with a wide variety of restaurants and clubs still going strong after midnight. This is true of North Beach as well with its many bars and coffee houses. There are always places to dance the night away, savor a glass of champagne in a mile-high setting above the City, or catch a rising star at any of the hot comedy or jazz clubs around. You just have to know where.

CABARETS

The Great American Music Hall
859 O'Farrell at Polk
885-0750

Since 1972, this has been a popular place for music and comedy. With its ornate and fanciful facade, it enjoys the distinction of being located in a structure built from the rubble of the '06 Quake. Today it hosts some of the most well-known big-name entertainment around. Call for a schedule.

LATE NIGHT

Contrary to popular belief, San Francisco, unlike New York, is not the "City That Never Sleeps". At 11 PM, restaurants are often closing, streets are emptying and "sensible" San Franciscans have gone home to bed.

Plush Room, York Hotel
940 Sutter
885-2800

One of San Francisco's premier cabarets, offering live performances from nationally recognized entertainers. I saw the young(er) Michael Feinstein do one of his first concerts in the intimacy of the Plush Room's small, but well-designed nightclub atmosphere.

Bimbo's 365 Club
1025 Columbus
474-0365

Despite this frankly off-putting name, Bimbo's has been a fixture on the supper club scene since 1931. Special events and live entertainment are offered in this popular North Beach locale on a regular basis. Call for schedule.

DANCING THE NIGHT AWAY

Paradise Lounge
1501 Folsom
861-6906

Relaxed comfortable environment with easy accessible parking. This SoMa club has lots of music going on nightly til 3 AM.

Club DV8
540 Howard
957-1730

Stylish, well-known club with 2 large dance floors on separate levels.

DNA Lounge
375 11th Street (at Harrison)
626-1409

Featuring dancing to new wave rock, with a wide range of slick, hip live entertainment.

Club 1015
1015 Folsom (at 6th)
431-0700

Three levels of dance floors means this place is always hopping. Different music and ambience nightly. Check it out.

Oasis
11th Street at Folsom
621-8119

Offers dancing Fri & Sat in main room and Egyptian Room. Available for private parties as well.

Rockin' Robin's
1840 Haight at Stanyan
221-1960

Features dancing to 50's & 60's music in vintage setting.

Slim's
333 11th St.
between Folsom and Harrison
621-3330

Huey Lewis is one of the partners in this happening night spot in SoMa. Live bands and special guest artists offer a wide variety of musical entertainment. The action starts at 9 PM most evenings. Call for schedule of upcoming gigs.

JAZZ ON TAP

These spots offer a wonderful atmosphere to relax and unwind after a busy day. They may not have the frenetic pace or non-stop action of a SoMa night club, but they do have an easy, sophisticated charm that many San Franciscans find attractive.

Bix
56 Gold Street (& Montgomery)
433-6300

This 40's style supper club is one of the most elegant spots around for live jazz nightly, full bar, and daily menu.

Cafe Bastille
22 Belden Place
986-5673

Great jazz is offered downstairs Thurs. through Sat. nights. A charmer of a coffee house bistro by day in a delightful location in the heart of the City.

Cafe Du Nord
2170 Market
861-5016

This intimate french bar and cafe also features wonderful jazz. Described as "walking into a James Dean movie".

Cafe Claude
7 Claude Lane
392-3505

Located off Bush Street, in the Financial District, this popular cafe is open nightly as well as in the mornings. Closed midday. Parties of 4 or more can make reservations. Enjoy coffee, wine tastings and french bistro fare in a delightful atmosphere. Tues through Fri, you can enjoy live jazz.

JAZZ IN THE EAST BAY

You may want to check out the thriving jazz scene in the East Bay. There are those who would strongly protest Gertrude Stein's infamous words about Oakland, "There is no there there"!

Kimball's East
5800 Shellmound
Emeryville
(510) 658-2555
One of the Bay Area's best jazz clubs with a wide-ranging menu of wonderful food offered Wed. through Sun.

Yoshi's
6030 Claremont Avenue
Oakland
(510) 652-9200
In addition to good Japanese cooking, there is also live jazz, singing and occasional dancing.

Kimball's
300 Grove Street (at Franklin)
861-5555

In the heart of the Civic Center, this has always been one of the hottest and most prevailingly popular jazz clubs in town. Open again for business in '93, Kimballs almost left the jazz scene, to the consternation of its enthusiastic followers.

Cava 555
555 Second Street
543-2282

Stylish bar, smart crowd and live jazz with a wonderful menu as well.

Lascaux
248 Sutter
391-1555

An intimate setting in the Union Square area offering Mediterranean-style cooking and some pretty terrific jazz served up Wed. through Sat. Lunch served daily.

Jazz at Pearls
256 Columbus
291-8255

Acoustic jazz nightly with some great local talent. Hearty appetizers are available, including the best babyback ribs going. Full bar as well. Opens at 4 PM through 2AM. Music starts happening at 9 PM.

Paragon
3251 Scott (at Greenwich)
922-2456

Bar & restaurant with American bistro-type food. Piano music during dinner. Mon through Wed you'll find jazz, blues and R&B starting at 9:30 PM.

SPORTS BARS

This is the place to be during any of the big televised sporting events. Whether it's a standard 49er's game (is there such a thing?) or the finals of Wimbledon or the America's Cup, sports bars are an easy place to hang out in during a big game on an otherwise lonely Sunday afternoon. Here are a few of the City's most popular spots.

The Bus Stop
1901 Union
567-6905

15 TVs, satellite hookup, 2 pool tables, 5 pinball machines. Wow! During the football season there could be 4 games going at once! Located on one of the best action-packed streets in the City. Full bar, hearty appetizers, but feel free to bring your own. Open year round.

Pat O'Shea's Mad Hatter
3848 Geary (at 3rd Ave)
752-3148

This local neighborhood bar serves a great Sunday brunch as well as lunch and dinner daily. Comes complete with satellite dish and eleven TVs for round the clock sports viewing.

Pierce Street Annex
3138 Fillmore
567-1400

This hopping singles hangout also caters to sports enthusiasts with its two big screen TVs and five monitors for the ultimate viewing experience.

Washington Square Bar & Grill
1707 Powell (in Washington Square)
982-8123

The historic "Wash Bag" is still a popular eating and drinking spot for old-timers, locals, tourists and the younger crowd as well. Lunch and dinner daily, brunch on Sunday with large screen TV in bar area.

Chestnut Street Grill
2231 Chestnut
922-5558

Brunches on Sat and Sun, lunch and dinner throughout the week and for sports fans, 2 TVs on a satellite dish.

The Boathouse
1 Harding Road on Lake Merced
681-2727

The perfect place for a drink and some televised sports action after a round of golf at Harding Golf Course! This well-known spot "on the other side of the park" serves up a great Sunday brunch along with 2 big-screen TVs and 12 monitors.

THE ULTIMATE ENTERTAINMENT

Beach Blanket Babylon
678 Green Street
421-4222

*"Beach Blanket Babylon" is the City's longest-running musical comedy review. See it once, and then like the natives, see it again and again. Located in the historic Club Fugazi in North Beach, you will want to sample any of the great Italian restaurants in the area including the hilarious **Caffe Sport** at 574 Green Street. One last thought. Steve Silver, creator and founder of BBB recently opened Cyril's in the basement of Club Fugazi. Named in memory of loyal patron and San Franciscan extraordinaire, Cyril Magnin, Cyril's features lively cabaret acts.*

*"Dying is easy.
Comedy is difficult."*
*–Actor Edmond Gwenn
on his deathbed*

COMEDY CLUBS

Cobb's Comedy Corner
2069 Chestnut at Fillmore
928-4320

Some of the best local comedy around on weekends. Amateur night is held during the week.

Holy City Zoo
408 Clement
386-4242

The City's oldest comedy club, offering live comedy as well as comedy workshops in this busy and eclectic SF neighborhood.

The Punch Line
444A Battery Street
397-7573

Featuring well-known entertainers, improv acts and "open mike" night at this popular comedy club, restaurant and bar, adjacent Embarcadero One. Shows throughout the week.

PERFORMING ARTS

Even in the heady, rollicking days of the gold rush, San Francisco loved its performing arts. At least fifteen legitimate theatres flourished in the 1850's amidst the rowdy saloons of the Barbary Coast. As the town flourished under the steady discovery of gold "in them thar hills", so too did the concert halls become increasingly ornate as the public clamored for more and more entertainment. Believe it or not, enthusiastic audiences threw gold nuggets at the feet of delighted performers!

Life in the performing arts has quieted down a bit since those early days, but San Franciscans are no less enthusiastic or supportive of their opera and ballet, theatre and symphony. There's still gold to be found on these stages...

THEATRE

Magic Theatre
Fort Mason
441-8822

This innovative theatre does straight dramatic works, many of which are new and are premiering at the Magic. It enjoys an illustrious reputation and many of its productions which originated here have received national attention. Sam Shepard was a playwright-in-residence and wrote and produced a number of his critically acclaimed works under the auspices of this fine theatre company.

A.C.T.
American Conservatory Theatre
749-2ACT

Artistic director, Carey Perloff, has promised and produced a fabulous season that is "vivid and visceral, outrageous and hilarious". ACT has enjoyed an illustrious history in San Francisco and continues this tradition in its 26th season. Call for information and season ticket sales.

ACT performs in the following theatres throughout its repertory season:

Stage Door Theatre
420 Mason at Geary

Marine's Memorial Theatre
609 Sutter

Orpheum Theatre
1192 Market

Still impacted by the '89 Quake, the original home of ACT on Geary remains closed and barred for costly earthquake-proofing, a lingering reminder of how close we live to the edge.

"BEST OF BROADWAY"
474-3800

Granted, Broadway shows don't head immediately for San Francisco once they hit the road. "The "Phantom of the Opera" has arrived at last- only seven years after it opened in London and almost six years after its Broadway premiere. But when we do get shows, they are first-rate productions with well-known performers.

Curran Theatre
445 Geary
Located in the heart of Union Square, the Curran is extremely convenient for theatre-goers, with ample parking garages and fine restaurants nearby.

Golden Gate Theatre
6th and Market at Golden Gate Ave.
One of the Grand Dames of concert halls which has been lovingly refurbished. Parking can sometimes be a challenge.

Orpheum Theatre
1192 Market
Another carefully restored architectural wonder which highlights many of the Best of Broadway shows. Parking is tough around here and so is the neighborhood. Use street smarts at night.

Theatre on the Square
450 Post
433-9500

This building was originally an Elks ballroom and was built in 1923 by the architect who designed the Orpheum Theatre. In 1981, it was bought by Jonathan Reinis and made into a theatre with original fixtures and fittings to resemble the thirties. A wide theatre, with an unusual thrust stage, it is well-suited to the many Broadway and off-Broadway productions it hosts throughout the year.

Young Performer's Theatre
Building C Fort Mason
at Marina Blvd & Buchanan
346-5550

Children's classics, adaptations and new works are performed for the whole family. Young actors work side by side with professionals to create magical productions. Weekend performances only.

George Coats
Performance Works
110 McAllister
863-8520

Internationally recognized avant garde performance ensemble specializing in imaginative and creative special effects.

THEATRE AL FRESCO

There is some pretty wonderful free music and theatre offered outdoors in the summer in San Francisco. Be sure and try the following:

San Francisco Mime Troupe
Various locations around the City
285-1717

This Tony-award winning troupe celebrates its thirtieth season with lively, original productions filled with song, dance and political jabs. Pack a picnic lunch, invite a friend, and enjoy this pleasure in the park. Call for complete schedule of performances and locations.

Stern Grove
Midsummer Music Festival
Sigmund Stern Grove
19th Avenue and Sloat
252-6252

The oldest continuous free midsummer music festival in the country, set in a natural amphitheater of redwoods and eucalyptus. Pack a lunch, arrive early, DRESS WARMLY and plan on thoroughly enjoying yourself. That was Rosalie Stern's intent when she bequeathed the land to the City of San Francisco for free concerts to be held there.

EVENTS LISTING

Check the "pink section" of the Sunday Chronicle/Examiner for upcoming events. I always hang on to mine from week to week because it is an excellent reference for all entertainment throughout the Bay Area.

Opera in the Park
Sharon Meadows
Golden Gate Park
861-4008

This free concert, normally in September, is sponsored by the San Francisco Examiner. Call for exact date and time of performance.

Summer Festival
of Performing Arts
Music Concourse, Golden Gate Park
474-3914

A three month concert series presenting a variety of music and dance for all ages from August through September. Held free to an appreciative public on Thursdays and Saturdays.

GOLDEN GATE PARK BAND

Music Concourse, Golden Gate Park
666-7107

Since 1882, the Golden Gate Park Band has performed regularly in the park. Pack a picnic, find a seat and join the enthusiastic crowd who comes out on Sunday afternoons at 1 PM to applaud this worthy group of musicians.

FREE SHAKESPEARE IN THE PARK

Golden Gate Park
666-2222

Find a shady spot (or a warm one, depending on the fog that day!) and settle in for something truly special. "A crust of bread, a jug of wine"... and Shakespeare in the Park. Call for more information.

MUSIC

San Francisco Opera
War Memorial Opera Hall
Van Ness and Grove
864-3330

The venerable SF Opera celebrated its seventieth season in 1993 and is a must among old-time San Franciscans and opera buffs anywhere. Tickets are prohibitively expensive and hard to come by, but to live in San Francisco is to attend the Opera at least once before you die.

San Francisco Blues Festival
Great Meadows, Fort Mason
762-BASS

The oldest blues festival in the country is held at the Great Meadows in Fort Mason with some of the finest talent coming together to make it happen.

▶ *There is a **free concert** to kick off the Blues Festival each **September** in Justin Herman Plaza in Embarcadero Four. Call for exact date of concert.*

San Francisco Performances
Herbst Theatre
War Memorial Veterans Building
Van Ness at McAllister
398-6449

More than thirty programs in chamber music, recitals, dance and jazz are performed in the intimate, gem-like setting of Herbst Theatre. You may also wish to attend the Midsummer Mozart Festival, a delightful taste of Mozart, including both orchestra and chamber music, held each summer in Herbst Theater. Call **392-4400** for more information.

San Francisco Symphony
Davies Hall
Van Ness & Grove (Civic Center)
864-6000

A ten million dollar acoustical modification project has finally transformed Davies Hall into one of the finest concert halls in the country. Check with the Symphony Box Office for complete programs and ticket availability.

San Francisco Symphony Pops
Civic Auditorium, 99 Grove Street
554-9671

Sponsored by the SF Arts Commission, the Pops has evolved into a tradition in which the SF Symphony joins with guest artists for a series of summer concerts.

FREE NOONTIME CONCERTS

Old St. Mary's Church
660 California in Chinatown
255-9410
A charming musical interlude set in this quaint and intimate sanctuary makes for a perfect mid-day break. On nice days, enjoy a picnic lunch across the street in St. Mary's Park.

Brown Bag Opera Concerts
One Bush Street, One Market Plaza
565-6434
Bring your lunch and a friend to savor these hour-long concerts featuring the SF Opera Center's Adler Fellows performing operatic arias and ensembles. At 12:15 each Friday at Bush Street and each Wednesday at Market Plaza.

DANCE

San Francisco Ballet
War Memorial Opera House
Van Ness and Grove
861-5600
Box office 703-9400

The San Francisco Ballet is the oldest professional ballet company in the country and celebrated its sixtieth season in 1993. It was the very first company to perform both Swan Lake and the Nutcracker.The Ballet has performed several world premiers by internationally recognized choreographers. The regular repertory season runs from February to early May under the direction of Helgi Thomassen.

▶ *Included among its many "firsts" for the San Francisco Ballet is the magnificent **Ballet Building** at 455 Franklin, the first one of its kind to house the ballet school, practice areas for the existing troupe and administrative offices all under one roof. **Tours** of the **Performing Arts Center** are offered every Monday from 10 AM to 2:30 PM. Phone 552-8338 for details.*

STBS

Provides only day-of-performance tickets for selected music, dance and theater at half-price (cash sales only however). They also handle advance full-price tickets to many events through BASS. No reservations or phone orders accepted. Located on Stockton side of Union Square, noon to 7:30 PM. Closed Sun & Mon. Dial 433-STBS.

TICKET RESERVATIONS

The advantage of the following agencies is that although you have to go there, you can study the seating plan and visually pick out the best seats.

BASS/TM Tickets
(510) 762-2277

To order by phone is certainly easier, but you take whatever the computer determines is the "best seat" at that moment. Call for ticket information and reservations. Conveniently located at:

STUBS, Union Square

Supermail, Four Embarcadero Center

Tower Video, 2278 Market

The Wherehouse, 2083 Union at Webster

Tower Records, Bay at Columbus

BOX OFFICES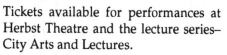

City Box Office
Sherman Clay & Co.
141 Kearny
392-4400

Tickets available for performances at Herbst Theatre and the lecture series– City Arts and Lectures.

Symphony Box Office
Davies Symphony Hall
Van Ness and Grove
431-5400

St. Francis Theatre and Sports Tickets
Westin St. Francis Hotel
Union Square
362-3500

FINE ARTS IN THE CITY

MUSEUMS

Asian Art Museum
The Avery Brundage Collection
Golden Gate Park
668-8921

When Avery Brundage selected San Francisco as the city to house his permanent collection of priceless Asian masterpieces, a specially constructed museum was constructed in 1966. The first floor houses the Chinese and Korean collections of more than a thousand magnificent examples of Asian art and the second floor contains works from India, Tibet, Nepal, Japan and Southeast Asia. First Wednesday and Saturday of month is free admission.

M.H. de Young
Memorial Museum
Golden Gate Park
750-3600

The City's most diverse art museum, containing twenty-two different galleries of American art ranging from the 17th century to contemporary exhibits. The museum also hosts a number of travelling exhibits throughout the year. Closed Mondays and Tuesdays. Admission first Wednesdays and Saturdays free. Call for additional information of schedules of special exhibits.

JUST THE TICKET

One admission charge will permit you to visit the Asian Art, the de Young and the Legion of Honor museums. Try to take advantage of the daily docent tours, they are informative and well-organized.

California Palace
of Legion
of Honor
Lincoln Park
750-3600

Museum closed until April of 1994 for renovation and seismic up-grading.

San Francisco Museum
of Modern Art
War Memorial Veterans Building
Van Ness Avenue & McAllister
252-4000

This is the only contemporary art museum in the City and it is busy planning to move into its dramatic new location, designed by famed Italian architect Mario Botta, near the Moscone Center in 1995. In the meantime, the museum boasts an excellent rotating permanent collection with special strengths in the area of photography as well as in abstract art, due to a major bequest by artist Clifford Still. There is an impressive schedule of visiting exhibits throughout the year as well. Docent tours are offered daily with a particular interest in making art fun and understandable for children.

▶ *You will definitely want to know about "Third Thursday at the Modern", a lively program which offers exhibition-related discussions, musical entertainment and light snacks on the third Thursday evening of every month. It's a great way to stay plugged into the art world and meet some pretty interesting people as well. Consider becoming a* **Friend of the Museum** *and take advantage of discount admission as well as special behind the scenes events.*

San Francisco Craft and Folk Art Museum
Building A, Fort Mason
775-0990

Elegant, beautifully-rendered exhibitions of contemporary crafts, traditional ethnic art and American folk art are on view at this space in Fort Mason. There is also a wonderful gift shop. Closed Mondays.

▷ *Speaking of crafts, be sure and mark your calendars in August for the Pacific States Craft Fair held in Fort Mason each summer. Fabulous designs in metal, textiles and jewelry are on display when over three hundred of the country's top craft artists gather for this lively annual fair. A must.*

ART GALLERIES

San Francisco is filled with wonderful art galleries, the most notable of which are still located around the Union Square area (although there is a thriving and exciting art scene South of Market). The following represent just a few of the most centrally located and highly regarded contemporary art galleries in the City.

The Allrich Gallery
251 Post Street
398-8896

Braunstein Gallery
250 Sutter Street
392-5532

Erika Meyerovich Gallery
231 Grant Avenue
421-9997

Gallery Paula Anglim
14 Geary Street
433-2710

Gumps Gallery
250 Post Street
982-1616

K. Kimpton Gallery
228 Grant Avenue
563-3846

Campbell Thiebaud Gallery
647 Chestnut Street
441-8680

John Berggruen Gallery
228 Grant Avenue
781-4629

Michael Dunev Fine Arts
533 Sutter Street
398-7300

Modernism
685 Market Street
571-0461

Pasquale Iannetti Art Galleries
522 Sutter Street
433-2771

Stephen Wirtz Gallery
49 Geary Street
433-6879

SF Museum of Modern Art Rental Gallery
Fort Mason
441-4777

It's A Small World After All

Raising children in an urban environment is a challenging endeavor. But when that environment is San Francisco, parenting also becomes an exciting adventure. If you have an infant, you will discover that it is not too  difficult to meet other new parents in support groups or at one of the many playgrounds scattered throughout the City. If you have active youngsters, there are some pretty terrific programs in sports, music, art or theatre. I hope the following chapter will help you to decide where to go, what to do and how to do it with kids in San Francisco.

NEW PARENTS SUPPORT GROUPS

 For new parents, there are several fine support groups to join which are geared towards parents and infants, toddlers and pre-schoolers.

Sunset Strollers/Small Change
1234 Ninth Avenue
566-1234

This informal group meets every Wednesday at 12:30 PM for a stroll in Golden Gate Park. A wonderful way to meet fellow parents and children. No strolling on wet or gloomy days!

FAMCAP
2266 Geary
202-3020

For members of Kaiser Permanente Health Plan, this service offers a number of excellent resources including pre-natal classes, post hospital visits by nurse practitioners and special sibling classes.

Parent's Place
3272 California Street
563-1041

Run by the Jewish Family and Children's Services, this organization offers excellent support groups and workshops for all parents and children from birth to six years of age. There is also a drop-in center for integrated play, a warm-line (931-WARM) for practical advice, information and resources, support groups for single moms and a special play group for dads and kids on Saturday mornings.

Natural Resources
4081-24th Street (Noe Valley)
550-2611

A pregnancy, childbirth and parenting resource center. There is a nominal membership fee which entitles you to use of extensive files and resource materials. Maternity clothes are for sale as well.

Partners & Babies
(formerly "Moms in the Morning")
346-BABY

California Pacific Medical Center sponsors special programs on both campuses for new parents and their babies age 0-6 months. There are selected topics, and often guest speakers, at each one-and-a-half hour meeting. Groups are informal and meet every week on a drop-in basis. Staffed by knowledgeable and enthusiastic nurses, this is a wonderful, reasonably-priced support group for moms or dads. There is also an community resource library in the hospital filled with information on parenting.

SF City College
Parent Education Programs
561-1921

There are a number of terrific parent-child observation and infant development classes under the auspices of City College. One of my favorites is held in St. Mary's Church at the corner of Union and Steiner. It is a great chance to meet other parents and to watch your baby in action in a group setting. Held in a cheerful room filled with play structures, educational toys and blocks, the class is supervised by a facilitator. It is tuition-free, although parents are urged to make a contribution at some level to this excellent resource group.

Gymboree
752-0634

Creative movement and developmental play classes for children ages three months to five years. Birthday parties are also available for infants and toddlers. Classes are held mornings, afternoons and evenings at two locations- M-Th at 30th and Geary, Wed-Sat in Daly City. Call for information.

CHILD-PROOFING

For parents who don't have the time to investigate every child-proof device on the shelves, there is a wonderful mail-order catalog called Perfectly Safe, which lists almost fifty pages of safety devices and products. You can also order the catalogue's All-In-One Home Safety Kit which offers a range of essentials as well as a prodigious book of child-proofing tips. To order the catalog, call (800) 837-5437.

SCHOOLS

San Francisco, unfortunately like many urban environments, suffers a dearth of top-quality public school education. Many families have considered private education for their children. Listed below are a range of private schools which represent the very best San Francisco has to offer. There will be recommendations for alternative public schools listed throughout this chapter whenever applicable.

PRE-SCHOOLS

The Little School
2507 Pine
567-0430

A developmentally-based program located in a large three-room building with a courtyard for outdoor play. Children are grouped according to age and attend on specific days. There is an optional hot lunch program and daycare is offered M/W/F. There is a long waiting list, so try to sign up at birth and do your touring and interviewing way ahead of time.

Calvary Presbyterian Church Nursery School
Jackson & Fillmore
346-4715

Half-day programs available in the mornings for ages three to five. This is a play-based curriculum with a roof-top playground. Multi-cultural in its mix of students. There is a small summer program available, separate from the school year. Long waiting list with preference given to siblings, legacies and church members.

St. Lukes
1755 Clay
474-9489

St. Lukes offers a five-day program of either a morning or afternoon session. Children aged two years, nine months attend morning session and older children attend afternoon. There is no day-care and the school is closed in the summer. This is an academically-oriented program combined with play time on a roof-top playground. There are fifty students (to five teachers) in each session. Parents are urged to register at birth, but there are some slots available for newcomers.

Children's Place
1868 Greenwich
931-7510

This is a small, non-academic program with fifteen children per session. There are two teachers with occasional dance and music specialists. You can sign up for any of the five days you wish your child to attend. There are morning classes only, as well as a lunch program. A five-week summer session is available.

SF Jewish Community Center Nursery School
3200 California
346-6040

The JCC offers four distinct programs on three separate sites which encourage young children to expand their social, physical and intellectual horizons and to feel good about their accomplishments and themselves. The Early Childhood Program offers pre-school, daycare, summer camp and pre-Kindergarten. All classes are in small groups with an excellent staff overseeing activities. There is an emphasis on Jewish culture, although the school is so popular, there is a long waiting list among Jewish and non-Jewish families. Siblings have preferential treatment, but other factors are considered.

Lone Mountain Children's Center
1738-9th Avenue
681-8250

In existence for eighteen years, Lone Mountain offers programs for children ages 2 years, 9 months to Pre-Kindergarten in the afternoon session. This is a developmental program with 31 children and three teachers and one aide. Special resource assistants are brought in for science and art. There is no extended daycare. Full playground facility on campus.

Park Presidio Montessori
788-8th Avenue
751-2790

An academically-based program with trained specialists in the Montessori approach to learning. The building itself was designed specifically for use as a Montessori school. The school has a unique advantage of its proximity to Golden Gate Park. Park facilities are a wonderful source of play and learning experiences for the kids.

One Fifty Parker
150 Parker
221-0294

Since 1954, Director Doris Welsh has presided over this developmentally-based pre-school in the Jordan Park area of the City. For children 2 years, nine months to Pre-K, the program encourages the individual child and offers a co-ed, multi-ethnic and diverse program. Highly-qualified and committed teaching staff.

EMERGENCY RESOURCES

Animal Bite Reporting
SF Department of Health
554-2840

SF Poison Control
1 (800) 523-2222
(24-hour hotline)

PRIMARY SCHOOLS

Katherine Delmar Burke School
7070 California
751-0177

A private K-8 school for girls. Uniforms are required, and always have been. The uniqueness of this school is its beautiful, country campus setting in the heart of the City. This includes a soccer field, full gym and tennis courts, all of which enhance its fine PE program. French and Spanish offered daily in upper grades as well as music, art and drama for all grades. There is a hot lunch program, day care and an after-school sports program as well as fairly small student-teacher ratio. There are also special education teachers on staff.

Town School
2750 Jackson
921-3747

This all-boys K-8 school in Pacific Heights has an excellent and energized staff and committed parent community. There is a full gym and rooftop play area. Computers are taught in all grades and language is offered daily for upper grades. A full PE program as well as art, music, drama and woodworking are all part of the curriculum. Learning resource specialists are on staff. No hot lunch program per se, it is parent assisted on Wednesdays. Day care and after school sports are optional. Competition for entry is keen.

San Francisco Day School
350 Masonic
931-2422

Conceived and started eleven years ago as an effort to create a K-8 co-ed learning experience in the City. There is an emphasis on dance, theater and drama as well as a strong academic, although non-traditional, approach to learning. Afternoon enrichment programs for all grades. Small classes, multi-ethnic and no dress code.

HOW TO BEAT THE BACK-TO-SCHOOL BLUES

- *Re-train your children to get up on time. Try waking them up fifteen minutes earlier every day until the desired time is reached.*

- *Update their medical records and make doctor's appointments well in advance of the September rush.*

- *Limit television and Nintendo viewing (slowly, so that your child doesn't go into withdrawal).*

- *Start a reading incentive program with interesting books placed in strategic locations next to their bed at night, by their cereal boxes at breakfast and in the bathroom (but not near the toothbrush, or they will never be noticed)!*

- *Shop for basics, such as underwear, socks and school supplies early.*

- *Enroll your child in a bicycle safety class if he or she rides to school. Make sure the bike has been serviced recently and the bike helmet wasn't last seen at a friend's sometime in July.*

The Hamlin School
2120 Broadway
922-0300

One of the oldest schools for girls in the City, located in the magnificent Flood Mansion on Broadway. There are four buildings connected by covered passages. Getting from class to class in the older grades can take on the feel of an endurance course! Uniforms are required in this traditional K-8 school. French is taught in all grades, as is computer, art and music. Drama is available in the middle school. There is a hot lunch program and day care.

Schools of the Sacred Heart
2222 Broadway
563-2900

- Convent of the Sacred Heart (Girls K-12)

- Stuart Hall (Boys K-8)

The girls and boys schools are in separate buildings next door to one another on Broadway. The buildings just happen to be elegant mansions with drop-dead views out over the Bay! Some facilities are shared by the two schools, each of which has three hundred children. Although 60% of the students are Catholic, catholic dogma is not taught. All students wear uniforms. This is a traditional teaching institution with state-of-the-art facilities, including two full gyms, two complete libraries and two new comprehensive science labs. There are computers in all classrooms. There is no hot lunch program and PE is taught off-campus. Day care through 6th grade is offered.

Cathedral School for Boys
1275 Sacramento
771-6600

An Episcopalian-based K-8 private boys school with traditional teaching methods. Uniforms are required. The curriculum is not religion-based, although all students do attend chapel three mornings a week where the emphasis is on morals and values. This is a literature-based program with a full-time reading specialist on staff. Large library with full-time librarian. Strong math program and computer skills are stressed, and there is a full science lab. Art, music and choir are offered and Spanish is required in the first five grades. Small student population, although classes, (approximately 24 boys), stay together for the entire 8+ years at the school.

French American International School
220 Buchanan
626-8564

It would be extremely helpful if the child is fluent in French, or comes from a family fluent in French, to succeed in this school. As a matter of fact, the primary school will not encourage a child to enroll beyond third grade without a good sense of the language. Note that the high school program does admit non-French speaking students. This is a co-ed program in which children change classes for each subject starting in second grade. There is a playground on campus and day care is available after school. No hot lunch program.

Brandeis Hillel Day School
655 Brotherhood Way
334-9841

A co-ed Jewish K-8 day school located in the same building as the Jewish Community Center (on the "Other Side of the Park"). Full use of the JCC facilities is allowed. No uniforms are required. One third of the curriculum is Hebrew studies and there is no other language taught. There is an emphasis on computer skills, as well as art, music and PE. There is a gifted program as well as a program for mainstreaming mildly learning-disabled kids. The school offers an extremely nurturing environment with small classes. Hot lunch program for all grades except Kindergarten. Daycare and after-school enrichment programs offered separately through the JCC.

ALTERNATIVE SCHOOLS

If you are interested in alternatives to private schools, there are some very fine public, or "alternative" schools, throughout the City. I would strongly suggest contacting the San Francisco Unified Public School District at 135 Van Ness Avenue. Or call 565-9000 for more information. For parents of gifted children, be sure to ask about:

The GATE program
(Gifted and Talented Education)
759-2930

Project 2061
(Science & Math high school program)
759-2767

TEEN PROGRAMS

San Francisco Recreation & Park
292-2008 Headquarters

The SF Rec. & Park offers fun and exciting programs for teens in various locations around the City. Personal enrichment activities include tutoring and special interest clubs. There are also cultural events, community service opportunities, fashion shows and carnivals as well as dances and social events. There's even a teen newspaper.

Young People's Teen
Musical Theater Company
Harvey Milk
Recreational Arts Bldg.
50 Scott St. (near Duboce Ave.)
554-9523

For 13-19 year-olds, this is a great opportunity to participate in an ongoing musical theater workshop. Auditions are in September, with classes in dance, drama and voice. Performances throughout the year.

Make-A-Circus
Fort Mason Bldg C
776-8477
There is a teen apprentice program in circus skills, theatre and technical skills for kids who have always been fascinated by circus life.

HIGH SCHOOL

The Urban School of San Francisco
1563 Page
626-2919

There are several unique aspects to Urban. First, it is an extremely small school of approximately 130 students located in an old converted firehouse with connecting buildings. Teaching is non-traditional and students are on a "Block System" of seven, five-week sessions. Students do not receive grades. At the end of each session, students and teachers do an evaluation of the student's progress and this is discussed. However, a GPA is kept for each student for college application use. There is a strong fine arts department, language program, a computer lab and a library-in-progress in conjunction with a parent-driven capital campaign. There is a full gym across the street and all students are encouraged to join the sports teams. Open campus policy during lunch or free classes.

Lowell High School
1101 Eucalyptus Drive
759-2730

Lowell is proof that a top public high school is alive, well and flourishing in San Francisco. The down side is that competition for entry is extremely high, even though Lowell is "public". It is also located on the outskirts of the City, so transportation is another consideration. It offers a strictly college-prep curriculum and you must be a resident of San Francisco to attend. There is an extensive language department, a strong music and drama program and a highly-competitive sports department. School population? 2800 students. Limited open campus. Students cannot go to nearby Stonestown Shopping Mall!

University High School
3065 Jackson
346-8400

A co-ed City school with a highly-regarded all-round academic program. A small school, with approximately one hundred students per grade. An excellent music, drama and fine arts program is offered. There is a strong sports program with a full gym on campus. All outdoor sports are off-campus at the playing fields in the Presidio and local stadiums or tennis courts. A variety of languages are taught and there is a large library on campus which is on-line. There are computer labs offered with every class, and a full-time college counselor on staff. This school is geared towards an academically-competitive student on a college track. "Open campus" policy (students can leave campus during lunch or free classes).

Convent of the Sacred Heart
2222 Broadway
563-2900

The Convent also offers a high school program for girls only. Uniforms are still required. The school offers fifteen advanced placement courses. Art is not offered, although art history is required. There is an "open campus" policy at high school level. See "Primary Schools" for more details.

St. Ignatius College Prep
2001-37th Avenue
731-7500

This large Jesuit school of 1375 students has been in existence since 1855. It has recently turned co-ed. There is a strong emphasis on community service and students are required to fill 100 hours of service. Classes in religion are taught, although there is no Catholic dogma. "SI" offers incredible extracurricular activities. There is every kind of club imaginable and the drama program is considered outstanding. There is also a large orchestra and music department. The school is recognized for having a very competitive all-sports program. The extensive 11 1/2 acre campus houses a full gym, pool, tennis courts and playing fields. Optional private bus service is offered. There are honors and advanced placement classes, but no real emphasis is placed on the counselling program. Tuition is more reasonably-priced than many of the other schools. No open campus.

Lick-Wilmerding High School
755 Ocean Avenue
333-4021

What was once a technical school is now a fast-track college prep high school with an outstanding reputation and one of the lowest tuitions around, thanks to a strong endowment fund. Because of its original technical arts facilities, students can take courses in wood, metal and machine shop, as well as drafting and pre-architecture. This is in addition to a strong fine arts and drama program. Complete computer labs throughout the school and freshman computer class is required. Small student body of approximately 345 kids, all of whom, (100%), go on to four-year colleges. Lick also competes in all inter-school sports except football. One drawback is its location out on Ocean Ave. Open campus policy during lunch or free classes.

USEFUL RESOURCES

Gifted and Talented Education Program (G.A.T.E.)
759-2930

This is a State program for public schools that can be adopted to any school. Children are tested in 2nd grade and enter the program the following year. It runs through the honors program in high school. It is up to the individual schools, who do their own testing under State guidelines, to offer this program. Children who test into this program must receive at least two hundred minutes of advanced training in special academic areas. In spite of the on-going budget cuts to education in the State of California, the GATE program is alive and well.

PROJECT 2061
759-2767

Introduced in 1985, the last time Haley's comet appeared, Project 2061 is named in honor of the Comet's next appearance in the 21st century. A long-term, multi-phase project which focuses on the math and science skills students should master by graduation. The San Francisco Unified School District is one of only six sites in the country to be selected for this long-range project. It will be an integrated math and science curriculum for all students K-12, the model of which is now being developed in conjunction with the American Association of Advancement of Science, the national government in DC and Stanford University.

EDUCATIONAL CONSULTANTS

Jackson, McClure & Mallory
3607 Sacramento
346-3660

This well-recommended group works on an individual basis with children from preschool to high school. Testing is done in aptitude and academics. College consulting is a specialty as well as counselling on boarding school choices and decisions.

Gary Holbrook & Associates
40 Rodeo Avenue, Sausalito
332-1577

Educational and career counselling programs for grade eight through adults. The comprehensive program covers areas including college prep, transferring colleges, graduate school planning and placement, career guidance and adult retirement activities. A full life-cycle consulting program!

TUTORING & TESTING

Garden Sullivan Learning and Development Program
2700 Geary & 3360 Geary
921-6171

This excellent program run under the auspices of California Pacific Medical Center offers a complete range of testing, treatment and tutoring for children from infancy to sixteen years of age. Whether it is a child who has a mild learning disability to one with severe learning problems, this program works wonders.

ENRICHMENT PROGRAMS

YOUTH ORGANIZATIONS

Big Brothers and Big Sisters of SF
414 Mason
434-4860

A wonderful organization which matches boys and girls, ages six to sixteen, from mostly single parent homes with adult "mentors". A one-on-one relationship is established that provides the child with an adult role model and companion. Adults volunteer for a minimum of one year and spend about four hours a week with the child. There are also programs for hearing-impaired children or kids with hearing-impaired parents. Special events throughout the year include the annual Bowlathon, which raises much-needed funds.

San Francisco Bay Girl Scout Council
1 (800) 447-4475

Call the above number to learn how to set up a troop, where to buy uniforms, or how to join an existing troop in your area. The program starts with the Daisies in Kindergarten and goes up to the Senior Scouts in grades 9-12.

B'nai Brith Youth Organization
259-9140

A leadership training program for Jewish boys and girls in grades 9-12. Kids concentrate on community service and hold special teen events. There are local chapters throughout the Bay Area.

Boy Scouts of America
124 Beale St Suite 402
543-8780

Call the above number for all information regarding how to set up a den or pack, how many adults are needed, where to get supplies, uniforms, manuals, etc. and how to run meetings. Dens are set up according to age group from youngest, Tiger Cubs, to Explorers, for boys & girls age 14-20.

YMCA of San Francisco
1530 Buchanan
931-9622

The "Y" offers a myriad of programs for children, from babies through boys and girls in high school. There are various locations around the City offering activities ranging from childcare and youth counselling to sports, exercise and dance activities. There are also a number of parent/child programs and workshops.

Enterprise for High School Students
921-6554

This highly-acclaimed organization places high school students in domestic and commercial job situations. All interested students must take a free workshop to qualify. Basic job interview and phone skills are learned as well as an appropriate work attitude, reliability, etc. Students must show proof of a "C" average or above to qualify and must provide a letter of recommendation from an academic teacher.

SPORTS

Organized sports activities are flourishing in San Francisco. Here are some suggested resources.

YOUTH ATHLETIC LEAGUES

At a certain age, usually around eight years old, boys and girls may choose to participate in competitive athletics. They play on teams for which there are try-outs, regular season games, uniforms, sponsors and enthusiastic parent support, often in the area of coaching. Most kids qualify to play and the emphasis is on, and should be on, team spirit, good sportsmanship and having a great time, win or lose.

BASEBALL

SF Youth Baseball League is organized under the auspices of:

The SF Rec. & Park Department

Play is available to boys and girls ages 6-14 who live in or go to school in San Francisco. Teams are organized according to geographic area, with games played throughout the City. For more information, contact Director Peter O'Quendo at 753-7029.

Police Athletic League

PAL baseball is offered to boys and girls age 6-14 who live in or go to school in the City. Play begins in April and is played on fields all over San Francisco. Sign-up begins in January. Call 753-7029.

SOCCER

SF Viking Soccer Club
3208 Irving
753-3111

For boys and girls ages 5-18. Players must live in the City. Registration is in May and June. Play is from Sept.-Dec. Teams are coached by volunteers, usually parents. You may join an existing team or form one of your own. Viking sponsors approximately 160 teams a year who play on different fields around the City.

CYO Soccer
(Catholic Youth Organization)
1 St Vincent Drive, San Rafael
507-4290

All SF and Marin programs are handled from this main office. League play is available to boys in grades 3-8. Players must live in the archdiocese of San Francisco.

TIP

Don't worry if you've recently arrived in town and the deadline has come and gone for registration. Most leagues will take that into consideration and if there is any room, they will try to accommodate your youngster.

"Simply Soccer"
995-4984

Gus Eadie, well-known soccer coach, offers soccer clinics and team play for kids in the City. He also runs an after-school program from September to June for boys and girls ages 5-14. His teams compete in the Viking league in the fall. Gus also runs summer soccer camps all around the Bay Area.

SF Rec and Park Soccer
753-7029

Soccer is offered only in the summer for boys and girls age 8-17. Games are organized according to age and geographic area.

FOOTBALL

SF Rec and Park
753-7029

Flag and Touch Football are offered to boys and girls ages 10-17. Teams are organized according to age, size and weight. Games are played throughout the City according to geographic area from September through November.

The Police Athletic League
695-6935

PAL sponsors tackle football for boys ages 8-14, (whose mothers will allow it!). Teams are organized according to age and weight. Sign-up is in April and practice begins in August, with play in Sept-Nov.

BASKETBALL

SF Rec and Park
753-7029

Play begins the second week of January and is offered to boys and girls ages 8-17. Games are organized according to age and geographic area. There is a separate girls league in the summer for Under 17 and Under 14.

PAL Basketball

Play is held in Oct & Nov, with a play-off in December, for boys and girls in grades 6-8. Games are held in gyms around the City.

CYO Basketball
507-4290

League play is offered to boys in grades 3-8 who live in the Arch Diocese of SF. Call for information on joining or forming a team.

VOLLEYBALL

The SF Rec and Park offers a volleyball program for girls in March and April. It is actually a tournament for two age groups-17 & Under and 14 & Under. Note: There are about a hundred rec centers throughout the City. Check into the programs at the one nearest you. Call 753-7029.

TIP

Girls, ages 5-15 may be interested in cheerleading during the above football games. Call PAL for more information.

SPORTS PROGRAMS

TENNIS

Gil Howard Tennis School
992-9192

Gil Howard is a skilled tournament player who teaches boys and girls age 8-18, from beginners to tournament players. He offers year-round private lessons at courts around the City and Bay Area. Clinics are at Washington High in the summer months.

Youth City-Wide Tennis Classes
SF Rec & Park Dept.
753-7032

Junior tennis clinics are held in the summer in Golden Gate Park and on courts throughout the City.

California Tennis Club
1770 Scott
346-3611

You do not have to be a member of this exclusive club to enroll your junior player in any of the clinics for children in grades 2-12. Teams are also formed within the club to play matches against each other. There is a Junior Membership for a reduced fee. Five co-sponsors from club members are required, and there is a one year's waiting list.

San Francisco Tennis Club
5th & Brannan
777-9012

Private lessons and a number of fine clinics are available for children. Must be a member of the club.

GYMNASTICS

Gymboree
First United Lutheran Church
Geary & 30th Ave.
752-0634

Classes are held for pre-schoolers from three months of age to five years. An emphasis is placed on creative movement and developmental play. Drama programs are also offered to 4-5-year olds, and you may want to look into GymKids. Note: This is a great idea for a birthday party! Call for more information.

Gymnastics at the JCC
SF Jewish Community Center
3200 California St.
346-6040

• Kindergym is geared towards the ten-month to two-year-old set. Half the parents and children interact on mats and equipment while the other half do exercise and songs. Pre-School Gym is for 3-4 year-olds. Kids do modified tumbling, balance beam and ring work.
• There are also programs for girls only, including gymnastics for girls grades 1-8 and acrobatics for K-5.

American Gymnastics Club
2520 Judah
731-1400

Gymnastics classes are offered to children age two through adults. The club sponsors a boys and girls team which competes through USGF level 10.

KARATE & JUDO

Karate USA
2849 California
552-7283

Classes are available for boys and girls ages 3 1/2 to 13.

PAL Sports Judo Classes
Hall of Justice, 5th floor gym
850 Bryant
695-6935

Judo classes are held year-round at the Hall of Justice on M/W/F, from 5-6:30 PM, for boys and girls ages seven to eighteen.

SWIMMING

SF Rec & Park Aquatics
753-7026

(Ask for Pablo)
The Rec & Park Dept. offers an excellent swimming program throughout the City, with eight indoor pools and one outdoor. Call the above number for all activities and programs as well as schedules for all public pools in San Francisco.

SF JCC
3200 California
346-6040

The JCC offers a variety of junior swim programs in its indoor pool. "Mommy & Me" is a swim program geared especially for tiny tots and parents and lessons start at age four months and up.There is also a junior swim team which participates in meets throughout the Bay Area.

Rossi Pool
Arguello Blvd. & Anza
666-7014

This indoor public pool offers swim lessons for infants to adults. It is also open to children for recreational swimming 1:30-3 PM Saturday through Thursday.

Hamilton Pool
Geary, off Steiner
292-2001 (Ask for Bob)

This indoor public pool has swimming lessons for infants through adults, sponsored by the SF Rec & Park. It is one of two pools that fields a junior swim team which trains and competes year-round.

Sava Pool
19th & Wawona
753-7000

This beautiful facility also offers indoor swim lessons for infants through adults sponsored by the SF Rec & Park Dept. Children must be accompanied by an adult. Sava also has a junior swim team for kids 8-18, to practice and compete year-round.

SWIMMING IN MARIN

Try getting out of the City in the summer and sign up your youngster at one of the two highly-recommended swim programs in Marin County:

Ann Curtis Swim School
25 Golden Hinde Blvd, San Rafael
479-9131

Ross Valley Swim & Tennis Club
235 Bon Air Rd, Kentfield
461-5431

HORSEBACK RIDING

Golden Gate Park Stables
668-7360

Lessons are available for boys and girls age eight and up. Kids are taught basic riding skills right up through jumping. Guided trail rides throughout the Park are also available for hire.

SAILING & ROWING

Sea Explorers
543-8780

Classes are offered in sailing and rowing for boys and girls ages 14-20. You do not need your own boat. Sailing classes are located on the dock at the end of Van Ness. Rowing is done in 8-man shells at Lake Merced.

GOLF

Harding Park Golf Course
34 & Clement
664-4690

Junior golf lessons and clinics are available for boys and girls ages 7-18. Offered in summer only.

SKIING

Mogul Ski Club
456-1000

Mogul is the name of the game if you want your child to participate in day, weekend or holiday trips to Tahoe without you! Mogul enjoys a fine reputation for busing kids up to Tahoe, making sure they are safe, sound and skiing in the appropriate group and getting them home in one piece again! Kids participate from all over the Bay Area. Pick-up point in the City is Laurel Village at 4 AM!

AROUND THE BAY

On windy San Francisco days, try the **Marina Green** *for kite-flying, or* **Fort Funston** *for watching hang gliders!*

◆

Don't miss the annual **All-American Sports Collectors Convention** *every Labor Day Weekend at Moscone Center, 747 Howard Street. It's one of the biggest baseball card shows in the United States. For little boys (and big), it's a dream come true.*

◆

Boys & Girls who love baseball may want to join the **Giants Orange & Black Kids Club.** *Membership entitles you to passes, clinics and souvenirs. For information, call 330-2516.*

ART

SF Jewish Community Center
3200 California St.
346-6040

Art classes are offered for all ages at the JCC both after school and in the summer, as well as holiday programs.

SF Children's Art Center
Fort Mason Bldg C
771-0292

Multi-media classes are available for kids and include drawing, painting and sculpture.

Art for Children
MH deYoung Memorial Museum
Golden Gate Park
750-3658

Two special Saturday morning programs are offered, one for pre-schoolers and parents and the other for older children. There are docent-led tours and studio art workshops for kids 4 years and up.

Randall Museum
199 Museum Way
554-9600

Classes are available for the whole family in arts and crafts in this delightful museum near Buena Vista Park.

SF Museum of Modern Art
401 Van Ness
863-8800

Docent-led tours of both permanent and special exhibits are available to schools as an art-related field trip. Art projects are included in tour. Interested schools must sign up well in advance as this is a popular program which fills up quickly.

ARTISTIC BIRTHDAY PARTY

The Children's Art Center also offers Special "Art Birthday Parties for ages 2-12. Offered on Sundays for two hours for up to ten kids. All guests create their own cards with print-making equipment, as well as other art projects, under the supervision of two staff members. Art supplies provided. You bring the food. Call 389-1090 for more information.

MUSIC

San Francisco Community Music Center

Main Office

741-30th Avenue
221-4515

544 Capp St.
647-6015

At this non-profit music center, children, age 4-8, can play games using instruments and experiment with songwriting. The center also conducts a children's chorus during the school year for youths 8-14.

Co-Stars School of Music & Performing Arts
1221 Vicente
731-0773

Formerly Young's Music School, this school for ages three through adult, has a "yamaha-based" philosophy for keyboard. Group classes and private instruction are offered in piano, guitar, strings, woodwind and percussions instruments, as well as voice. It also has musical theater and a rock 'n roll workshop for teens.

SF Girls Chorus
1100 Ellis
673-1511

Girls age, 7-16, receive choral and theory training in classes on Tuesdays and Thursdays from 4-6 PM. Auditions are held three times a year.

YOUTH ORCHESTRA

The San Francisco Symphony Youth Orchestra. For young people interested in auditioning, call 552-8000, ext.

SF Children's Opera
245-10th Avenue
386-9622

This unique program offers opera classes for kids age 7-14. Five fully-staged operatic performances are presented yearly. All classes are free.

Bay Area Youth Opera
431-2027

Students, 7-15, learn acting, dancing, mime and singing at Saturday workshops. Semesters culminate in a performance. Call for location.

Guitar Solo
1411 Clement
386-0395

Guitarist and singer Irene Siegel teaches guitar for boys and girls age 8 and up in this sheet music store on Clement.

SF Conservatory of Music
1201 Ortega
665-3818

After-school and weekend programs are available for children age 4-18. Youngest children start with "music sharing", then on to pre-instruments for 6-8 year-olds. Parents and children are interviewed for this program. After age 8, children are tested for musical sensitivity or must be interviewed for the continuing program. The Conservatory also has "Summer Music West" for ninety students offering a comprehensive music program for children in their chosen field.

SF Boys Chorus
801 Portola Dr.
665-2330

Boys, age 7-11 (or until the voice changes!), can audition. No experience necessary and auditions are held three times a year. Choral and theory are taught using the Kodaly theory of sight singing.

Music Time School
301 Balboa
386-7374

This school offers interactive music classes for babies from ten months to 8 year olds (all of whom must be accompanied by a parent!). Music theory is introduced through song, dance and creative movement. The school also has a store that sells music, small-scale instruments and tapes for little children.

DANCE

Star Dance
1883-10th Ave.
This well-known dance school has been around since 1950 and specializes in classes for boys and girls from 3 1/2 years of age through high school. Beginners learn ballet, tap and acrobatics, and classes advance from there in complexity and rate of attendance.

Lorna Fordyce School of Dance
1926 Lawton
681-2150

Classes are taught in ballet, tap, jazz and acrobatics for boys and girls in pre-school on up, as well as for adult professional dancers.

San Francisco Ballet School
455 Franklin
553-4642

This is the official school of The San Francisco Ballet located in its state-of-the-art facility on Franklin. Classes are available to boys and girls age 8-10 with no previous experience and begin in September. Call for more detailed information for classes for older children. Helgi Tomasson is the Artistic Director of this world-class school and ballet.

Academy of Ballet
2120 Market St
552-1166

Classical ballet is taught to children through adults. Pre-ballet is available to five-year-olds and up.

DRAMATIC ARTS

ACT Young Conservatory Theatre
450 Geary
749-2350

This nationally-recognized theatre company offers theatre training for youths 8-18. Year-round classes including acting, improvisation, musical theatre and playwriting are offered for all levels.

Kids on Camera Acting School
240 Steuart
882-9878

This acting school for boys and girls, age 4-17, offers training in film and television acting, as well as modeling, using videotape as an educational tool. There is an emphasis on developing self-esteem.

LIBRARIES

Libraries offer a variety of activities for children. Even with the continuing cutbacks from the State, libraries in San Francisco seem determined to maintain summer reading programs, story times, plays, puppet shows, and preschool programs. Check the libraries nearest you for a schedule of events. Main Branch 557-4400.

The New Conservatory
25 Van Ness at Market
861-4914

This performing arts school offers year-round theatre for boys and girls age 4-19. Students enjoy hands-on experience and instruction in theatre, dance, music, costuming and lighting design. Summer sessions are also available. Call for complete schedule.

Young Performers Theatre
Fort Mason Bldg. C
Marina Blvd
346-5550

Theatre production, acting, musical theatre and technique are just a few of the classes offered to children age 3-18. There are open auditions for kids interested in acting in any of the productions.

Make-A-Circus
Fort Mason Bldg. C
776-8477

The Make-A-Circus cast travels regularly to Bay Area parks to present a circus show and hold post-performance workshops for kids in circus skills. Children can exhibit their skills in the grand finale. A special year-round program for disabled kids is also available.

MUSEUM PROGRAMS FOR KIDS

Randall Museum
199 Museum Way
554-9600

This small natural science museum is geared especially for kids. There are live animal exhibitions, dinosaur bones, a gem display, art studios and a Petting Corral. Classes are offered for the whole family in arts and crafts, ceramics, woodwork and much more.

Exploratorium
Palace of Fine Arts
3601 Lyon
563-7337

Over six hundred hands-on exhibits to challenge the senses can be found at this innovative science museum. Be sure and visit the Tactile Dome, a reservation-only, crawl-through exhibit exploring the sense of touch.

California Academy of Sciences
Junior Academy
Golden Gate Park
750-7100

A year-round program for youths age 6-18 including workshops, labs and field studies about astronomy, chemistry and marine biology. Field trips to Sonoma or Big Sur are offered to study California history. Also sessions in summer and during holiday breaks.

Marine Mammal Center
West end of Bunker Road
Golden Gate National
Recreation Area, Sausalito
289-7325

It is worth the short hop over the Bridge to enroll your child in any number of excellent classes centering on marine mammals, such as dolphins, sea lions, whales and plant life native to the Marin Headlands. Summer camps are also available.

Terwilliger Nature Education Center
50 El Camino Drive,
Corte Madera
927-1670

Every child in the Bay Area should have the chance to experience the extraordinary "Mrs. T" in action! Whether it's the famous Mrs. Terwilliger leading year-round nature outings all over Marin, or any of the knowledgeable naturalists, these excursions in natural habitats are a must. Children, ages 3-7, learn about environmental issues and ecology on their treks. Special programs include summer nature camps, after-school programs and "tot-walks".

ESSENTIALS FOR KIDS

SHOES

Junior Boot Shop
3555 California
751-5444

This shop has been professionally fitting boys and girls with shoes for almost a half century. It is a landmark for parents with almost-ready-to-walk little ones. As I now gape at my thirteen-year-old's giant Reeboks, I can't believe he once toddled proudly across the floor of the Junior Boot Shop to the applause of one and all.

Lombardi's
152 Clement
387-0600

Speaking of Reeboks, Lombardi's specializes in athletic shoes, clothes and equipment.

Nordstrom
Stonestown Galleria
753-1344

865 Market
243-1344

Nordstrom has long been recognized as a good source for children's shoes and clothes. There is a full range of styles and sizes.

▶ *I always check out the sales rack in the boys department nearby. You can usually find some good buys, especially since it seems boys wear basically the same clothes year round.*

CHILDREN'S CLOTHES

Dottie Doolittle
3680 Sacramento
563-3244

The most famous little girls store in the City. Also carry a smaller boys line (as well as shoes across the street). Specialize in unique children's clothes, hand-made sweaters and hand-smocked dresses.

Bellini
418 Sutter
391-5417

Imported Italian furniture and clothing for babies and children, as well as baby gifts and accessories.

Yountville
2416 Fillmore
922-5050

Full line of U.S. designer clothes for children, age newborn to size 10.

CitiKids Baby News
1160 Post at Van Ness
673-5437

A "soup to nuts" store for babies and toddlers. All the basics from diapers to strollers. Good News-validated parking!

Gap Kids and Baby Gap!
100 Post
421-4906
Laurel Village
386-7517

A Gap wardrobe is practically a uniform for many SF kids. Durable, fairly reasonably-priced, great style and color. If you don't mind your child meeting himself coming and going, Gap clothes are great! Several other locations around the City.

Esprit Outlet
499 Illinois
957-2550

This is the continuing favorite among outlet shoppers, particularly teenage girls and their moms. A full line of first quality clothing from infants and toddlers through teens and adults. Also carry shoes and accessories as well. 30% off retail with new shipments arriving every two weeks. Grab a bite to eat in the Esprit Cafe and be sure to wander through the sculpture garden.

Patagonia
770 Northpoint
771-2050

The variety of unique clothes for kids is mind-boggling at this upscale store on Northpoint. You will discover an extensive line of cold-weather gear, active-wear, rainwear, climbing and nature gear, neoprene shorts and tops for surfing and water sports and even equestrian clothes and fishing vests. A must-see!

Young Man's Fancy
3527 California
221-4230

Clothes for boys and men, from underwear and pajamas to suits and sweaters. YMF has been fitting young boys with their first blue blazers and gray flannel pants for generations. It's kind of comforting that styles come and go, but the clothes at YMF are eternally classic.

Mudpie
1694 Union
771-9262

Unique, one of a kind children's clothes. A grandma's delight!

Ragamuffin
3048 Fillmore
563-7140

Imported and domestic fine children's wear. Many items are 100% cotton. For boys and girls, newborn to ten.

Jessica McClintock Boutique
353 Sutter
397-0987

Special occasion dresses for girls through adults. Especially good for those hard-to-fit pre-teen girls. You'll find the perfect graduation dress here as well.

TIP

You may luck out and find similar dresses at the Gunne Sax outlet store located at 634-2nd Street, 495-3362. Call for information on the latest shipments and sale items. You'll find fantastic savings!

HAIRCUTS FOR KIDS

Zippy's Hair Studio
3661A Sacramento
921-2192

Haircuts for toddlers to adults. All operators are happy to work on children. Located right across the street from Dottie Doolittle, you will find the prices for cuts very reasonable. Appointment necessary.

Asano Barber Shop
3312 Sacramento
567-3335

For boys and men only. Appointments are definitely required.

diPietro Todd
177 Post
397-0177

Chad or Megan will cut kids' hair, but prefer not to do toddlers. Haircuts are at a reduced price for children, but still expensive.

Masa Hair Salon
2536 California
921-4033

Masa will happily cut children's hair, including little ones getting their first hair cut. Appointment necessary a week ahead.

BRIGHT IDEA!

There really is a need for a first-class, kids-only, reasonably-priced hair-cutting salon in the City. Picture VCRs playing "Beauty and the Beast", healthy snacks or sugar-free lollipops, children's books and games and toys available for kids who are waiting, and most of all, qualified cutters who are trained to deal with squirmy, wiggly toddlers. Sounds like a good business to me!

"There's only one pretty child in the world, and every mother has it."
—Chinese proverb

TOY STORES

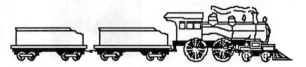

San Francisco Art Supply
5221 Geary
387-5354

This store carries every possible art supply in every size and color your child will ever need to complete any school project! Extensive line of items available. Student discounts given.

FAO Schwartz
48 Stockton
394-8700

The ultimate high-end toy store. Fun to visit, with or without kids, even if you don't buy anything. The animated decor makes shopping an exciting experience for young and old.

Toys R Us
2400 O'Farrell Street
(Entrance on Geary & Masonic)
931-8896

Open seven days a week, until 9:30 PM, it's about time this giant mega-discount toy store has come to San Francisco. All items, including the basics, discounted for perfect one-stop shopping.

Quinby's
3411 California
751-7727

Great art supplies, books, educational games and party favors aimed at kids from infants to 10 years old.

Hobby Company of San Francisco
5150 Geary
386-2802

A SF landmark for all sorts of hobby and craft items including model boats and planes, doll houses and miniatures, craft tools and supplies, and model railroads and accessories.

Chan's Trains and Hobbies
2450 Van Ness
885-2899

Huge selection of trains in all gauges and accessories. They also buy and sell old trains and toys.

Imaginarium
3535 California
387-9885

Known as a "toy store kids can handle", with play stations throughout the store, so kids and adults can play with the toys. The staff is trained to know age-appropriate toys and help customers with selections. Free gift wrap. There is a "Story Time" every Thursday at 4:30 PM for 4-5 year-olds. Educational games also available.

Discovery Toys
664-7011

The tupperware method of selling high-quality, often unique, educational toys and games in private homes.

KID-FRIENDLY RESTAURANTS

Pizzeria Uno
2200 Lombard at Steiner
563-3144

Kids love pizza and Uno's fills the bill with its Chicago-style pizzas and easy atmosphere. Open daily for lunch or dinner, or take it out.

Chevy's
2 Embarcadero Center
391-2323

Chevy's can be found in several locations around the City. At each one, however, you will find the food appealing and of high quality. Kids love the bustling, noisy atmosphere and you will see high chairs everywhere. A big favorite among the ten and under set is to watch the tortilla machine and beg for freebies!

MacArthur Park
607 Front
398-5700

The ribs here are a popular menu item with kids. They also love the fresh crayons and blank menus to color on. The staff is particularly patient with the little ones, and the food can come as fast as you like.

Flower Lounge
5322 Geary
668-8998

Great family spot for Chinese food. Kids are apt to be running around everywhere. High chairs are common and kids love peering into the tanks of fish. Dim sum served at lunch. Early dinners start at 5 P.M.

Mel's Drive In
3355 Geary
387-2244
2165 Lombard
921-3039

There actually is drive-in service at the Lombard St location in the summer only. Mel's is a fun, laid-back, fifties-style restaurant with an all-American hearty menu and blaring juke boxes. Kids love it!

Bill's Place
2315 Clement
221-5262

A landmark, since 1959, for great burgers, shakes and sundaes.

Hard Rock Cafe
1699 Van Ness
885-1699

A favorite among the teen and adolescent set, with its throbbing rock and roll music, all-American food, t-shirts and sweatshirts for sale and hip atmosphere. Tourists congregate here in the summer and there are often long lines to get in.

PLACES TO GO WITH KIDS

Basic Brown Bear Factory
444 DeHaro St. at Mariposa
626-0781

One of the few stuffed animal factories still operating in the US. Children can tour the sewing and cutting rooms and even stuff their own bears. Call for schedule of tours.

Golden Gate Fortune Cookie Company
56 Ross Alley
between Jackson & Washington

Children enjoy watching fortune cookies being created right before their very eyes. All work done by hand. Open daily 10 AM -8 PM.

Lawrence Hall of Science
Centennial Drive near Grizzly Peak Blvd., Berkeley
(510) 642-5133

This is a must-visit and well worth the winding route across the Bay to get there. This renowned science museum houses revolving and permanent exhibits as well as hands-on displays. Special exhibits and workshops are offered year-round. Call for more information.

Raging Waters
Capitol Expressway & Tully Rd.
San Jose
(408) 270-8000

Water slides par excellence and well worth the drive to San Jose. Available in the summer months only. Great for kids of all ages.

Children's Fairyland
Grand & Bellevue Streets
Lakeside Park, Oakland
(510) 832-3609

Every youngster should visit Fairyland at least once, where nursery rhymes and fairy tales come alive on this seven-acre fairybook park in Oakland. An old-fashioned carousel, free puppet shows, art contests and special events are offered on a seasonal basis. The perfect birthday party site for little ones.

Marine World/Africa USA
Marine World Parkway, Vallejo
(707) 644-4000

It's a bit of a trek to Vallejo, but well worth it to see some wonderful shows with whales, birds, big cats and water skiers, to name a few! A full day's outing and lots of fun for the entire family.

Alcatraz Island
495-4089

Take the ferry out to the "Rock" for a complete two-hour guided tour of the island's history.

Golden Gate Park
General Information: **666-7201**

There's the children's playground and carousel, the Japanese Tea Gardens, The California Academy of Science including the Morrison Planetarium. The Park is closed to vehicular traffic on Sundays, so rollerblading, strollers and bikers abound. One of the last great urban parklands in the country.

PARTY ENTERTAINMENT & SITES

"The Ultimate Bubble Man"
331-4556

Louis Pearl, the Bubble Man, creates magic out of bubbles. His party package includesa half-hour show, packages of bubble-related toys for each guest and individual demonstrations with each child. Perfect for any party, regardless of age.

Joan Sutton "Story Teller Extraordinaire"
752-0821

Joan enacts an exciting and varied one-hour program of original works and stories from all over the world, using costumes, props and puppets. Best age group for this type of entertainment is 3-6 years.

Discovery Zone
123 Colma Blvd., Colma
992-777

The ultimate high-tech, action-oriented indoor playground. There are no video games or bumper cars but there are marvelous activities for little bodies to hurtle into including a moon bounce, water walk, cube climb. All structures are geared to different age groups. Birthday parties are welcome and children must be accompanied by adults, who are allowed in free!

Dance Dreams
664-7993

This is an imaginative addition to any birthday party for girls and boys age 3-12. There is usually a theme with props. Children are taught simple routines to their favorite music and the party ends with face painting. Older children learn to choreograph their own routines and then perform.

SF Zoo
Sloat at Pacific Ocean
753-7061

Birthdays parties are a snap at the Zoo. Geared towards children under six, the party package includes admission to zoo and children's zoo, ice cream, drinks, favors and rides on the carousel for 11-15 kids. There is a substantial savings for zoo members.

SF Children's Art Center
Fort Mason
771-0292

See Artistic Birthday Party on page 100 for more information.

CAMPS AND SUMMER PROGRAMS

LOCAL AREA DAY CAMPS

Club Earth Trek
Katherine Delmar Burke School
7070 California
751-0177

Run for many years by Director Bobbi Meyer, this excellent day camp is located on the beautiful and expansive site of the Burke's School. Camp is held in one-week sessions from June 21 to July 21 for boys and girls in grade K-8. There is an emphasis on learning about other countries in the world through camp activities. Extended day care is available. There is also a great Junior Counselor program for kids grades 6-8.

SF JCC
3200 California
346-6040

Day camp for pre-school through grade 8. All camps have a Jewish theme complementing the creative programming from swimming to nature and ecology. There are also two new adventure camps for kids in grades 3-7:

• KIMTU is a 5-day rafting and kayaking trip on the Trinity River.

• Elkus Ranch is offered in two-week day camp sessions. Campers make daily visits to a working ranch in Half Moon and participate actively in ranch life.

Adventure Camp
P.O. Box 2216
Mill Valley
332-2521

Since 1971, this wonderful mobile day camp serves boys and girls, ages 4 1/2-13, who live in the City and Marin. It also offers after-school activities, vacation camp and a Saturday morning camp.

▶ *San Francisco Day School is the site for a yearly "Camp Night" where parents and kids can wander around, talk to many representative camps throughout California, and collect videos, brochures and valuable information. Held every year in February. Call for exact date. 931-2422*

CAMP & TRIP ADVISORS

A wonderful resource to take advantage of is Student Camp & Trip Advisors. This is a complimentary service which will help you and your youngster decide which camp, summer school or travel experience is best. There are extensive teen programs, including travel and study abroad. Call Judy Wiesen at 454-5441 or Lois Levine at 592-7189 for information.

Family Camp or Bust

This past summer, we packed up two boys, three bikes, seventeen duffel bags, five Books on Tape and enough junk food to last well into the next century. We were going to Family Camp. In sunny Santa Barbara. We were embarking upon a six-hour car trip with two children who have been known to kill each other before getting out of the driveway.

I was determined to put myself in the appropriate mind-set. I would not Yell. I would not Scream. I would not further dislocate my left shoulder reaching behind me to mutilate or destroy feuding children. I would be Calm. A Maginot Line would be drawn down the center of the jeep. Neither child, conveniently plugged into individual walkmans, would be permitted to cross over. It was that simple.

We divided the trip into stages, so as not to tax the limited patience of our guests in the back seat. It is not many families who can turn a six-hour car trip into a two-day, $500 journey. I have a friend who thinks nothing of driving straight through to Montana with two kids and a couple of coloring books in the back seat. The husband flies out later. I don't relate to that.

The next afternoon, after brief stops in Monterey Aquarium ("Borrrrrrrring", said the nine-year-old) and Hearst Castle ("Awesome!" exclaimed the twelve-year-old), I arrived at Family Camp. Shoulder Intact. Smiling. Victorious!

Now a few comments must be made about Family Camps, an institution I find at best bewildering. Why should the whole family pack up and go off to camp? Where I grew up back east, children were shipped off uncomplainingly to camp for eight weeks. My parents would have been horrified at the notion that we all go off to camp together. So what was I doing at Family Camp? I guess I had to see it to believe it.

I've seen it. I believe it. And it isn't me. My goal of the week quickly became Being A Good Sport. Dorms were fun! Doesn't every forty-year-old woman want to spend her vacation sleeping in a bunk bed?

"You should have seen this place a few years ago", intoned a robust Southern Californian named Howard. I hate Southern Californians named Howard. "It's luxurious now compared to then. Black Widow spiders in the showers, no hot water, lumpy beds, rotten food...

Daytime activities centered around Family Bike Rides, Family Rope Climbing Expeditions, Family Swim Meets and Family Olympic Day. Wherever I was, I felt guilty that I should be somewhere else. And sunny Santa Barbara was humid, foggy, windy and gray.

"This is the worst weather we've had all summer!", I kept hearing. It figures.

Evening activities consisted of Skit Night, Bingo Night, Pantomime Night and Campfire Night. I looked around in amazement. Everyone loved Skit Night. I loved being back in my dorm room curled up with a good book.

At the end of Family Camp, as we piled into the car for the long ride home, I said to my husband and sons with feigned enthusiasm,

"That was certainly an experience! Want to do it again next year?"

There was a pause, and the Older Son said he thought Hawaii might be nice. Nods of agreement followed. I could have hugged them. I did hug them, as I absently planned how to keep two boys occupied on a six-hour flight to Hawaii without stopping...

FAMILY CAMPS

Stanford Camp
Fallen Leaf Lake
(916) 541-1244

Set on this lovely lake, near Lake Tahoe, is a camp primarily for Stanford alums and their families, although non-alumni can join the Alumni Association. Applications are chosen by lottery. This is a one-week camp, Sat. to Sat., from June to Sept. There are 48 cabins of varying sizes, all of which have private baths. Three meals a day, as well as all activities, are included in the weekly rate. There are organized activities for ages three and up. Stanford Camp is considered the most luxurious of all the family camps.

Cal Camp
Lair of the Bear
(510) 642-0221

This is a much more rustic environment than Stanford, located about twenty minutes from Pine Crest Lake. You must be a member of the Alumni Association. Applications are available for one-week sessions throughout the summer. There are "tent cabins", community bathrooms and families should bring their own bedding. Programs are enthusiastically staffed by Cal students and include organized activities for kids age 2-17. There is also tennis, volleyball, swimming, hiking, arts and crafts, etc. Three meals a day are offered family-style in the lodge where the hub of all the activities take place, including evening programs.

DAY CAMPS IN MARIN

You may want to consider sending your youngster over the Bridge this summer to Marin. The weather can be as much as twenty degrees warmer. Many of the following camps offer optional bus service.

Marin JCC
200 North San Pedro Road
San Rafael
479-6522

The program is geared towards boys and girls age 9-16. Extended daycare is available. There is an extensive swim program in its beautiful pool area, as well as a state-of-the-art gym, playing fields and air-conditioned activity rooms. Overnights and field trips are offered to older children. Optional bus service from the City.

Camp Sea Star
Headlands Institute
Marin Headlands
332-5771

Five-day camp for boys and girls age 6-12 (who mix with "residential" or sleep-over campers age 8-12). Located in the beautiful Marin Headlands, the focus here is marine science and coastal ecology. There is also a full science lab to study the day's finds.

Marin Country Day School Camp
5221 Paradise Drive, Corte Madera
924-3743

The extensive grounds of this well-known school is the setting for Summer Adventure Camp for boys and girls ages 4-10. Campers enjoy a special over-night each session. Optional bus service available.

Simply Single

Single in San Francisco?
That's good news and bad news.

The good news is that there is so much to do in the Bay Area, either alone or with a friend, that you could be busy every moment. The bad news is that as fulfilled as you may find your life, your career and your circle of friends, alone can be lonely at times. Being involved in dozens of varied activities doesn't necessarily mean they will lead to love and commitment.

The good news is that the weather isn't a negative factor here. You're not inside all winter, surrounded by eight foot drifts of snow, just making it from home to work and back again. Nor are you driven out of your mind in the summer by double-digit humidity and triple-digit temperature readings. The bad news is that summers in the City can be gray and relentlessly foggy for days on end.

The good news? Get out of the City on weekends! The differential in temperature between San Francisco and Marin, the East Bay or the Peninsula can be as much as thirty degrees. The bad news? Finding someone to get out of the City with.

The good news is that the following ideas and recommendations in this chapter are specifically geared to Singles. So, think of this chapter as one more piece of the puzzle in Surviving in San Francisco in the Nineties! The good news is that you are taking charge of your life. There is no bad news...

LOVE IN THE CLASSROOM

Classes, lectures and seminars are a great way to get out, pursue a special interest and meet other people with similar interests in a relaxed, user-friendly setting. There are classes of every possible kind offered throughout the City on a daily basis, and many of them are targeted towards singles. Instead of sitting home, try to enroll in a class which sounds unusual, fascinating or which addresses a concern you face.

ALSO AT THE JCC

Sunday Singles Workshops

These four-hour Sunday workshops throughout the year, tackle a number of relevant issues facing singles today such as "Why Men & Women Can't Talk". Hands-on approach taught by professional facilitators.

Cooking for Singles

Classes such as "Easily Prepared Meals for Singles" or "Nouvelle Pizza" are popular and fun to join.

Tempting Tuesdays

Weekly events on a drop-in basis in a wide variety of subjects such as "Inner Bonding", "Personal Style", "Overcoming Fear of Rejection" and the ultimate question, "Sex. Is It Worth It?"

SF Jewish Community Center
3200 California Street
346-6040

The JCC offers some of the most interesting, reasonably priced and well-run series of classes going! Tailored especially for singles, these programs range from "A Busy Person's Guide to Finding Romance Before Winter" to "Bridging the Gap to Relationships". You name it, you'll probably find it at the JCC–and you don't have to be Jewish! Many of the classes are drop-in and are offered to non-members for a slightly increased fee. For more details, stop by the JCC on California Street and pick up a monthly catalogue or call Danny Schwager, Director of Singles Events. He is a wealth of information!

"You never get a second chance to make a first impression."
–Will Rogers

The Learning Annex
788-5500

The Learning Annex considers itself the largest adult education seminar organization in California. Its hundreds of fascinating classes and workshops appeal to "busy baby boomers" and classes are practical, useful and up-to-date. All classes are taught by prominent experts in their fields. There are often "celebrity" speakers, many of whom are writers, who specialize in the "how-to" approach. Topics are specifically geared towards intimacy, relationships, business networking, finance and leisure activities. In a recent seminar titled "The Art of Courtship", 2/3 of the class were men! There are a series of "Getting to Meet You" parties offered throughout the year as well as many single-oriented events. Classes are fairly reasonably priced and your satisfaction is guaranteed! Pick up a complimentary copy of monthly events or call for information.

"Being single doesn't necessarily mean I am only interested in things that revolve around meeting other unattached individuals. I am always interested in what is the best of anything, whether it may attract other singles or not."

–Ruth Preucell

Third Thursday at The Modern
252-4000

Something's always happening at The San Francisco Museum of Modern Art, on Van Ness at McAllister, on the third Thursday of every month from 5-9 PM. There are spirited discussions about contemporary art, live music and exotic cuisine. A special Two-For-One admission price is offered, so it's a great opportunity to invite a friend to come along. On designated Wednesdays there are brown bag luncheon lectures, and the first Tuesday of every month is "Free Tuesday", when there is no admission charge. For more information call SFMMA.

University of California Extension Life-long Learning Classes
55 Laguna (at Market)
150-4th St. (near Moscone Center)
(510) 642-4111

UC Extension has eight locations throughout the Bay Area, including two in the City. It offers 750 accredited and non-accredited programs during the year ranging from Business & Management to Fly-fishing. Also included are a range of personal development classes such as Sexuality in America or Gender & Relationships. Classes vary in length. Call for a free brochure or information.

SINGLES CLUBS

There are a huge number of singles clubs, each of which have something a little different to offer. Many singles who attend these clubs are in their forties and women tend to predominate, but there are also a number of groups for younger members as well. In any club you'll find a cross-sampling of people with similar interests. It is certainly worth investigating and attending a few meetings.

Pacific Heights Club
641-4909

With chapters all around the Bay Area, this club attracts members who are in the 35-55 age range. There are two to four dance parties held a month, with an average of 200-400 people attending. Admission price is $15-$20.

Positive Connections
826-7234

This SF club holds one to two events a month, including progressive dinners, and draws a crowd which is about 50% Asian. Average age is in the 25-45 range. Party sizes average 50-125 people and admission is $35 including dinner.

San Francisco Club
681-7525

Dance parties, sponsored by this club, are held once every six to eight weeks in San Francisco bars and restaurants from 7 PM to midnight. The average age is 35-55, admission is $20-$25, and 150-250 attend. Call for schedule.

Spinsters

The Spinsters are a group of young single women under the age of thirty-five who raise money for a variety of worthwhile charities. They also know how to put on some pretty terrific parties which are held every two to three months. For information about joining the Spinsters, you can write to 1850 Union Street, #102, SF 94123.

Stanford Bachelors

Located throughout the Bay Area, the Bachelors are a group of Stanford alumni numbering 250-300 unattached men. But be aware that at any given event there will only 50 or 75 of them in attendance! There are two or three events a month and dance parties with live bands can attract from 200 to 2000 people. For information, write The Bachelors, P.O. Box 2345, Stanford, Ca. 94305.

PROGRESSIVE DINNERS

Progressive dinners have been called "the singles bars of the Nineties", in the sense that they are the latest "in" way to meet people. The dinners take place in a restaurant attended by equal numbers of men and women. After each course, you change tables so that by the end of the evening, you have met at least three new people.

Learning Annex
788-5500

The Learning Annex hosts progressive dinners every other month at different restaurants around the City. There are usually 30 to 40 men and women who attend, and dinner begins at 6:30.

Singles Supper Club
327-4645

This club has been in existence for over six years and has 550 members from all over the Bay Area who pay an annual fee of $100 to join. There are two dinners a month in the City at different restaurants and one of the dinners is reserved strictly for the "Under forties" group. Dinners range from $30-$50 a person with 16 to 60 men and women attending.

Dining Out Club
731-8026

Cookbook author/restaurant reviewer Marti Sousanis runs a dining club devoted to exploring and enjoying some of the Bay Area's finest restaurants, wineries and micro-breweries. About 150 members who pay an annual fee of $75 a year. Most members are single, in the 35-55 age range. Dinners offer eclectic menus and focus on fine dining.

CLUBS OF INTEREST

Professional & Arts Society
777-0149

Events are organized around cultural entertainment such as the theatre or ballet, and are preceded by a cocktail party. There is one event every two to three months with between 25 to 80 people attending. Membership is $35 a year. Call for more information.

Vintners Club
485-1166

Located in the Bedford Hotel in the City, the Vintners Club hosts between three to four wine tastings a month, held at 4:30 PM. Membership fee is $300 and there are monthly dues.

IN THE KNOW!

You may want to subscribe to a wonderful newsletter especially for Singles. This is the only subscription-based periodical that lists events from all the singles organizations in the Bay Area. To find out what's hot, what's in and where you should be, write or call

IN THE KNOW
634 Broderick, SF 94117
(415) 346-7783

Party Fax

All you need is a fax to subscribe to this electronic newsletter that will instantly provide you with what's happening on the social scene for singles in any given week. For information, fax 765-5320.

City Democratic Club
771-7229

For those interested in the Democratic party, and this is certainly a good year for it, you can join this club for a nominal membership of $25. Meetings are held at the Press Club, 555 Post Street, every third or fourth Thursday of the month. Groups average about 25-75 people in the 35-45 age range. There is a different speaker every meeting.

Mariana Nune's Professional Breakfasts
673-6775

These breakfasts are held for entrepreneurs and professionals at the Press Club, 555 Post Street, once a month on Saturdays. 60% of those attending are women who enjoy coming together to network and socialize. About 50 to 100 people attend.

Young Republicans
761-7970

One of the younger groups around, Young Republicans host one to three events in the City a month, with 40-140 people attending. Membership is $25 yearly. Call for more information.

Oz Business Connection
774-0116

Located on the top floor of the St. Francis Hotel in Union Square, this is a social/networking group that meets once a month from 6-9 PM. Admission is nominal and a maximum of 250 people may attend. Age group is 25 to 55.

Golden Gate Tip Toppers
841-TALL

What's the criterion and common interest??? Men must be over 6'2" tall and women must be over 5'10"! Located mainly in the City, there is usually one dance a month as well as other "smaller" (!) events. Parties attract tall people in the 35-45 age range and between 75-150 people attend.

Musical Theatre Lovers United
552-2222

Ever have musical theatre aspirations? This club hosts monthly sing-alongs as well as other events. This eclectic group consists of a wide age range. Membership is nominal as is the admission price. 25-100 people who like to sing Broadway show tunes are likely to attend any given event. Call for a newsletter.

Toastmasters
681-1047

There are chapters located all around the Bay, with members ranging in age from 25 to 75 years old. All share one thing in common, an enjoyment of speaking in front of groups and a willingness to learn to be a better public speaker.

RELIGIOUS CLUBS

The Lafayette Orinda Presbyterian Church
49 Knox Drive, Lafayette
(510) 283-8722

This Church is the site for one of the most well-known singles clubs in the Bay Area. Activities take place every day of the week. A Sunday Night Orientation divides prospective members into the following age groups, each has a hotline for upcoming events:

Islanders-for all people born since 1955. Call 284-1425.

Shipmates- for all people born between 1940 & 1955. Call 283-5699.

Single Ships for all people who are 50 or older. Call 283-2535.

Jewish Community Federation
121 Steuart Street
777-0411

Contact The Young Adult Division for information on social events within the Jewish community if you are between the ages of 25 and 40 years old and single. There are social events like the popular "Blue Mondays" which are held once a month in different restaurants around the City and attract up to 250 people. There is also a Newcomers Committee who will work closely with people who are new to the area.

DANCE THE NIGHT AWAY

Adrian Flores
652-6240

Adrian Flores holds Dance Extravaganzas every two or three months, usually at Caesar's on Mission Street, on a Sunday evening. Dances feature different styles of ballroom dancing.

Avenue Ballroom
603 Taravel at 16th Street
681-2882

Classes are offered during the week in Swing, Latin, Ballroom and Western. Change partners often during the course of the class. On weekends, lessons are on a drop-in basis and can attract as many as 100 people.

Bimbo's
1025 Columbus
474-0365

Since the mid-eighties, Bimbo's has been featuring monthly dance parties. Often big band affairs include an hour's dance lesson. This is a wonderful opportunity to dress up and dance the night away.

Hyatt Regency
Embarcadero Five
788-1234

There are free Tea Dances every Friday afternoon from 5:30-8:30 PM. Sometimes a big band sound and more often a rock and roll format, so be sure and check out the type of music you would prefer.

SPORTS UPDATE FOR SINGLES

*The **Sports and Fitness** chapter on page 23 gives you just about everything you need to know about athletics, exercise and fitness. The following tips, however, are specifically geared to Singles, and the information below will provide you with ideas where other people are gathering to play or work out.*

TENNIS

Tuesday Nite Tennis For Singles
332-6669

This friendly group meets in the summer in Golden Gate Park for mixed doubles activity in a relaxed and easy format. Ability level at "B" or above is preferred. You must join the league, at approximately $100 for the season, which includes dinner afterwards in private homes. It is a source of delight among this ever-changing group of tennis enthusiasts that they celebrate at least one wedding a year as a result of Tuesday Night Tennis in the Park! For more information, call Kirk Lee.

TENNIS MATCHMAKERS

Tennis Match Makers offers social tennis for single professional people all over the Bay Area in private tennis clubs. It's an easy, comfortable way to meet people who can play at your ability level. This non-profit USTA-member organization charges an entry fee for each event and membership is free. For more information, call Beverly Doan at (510) 548-6240.

BIKING

Single Cyclists
258-8067

This group meets to ride in Marin and hosts two to four events a month. The group size can vary from 10 to 100. The age range seems to be 25-45.

GOLF

Fairway Singles
349-8191

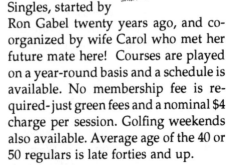

For the more senior single golfers around, there's a wonderful club called Fairway Singles, started by Ron Gabel twenty years ago, and co-organized by wife Carol who met her future mate here! Courses are played on a year-round basis and a schedule is available. No membership fee is required-just green fees and a nominal $4 charge per session. Golfing weekends also available. Average age of the 40 or 50 regulars is late forties and up.

FITNESS CLUBS

The San Francisco Bay Club
150 Greenwich
433-2200

This private club is considered one of the most popular singles workout facilities in the City. There are two rooftop tennis courts, racketball, squash, basketball, a pool, aerobic clinics, health and beauty services and a wide range of classes, seminars and parties throughout the year.

The Telegraph Hill Club
1850 Kearny
982-4700

A multi-purpose, members-only gym which attracts a large number of fitness-minded singles, many if whom work out regularly and take advatage of all the activities offered here. Smaller and less expensive than the Bay Club, it prides itself on a warm and friendly atmoshere.

VOLLEYBALL

SF Rec. & Park Dept.
753-7027

Monday nights at Kezar Pavilion, between Stanyan and Beulah, is a great place to find a game of volleyball. Starting at 7 PM and ending around 9:30 PM, these pick-up games are year-round depending on weather. Summer schedule switches to Tuesdays. Games tend to attract the 20-30 year olds.

RUNNING

The Tamalpa Runners
P.O. Box 701
Corte Madera,
CA 94976

This Marin-based running club offers several good reasons to join. First, among its thousand-plus members, you'll find quite a few singles of all ability levels. Second, it's a wonderful excuse to get out of the City on a foggy summer weekend. Third, you'll find a ton of activities with fellow running enthusiasts which include interval workouts, track meets, fun runs and frequent parties.

Mingling at the Marina Green!

Even if you never meet a single potentially interesting person while jogging the Marina Green, you can't complain about the view! There's jogging, kite-flying, dog-walking and rollerblading. Do linger for a few extra moments at the warm-up end of the Green where everyone goes to stretch before and after a run. Glance around as you limber up. And Smile!

SINGLES SHOPPING TIP

Be sure and do your grocery shopping across the street at the Marina Safeway-The place where Singles shop. After work or on weekends is the best time to stock up and check out items besides granola and low-fat milk!

HIKING & BACKPACKING

Sierra Singles
(510) 658-9977

This popular section of the Bay chapter of the Sierra Club, is a "must-join". Sierra Singles attracts people in the 21-40 year old age group and centers around activities "which promote an appreciation of nature and the environment". But what it really boils down to is some great hiking, biking and backpacking experiences around the Bay Area. Count on a variety of cultural and social opportunities as well. There is a monthly newsletter of all activities. Membership in the Sierra Club is encouraged. Call (510) 658-9977 for information on the Sierra Club.

Sierra Solos

Most people don't realize there is also a singles club called Sierra Solos, aimed at a more open age group, and which tends to attract people who are 35-50. Between Sierra Singles and Sierra Solos, there are between fifteen to twenty events a month covering the Bay Area. Some of them are purely social, such as a theatre evening. Exchange those hiking boots for high heels and that sunblock for lipstick.

SAILING

The Oceanic Society
441-5970

This is one way of getting on the Bay without owning a boat! The Oceanic Society is involved in the preservation of the Bay and the Farallone Islands, as well as purely social events. Meetings are at Fort Mason each month. Majority of the members are over forty.

Cal Sailing & Windsurfing Club
Across from Berkeley Marina
Berkeley
(510) 527-7245

This is a popular sailing school for the younger would-be sailors. For a nominal cost, a three-month membership permits you to take advantage of unlimited sailing instruction and equipment use. Take along a friend or go solo to the monthly Open Houses which offer free introductory classes.

SKI LEAGUES FOR SINGLES

There are several good Single Ski Leagues around the Bay and they meet every week of the year. Volunteers take calls regarding membership, so if these numbers are out of date, look for updated listings in CITY SPORTS MAGAZINE, available monthly.

San Francisco Club 771-3824

Powder Hounds (Oakland) 452-2449

Fall Line (Larkspur) 479-7796

In Skiers (San Mateo) 365-0789

Rusty Bindings (Walnut Creek) 254-5983

FAVORITE RESTAURANTS

Good food, fine service and ambience are always the top criteria for San Franciscans, single or otherwise. But there are restaurants in the City that are particularly popular Singles hangouts, like the recommendations below.

Johnny Love's
1500 Broadway
931-6053

Amidst the dating frenzy in many of the City's new "in" restaurants, there exists a remarkably good kitchen to be found at Johnny Love's new bar, dance spot and eatery in town. The courting is hot and heavy, but if things don't pan out, you can have a remarkably good meal. So good, in fact, that if you are coming just to eat, arrive early at this high-spirited, high-ceilinged watering hole on Polk & Broadway.

Cypress Club
500 Jackson Street
296-8533

Stylish and elegant supper club located in the charming Jackson Square area of the Financial District.

MacArthur Park
607 Front Street
398-5700

An enduring favorite among the single professionals in the area, and still some of the best barbecue ribs going!

Gordon Biersch Brewery
2 Harrison Street
243-8246

Located in the renovated Hills Plaza complex on the border of the Financial District, this has become *the place* to meet and mingle. One experienced observer of the singles scene in SF has dubbed Gordon Biersch the "Perry's" of the nineties, the perfect place for upscale professionals to come together. The lower hall is all bar and lounge and a single person can feel relaxed and comfortable sipping a superb glass of frosty beer and checking out the scene and the spectacular Bay views! At times, there are literally lines of people waiting to get in! It's not hard to figure out why.

Harry Denton's
161 Steuart Street
882-1333

Continental/ California cuisine with live music nightly, dancing on weekends. With its beautiful setting, bay views and lots of action, Harry Denton's is a popular spot for drinks, dinner or dancing.

THE BERMUDA TRIANGLE

Younger Singles have been known to wander into this labyrinth of swinging bars and restaurants and have never been seen again. Hence, its somewhat whimsical name. The whole area between Union, Filbert and Fillmore Street has come to be called "The Triangle". Listed below are the three restaurants which comprise this "notorious" title. Enter at your own risk!

△ *Balboa Cafe*
3199 Fillmore
921-3944

For a great burger and a noisy crowd, consider the renowned Balboa, king of Fillmore Street.

△ *Golden Gate Grill*
3200 Fillmore
931-4600

Great grilled food at moderate prices. Lively bar scene.

△ *Pierce Street Annex*
3138 Fillmore
567-1400

This well-known bar has been around for thirty years and keeps on attracting a young and enthusiastic crowd.

Cafe Jacqueline
1454 Grant
981-5565

One of the most romantic restaurants in the City. Tucked away on upper Grant, this is the place to eat with that someone special. Save room for Jacqueline's white chocolate souffles!

Bix
56 Gold Street
433-6300

A bustling jazz supper club and elegant restaurant tucked away in the famous Barbary Coast area of San Francisco. Drinking, dancing and torch songs will lift even the most despondent of souls.

Spinelli's Coffee
2455 Fillmore
929-8808

Drop by for a latte after a brisk exercise class, a challenging bike ride or a walk in the park with your dog. Check out the action at this popular coffee bar where cleats, pets and bikes are parked at the front door on any given morning.

IDEAS FOR AN EVENING OUT ALONE

Not looking forward to another night, home alone with Lean Cuisine?

Try going solo to a restaurant like Max's Deli or Spuntino, if you're in the blue jeans and turtleneck mood. Or sink your teeth into the world's greatest hot dog at the bar at Stars if you're willing to dress up a notch.

Afterwards, take a short walk to A Clean Well-Lighted Place for Books in Opera Plaza. Always filled with interesting-looking people, it is the ideal place to browse and strike up a conversation. Open nightly until 11 PM and midnight on Fridays and Saturdays. What does that tell you? Pick up a monthly schedule of literary events or put yourself on the mailing list.

MATCHMAKER MATCHMAKER

The Dating Game

Okay, you've gone to lectures at the Modern, attended dances sponsored by the Guardsmen, played in mixed doubles at the SF Tennis Club, joined in a coed volleyball game at Kezar Stadium, jogged the Marina Green and purchased basic provisions at the Marina Safeway on a Sunday morning. You've wandered around A Clean, Well-Lighted Place for Books at 10 PM looking appropriately literary, and have volunteered your time helping out at the Special Olympics. The weekend is approaching, and you are tired of cheerfully marching out to go it alone...again.

DATING SERVICES

Dating services have come a long way from the days of Yenta the Matchmaker, and there is a wide variety of services to consider, ranging from the inexpensive to ones requiring an outlay of thousands of dollars.

Computer Dating

In computer dating, you fill out a questionnaire describing yourself and the person you are interested in meeting. You are then matched electronically and are given the names and phone numbers of your "match". The main advantage to this system is that it is often quite cheap and comprehensive because of the vast data which can be entered and analyzed. Of course, there is that old saying, "garbage in, garbage out". The system only works if all applicants are brutally honest!

Photo & Video Dating Services

The unfailing logic behind these services is that you can see what you are getting into! There is a video or photograph besides the extensive bio of each candidate. When you see someone interesting, the club contacts them on your behalf so that they can then come down and see your bio. The big question to ask, of course, is how current is the video or photo and does it unduly romanticize its subject?

> *"It is a truth universally acknowledged that a single man in possession of a good fortune must be in want of a wife."*
>
> *–Jane Austen*
> *"Pride & Prejudice"*

PERSONAL INTRODUCTION SERVICES

These types of dating services tend to be more expensive. They pride themselves on providing the "human touch" and offer an active involvement in helping you find the perfect match. But you pay a steep fee, and you still have to rely on their intuitions and recommendations.

Listed here are a selection of services that have been researched and are recommended. The bottom line is a willingness on your part to give it a try, the determination to keep your perspective and the ability to have a sense of humor over the results!

Choosing the Best Dating Service for You

1. *Check the history and reputation of the service. What have other singles said about it? How long has it been around?*
2. *How many active members are there, and are they located in a geographic area reasonably close to you? What is the ratio of men to women?*
3. *Check out the age range. What percentage are in the age range you prefer?*
4. *What is the cost and how long is the membership? What are the limitations and/or advantages?*
5. *Are you comfortable with the process? Do you want your name and phone given out? Will you be willing to respond every time someone takes an interest in your resume/ photo?*

The Patricia Moore Group
777-9752

This highly-professional matchmaking service conducts the equivalent of an executive search in finding the appropriate mate for you and is "committed to searches which result in long-term relationships or marriage". That's the good news. The bad news is that you pay a flat fee of $4000 for this search. After an extensive interview (no photo or video), your information is passed on to the appropriate match. If he or she is interested, you review their "portfolio". It is up to the two of you to get together. There is a follow-up to discuss your reaction. You may also go "inactive" for a certain period of time, if you have met someone, allowing you to stay on file.

Perfect Strings
566-7774

This service was recommended by someone who had tried many such services and found this one refreshingly easy, very reasonably priced and attracted interesting prospects. Ideally, Perfect Strings is based on a mutual interest in music and in attending symphony, ballet, opera and other musically related fields. The matching up process is very casual, consisting of filling out two forms and paying a flat fee of $44. One form has your photo, bio, phone number (no address is suggested for women) and other relevant information. This is circulated to all members. Should you request the second form, you can purchase it for a dollar. A six-month listing can have as many as 400 names with monthly additions of 50 to sixty members.

New Partners
An Introduction Service of the SF Jewish Community Center
346-6040

The JCC offers a wonderful, hands-on, reasonably priced personalized introduction service for adults who want more control in how they meet other singles. The friendly atmosphere of this service, under the auspices of Danny Schwager, is almost a "throwback to an old-fashioned personalized approach of introducing people". There is a detailed open-ended questionnaire to fill out and an interview is taken as well. Clients can meet from 6-12 matches during the course of the six month membership. Open to all religions and the cost is $145 for members of the JCC and $195 for non-members.

Annual Singles Retreat

The JCC offers an annual weekend retreat for singles in a relaxed, social environment in locales around the Bay Area. The weekends include discussions led by a facilitator on a variety of personal relationship topics. There are also outdoor activities. All meals, lodging and transportation are included in the price. Call the JCC for further information or pick up a brochure at 3200 California St.

The Classifieds
This is considered the 'free fall" of unsupervised matchmaking! With movie spoofs like "Desperately Seeking Susan", the art of love through the "classifieds" can seem like a wild and woolly adventure. If approached carefully and sensibly, the classifieds become an interesting alternative.

RULES OF THE GAME

1. *Choose a classified ad in a periodical to which you can relate and in which you feel comfortable being advertised. The more upscale the readership, the more likelihood of your ad being seen by someone appropriate to your needs.*

2. *When you decide to place an ad, never leave a phone number (especially if you are a woman). Invest in a P.O. Box, and request all enquiries in writing with photos be sent there.*

3. *When an interested person responds to your ad, try to ascertain in your phone call with him/her, their address and place of work. Be sure and call there to verify this information. Honesty is one of the first criteria you want to establish!*

4. *Speaking of honesty, be specific about your requirements in the initial phone call, as well as what you can honestly offer. Don't waste each other's time.*

5. *Trust your intuition. Don't let things go beyond a phone call unless his/her voice sounds right and you're feeling good about the conversation.*

Let's Go Shopping

San Francisco is a shopper's paradise, small and compact enough to do in a day and yet sophisticated and varied enough to browse in for weeks. A good way to shop San Francisco is by neighborhood and each one has its own characteristic uniqueness. Perhaps the best place to start is with the world famous Union Square area.

UNION SQUARE

It is Madison Avenue, Rodeo Drive and Place Vendome all rolled into one compact area, punctuated by colorful flower stalls on every corner. Within a four-block radius, shoppers can purchase designer gowns or springer spaniel puppies, high-priced art or Beluga caviar. Major department stores include the Big Four:

I. Magnins
Geary & Stockton
362-2100

Neiman Marcus
Geary & Stockton
362-3900

Saks Fifth Avenue
Powell & Post
986-4300

Macy's
170 O'Farrell
397-3333

With its fabulous Armani AX boutique.

Macy's Men's and Childrens
Across the street from the main store on Geary & Stockton

POST STREET

An elegant street bordering Union Square and featuring world-class shops including:

Brooks Brothers
201 Post
397-4500

This famous men's clothiers also offers fashions for women. Featuring an entire range of formal and informal attire.

Escada
259 Post
391-3500

European designer fashions for women.

Gumps
250 Post
982-1616

One of the oldest shops in the City filled with unique one-of-a-kind gifts, furniture, china, art and jewelry.

Louis Vuitton
230 Post
391-6200

Leather goods for men & women.

The Polo Store
90 Post
567-7656

An architectural delight filled with classic Polo gear for men, women and kids, as well as beddings and accessories.

Tiffany & Co.
360 Post
781-7000

Located in its posh new site, Tiffany's contains the stuff of which dreams are made! Two floors of dazzling delights.

TSE Cashmere
171 Post
391-1112

Luxurious modern cashmere clothes for men, women and even kids.

Williams Sonoma
150 Post
362-6904

The "compleat" kitchen & culinary accessory shop for upscale cooks.

GRANT AVENUE

Made famous in the movie "Flower Drum Song", Grant Avenue is the gateway to Chinatown. Don't miss out on the following first class shops:

Banana Republic
256 Grant
788-3087

The last word in casual, good looking and easy to wear clothes.

Crate & Barrel
125 Grant
986-4000

Well-priced, colorful housewares and home supplies including glasses, ceramic tableware, pottery, linens and much more.

"What I've found does the most good is just to get into a taxi and go to Tiffany's..."
—Truman Capote
"Breakfast at Tiffany's"

SUTTER STREET

Located up the hill from Union Square is one of the most popular shopping areas in town. Shops on Sutter include:

Go-Silk
424 Sutter
391-2474

Pure elegance for men & women in washable silk classics. Go-see!

Jeanne Marc
262 Sutter
362-1121

Bold colors and striking prints characterize the Jeann-Marc look.

Jessica McClintock
353 Sutter
397-0987

A romantic, delicate look in this distinctive line of clothes for women in this visually dramatic shop on Sutter.

Obiko
794 Sutter
775-2882

A tiny gem of a shop for one-of-a-kind hand-made woven wear.

Wilkes Bashford
375 Sutter
986-4380

Local boy turns hot retailer in this elegant shop on Sutter with the latest in designer clothes for men and women.

GEARY STREET

Renowned as "Theatre Row", Geary is also host to a bevy of luxury retail shops including:

Bottega Veneta
108 Geary
981-1700

The consummate high-end Italian leather goods shop.

Bruno Magli
285 Geary
421-0356

The only franchised store in the US for this famed shoe designer.

North Beach Leather
190 Geary
362-8300

Luxurious up-to-the-moment, nationally-recognized leather fashions.

Be sure and wander along Maiden Lane.

A two-block walking street between Stockton and Kearny, filled with charming shops, hair salons and art galleries. These include J.S. Banks Clothiers at 125 Maiden Lane, Chanel at 155 Maiden Lane and Robison's Pet Shop, the oldest pet store in America, established in 1849, at 135 Maiden Lane and Pierre Dieux, relocated from Sutter to 120 Maiden Lane. This quaint street has a colorful history! Prior to the '06 Quake, it was known as Morton Street, the Barbary Coast's red-light district.

SHOPPING STREETS

UNION STREET

I had to learn the hard way that Union Street bears absolutely no relationship to Union Square! But that doesn't mean that popular Union Street doesn't share equal billing with its great places to shop and fine restaurants. Many of the surrounding Victorians have been transformed into shopping compounds bordered by trendy boutiques and galleries. Some of the best people-watching can be found here in any of the outdoor sidewalk coffee houses day or night.

There are some wonderful children's shops along the street including:

Ragamuffin
3044 Union

Mudpie
1699 Union

Check out:

An American Girl in Italy
2163 Union

The Smile Gallery
1750 Union

SACRAMENTO STREET

What was formerly a basic utilitarian shopping street for neighboring Presidio Heights has blossomed into one of the loveliest shopping, browsing, eating and movie-going streets in town. And it's delightfully flat! The parking is a challenge but it's worth it to shop in such stores as:

Sue Fisher King
3075 Sacramento

The latest in Italian ceramics and linens.

Susan of Burlingame
3685 Sacramento

Elegantly expensive womens fashions.

Forrest Jones
3274 Sacramento

Tops for housewares.

Dottie Doolittle
3680 Sacramento

The most famous little girls shop in San Francisco. Check out its new shoe store for girls across the street.

*Good Italian fare can be found at **Prego** at 2000 Union. For wonderful breakfasts, try **Doidge's Kitchen** at 2217 Union. Don't miss the pomme fritte at **L'Entrecote de Paris** at 2032 Union. Head for the **Balboa Cafe** at 3199 Fillmore for great hamburgers.*

"When you get tired of walking around San Francisco, you can always lean up against it."

–Anonymous

Button Down
3640 Sacramento

For up-dated classic clothing.

Brava Strada
3247 Sacramento

For Fine Italian leather.

The Virginia Breier Gallery
3091 Sacramento

A must see for fabulous ceramics, jewelry and crafts.

I could go on and on. Unlike Union Street's trendier, slicker look, the shops of Sacramento Street spell pure class.

Some super places to eat would include: Rosemarino, a chic little Italian eatery at 3665 Sacramento, (and smell the exotic blooms at Yoko next door at 3661). You may be sorry if you don't try Garibaldi at 347 Presidio & Sacto. Or Le Castel, elegant and expensive, at 3235 Sacramento. For lunch, try the Tuba Garden at 3634 Sacramento or Tortola, for a quick Mexican fix at 3640 Sacramento.

FILLMORE STREET

What was once run-down, shabby and rarely frequented by the natives is now Hot, Hot, Hot. There is a concentration of wonderful shops including:

Fillamento
2185 Fillmore

Fredericksen's Hardware
3029 Fillmore

Jim-Elle
2237 Fillmore

For contemporary women's fashion.

Yountville
2416 Fillmore

For all-American kids gear.

▷ *To buy or sell consignment clothes, one of the best shops around is the Junior League's Next to New Shop at 2226 Fillmore, and it supports a worthy cause.*

Some of the best eating in the City can be found on this upscale street including Pacific Heights Bar and Grill on 2001 Fillmore for fabulous fresh oysters. Don't miss The Elite Cafe at 2049 Fillmore for a taste of New Orleans in San Francisco. Some great Italian eating can be found at Jackson Fillmore Trattoria at 2506 Fillmore. Oritalia is the place for Italian with an Oriental twist at 1915 Fillmore. How about the greatest bagels? Gotta be Holey Bagels at 3218 Fillmore. Best ice cream cone? Rory's Twisted Scoop on 2015 Fillmore.

Warning: Parking on Fillmore is a colossal hassle.

BOOK STORES

My favorite book stores in San Francisco aren't necessarily the big chains or the heavily-discounted mega-stores. I like book stores with personality, whose staff care about their shoppers and look fondly upon browsers; who take pride in their children's section and enjoy working with kids. In the best of all worlds, my favorite book stores have a small cafe in-house where you can hunker down with a bowl of home-made soup or freshly-ground coffee and peruse the New York Times or linger over your new book. The following come awfully close!

A Clean Well-Lighted Place for Books
Opera Plaza, 601 Van Ness
441-6670

Oft-mentioned in this guide, this popular book store is open seven days a week from 10 am to 11 pm. Books for every age and interest are available and there are lively literary events each month.

The Green Apple
506 Clement
387-2272

Out in the Avenues is a funky, bustling book store with three floors filled with a huge, eclectic collection of new and used books. For twenty years, this has been a premier neighborhood book store.

"Where is human nature so weak as in a bookstore!"

–Anonymous

City Lights
261 Columbus
362-8193

A literary meeting place since 1953 and made famous by the Beat Generation. Owner-poet in residence Lawrence Ferlinghetti presides over one of the most beloved places for books in the City. Open every day from 10 am to midnight.

Cover to Cover
3910 24th Street
282-8080

A wonderful full-service book store in Noe Valley and one of the outstanding sources for children's books. Open seven days a week.

Old Wives Tales Bookstore
1009 Valencia
821-4675

Stocks both adult and kids books and offers a special discount card for discounts on all books.

Writers Bookstore
2848 Webster
921-2620

If you can find a parking spot near this delightful little book store off Union Street, you will find great deals on hardcover books, often up to 30% off, as well as a wonderful selection of "gently used" books.

Books, Inc.
140 Powell
397-1555
and
3515 California
221-3666

Since 1851, Books, Inc. has been offering a wide variety of books on every subject imaginable, including a wonderful children's section.

Alexander Book Co.
50 Second Street
495-2992

An old-fashioned full-service independent book store in downtown San Francisco. Handsomely appointed, it has an extensive children's section and offers monthly literary readings.

"The test of a first-rate bookstore is: Could you fall in love there? Say, the way Fred Astaire fell in love with Audrey Hepburn in 'Funny Face' or whatshisname with Amy Irving in 'Crossing Delancey' or Rod Taylor with Maggie Smith in 'Young Cassidy'?... Even the best of the new stores cannot match the old treasure caves."

–Roger Rosenblatt in the New Republic

BEST BARGAIN SHOPPING IN THE BAY AREA

Everyone likes a bargain. It's just a question of how far you are willing to go to seek them out. Listed below are a few recommendations that only begin to scratch the surface!

FASHION FINDS

Kutler Clothiers
625 Howard
543-7770

Top-quality designer mens clothing is sold in the elegant new site of an old San Francisco clothier at savings of up to 50% or more.

Jeanne-Marc-Downs
508 Third Street
243-4396

To Jeanne-Marc fans, this is Mecca indeed! The outlet store of this fabulous designer sells popular designs three seasons behind at excellent savings.

Esprit Outlet
499 Illinois St. at 16th
957-2550

One of the largest selections of Esprit merchandise includes clothes and shoes for women and juniors, activewear for kids and toddlers, bed and bath linens for the home. Discounts are 30% or more with a new shipment every two weeks.

Be sure and stop by the Esprit Cafe for breakfast or lunch, open everyday except Sunday. On sunny days, consider a picnic in the sculpture garden.

Yerba Buena Square
899 Howard Street
974-5136

For the consummate discount shopper, why not make a trip to the City's largest off-price factory mall. More than a 100,000 square feet of bargains, many of which are discounted up to 75%. Plenty of parking nearby.
Open 9:30 AM to 8 PM daily.

San Francisco Mercantile
2915 Sacramento
563-0113

This charming Eileen West Outlet, located in the middle of Presidio Heights, carries mostly flannel and cotton nightwear available at a discounted price from this popular designer.

Loehmanns
222 Sutter
985-3215

Loehmanns is synonymous with wholesale womens designer fashion. With this convenient downtown location, it's worth popping in as you are hurrying down Sutter or parking nearby in the Sutter Stockton Garage.

MARINA SQUARE SHOPPING CENTER

Okay, so maybe San Leandro is one spot on earth you could skip. But you may want to think twice when you consider some of the outlet shops you can cover in one trip to this East Bay discount mall:

Talbots
1235 Marina Blvd.
San Leandro
(510) 614-1090

The only Talbots outlet on the West Coast carrying merchandise at bargain basement prices. Quality is high, as it is company policy not to sell imperfect merchandise.

Eddie Bauer Outlet Store
1295 Marina Blvd.
San Leandro
(510) 895-1484

Over-stocked, discontinued and out of season items can all be had at fantastic savings in mens and womens activewear.

Audrey Jones Outlet
1221 Marina Blvd.
San Leandro
(510) 352-8337

Full-figure fashions can be had for fabulous buys here from a number of nationally recognized designers. New merchandise arrives every week at tremendous mark-downs, with loyal customers flying or driving in from all over the state to shop here.

LINENS

The Linen Factory Outlet
475 Ninth St.
861-1511

The perfect place to pick up discontinued linen lines and seconds in all kinds of home textiles including tablecloths, towels, blankets, down beddings, etc.

Bed Bath and Beyond Superstore
555 Ninth St.
252-0490

A huge selection of bed, bath and household linens at discounted prices. A one-stop shopping expedition for all household needs.

THE ULTIMATE REFERENCE BOOK

For a wonderful resource guide on discount shopping around the Bay Area, the ultimate reference book is "Bargain Hunting in the Bay Area" by Sally Socolich. $11.95

SHOPPER STOPPER
DISCOUNT SHOPPING TOURS
(707) 829-1597

This 6+ hour bus tour covers just about all the bases of discount, hassle-free shopping including some closed-to-the public warehouses. A full day of door to door bargain hunting delights.

WALLPAPER

WallStreet
2690 Harrison
285-0870

This wallpaper factory outlet located in the Mission stocks a dazzling array of more than a thousand papers from well-known manufacturers and at a savings of 40-50% off retail.

OPTICAL OUTLETS

Four Eyes
361 Sutter
781-2002

and
401 Washington
391-5300

With these convenient locations in the heart of San Francisco, it's easy to take advantage of wholesale prescription frames.

The Optical Outlet
951 Market
982-5106

This amazing Market Street shop carries "salesmen samples", over-runs and discontinued styles at bargain prices.

APPLIANCES

Cherins
727-2111

Call by phone for competitive prices on large and small household appliances. Cherins will take your order, deliver it and beat any price going, if possible. Very reliable, old San Francisco retailer/wholesaler.

FLOWERS

San Francisco Mart
690 Brannan at 6th

Although primarily a facility for wholesalers or those in the trade, there are retail shops within the mart which offer discounted prices on a variety of flowers and related items including baskets, ribbons, wrapping paper and much more. Or tag along with a professional and take advantage of the really big savings available.

KIDS GEAR

Biobottoms
620 Petaluma Blvd.
Petaluma
(707) 778-1948

If you're heading up to Napa or Sonoma, be sure and stop off in Petaluma to visit this outlet which sells "fresh air wear for kids". There is always a large selection of samples, seconds and discontinued lines at great savings.

Cary Children's Clothes
2390 Fourth Street
Berkeley
(510) 841-5700

Samples, seconds and over-runs of these perfect party dresses for little girls are snapped up as quickly as they are put out in this outlet whose dresses are known for exquisite detailing and fine fabrics. If you get on the mailing list, you will receive monthly notices of special events and sales. You can also pick up over-runs on fabrics, buttons and trims at great savings.

GOLF

**Nevada Bob's
Discount Golf**
1500 Monument Blvd.
Concord
(510) 680-0111

For value, price and
first class service, try Nevada Bob's.
Clothing and accessories are also sold
there and it's worth the drive.

SKIS

The key to buying skis is to shop during
the annual sales. Best bets are
Lombardi's whose sale is usually held
in mid-November, and **Any Mountain**
for their yearly Labor Day Sale.

Lombardi's
152 Clement Street
387-0600

Any Mountain Ltd.
71 Tamal Vista Blvd.
Corte Madera
927-0170

Located in a charming shopping center
in Marin, this shop is tops for skis, clothes
and accessories.

North Face Factory Outlet
1325 Howard
626-6444

While we're on the subject of skiing,
make a point of visiting this great outlet
store – manufacturers of rain and snow
gear, down parkas, ski wear, sleeping
bags, tents and backpacks. All items are
seconds, over runs or discontinued lines
at significant discounts.

TENNIS

Fry's Warehouse
352 E, Grand Ave.
So. San Francisco
761-5112

or

1495 E. Francisco Blvd.
San Rafael
453-3566

The best buys can be found at Fry's
which buys its merchandise in bulk to
allow for substantial discounts.

MOUNTAIN BIKES

**Windsurf Bicycle Snowboard
Warehouse**
428 S. Airport Blvd.
588-1714

Huge warehouse filled with wide array
of equipment. If you find a bike at a
lower price elsewhere, they will beat
the price by 10% of the difference.

**Marin Mountain Bike
Factory Outlet**
400 Francisco Blvd.
San Rafael
457-1222

This is worth a ride to Marin to check
out this spacious, beautifully merchan-
dised new store offering a low-priced
alternative to big name manufacturers.

COMPUTER SHOPPING

CompUSA
1250 El Camino Real
San Bruno
244-9990

Considered one of the best local "superstores" for computers. They claim to beat any price, so bring ads from competing vendors with you.

Frys' Electronics
340 Portage Ave.
Palo Alto
496-6000

If you are willing to venture as far as Palo Alto, you can find some unbelievably good buys at Fry's. With an ambience that is half Sharper Image and half K-Mart, you'll find the prices here are almost as cheap as the mail order catalogues.

Computer Attic
2750 El Camino Real
Redwood City
332-0639

One of the best local stores with consistently low prices, thirty thousand square feet of hardware and excellent technical support.

Whole Earth Access
401 Bayshore Blvd.
285-5244

863 E. Francisco Blvd. San Rafael
459-3533

Whole Earth is highly recommended for its competitive prices and knowledgeable sales staff. Every effort is made to satisfy its customers.

ELECTRONICS

Video Only
1199 Van Ness
563-5200

An 18-store national chain that keeps its prices consistently low, its sales staff small and does little advertising, but its merchandise is often the best value in town for certain items.

RETAIL BARGAINING

One of the electronic industry's best-kept secrets is that many retail stores are receptive to bargaining. Competition is so intense that not only will they match each other's prices, often they will undercut them. So do your research and be prepared to haggle!

RECYCLING

*If you have a laser printer, here's a way of recycling your existing toner cartridge for considerably less than buying a new one. Call **Cartridge Express** at 833 Market (979-0626), a dependable vendor who will unconditionally guarantee the refilling of your current cartridge and pick up and deliver.*

Taking The Byte

*I am convinced we are the last family
in America to buy a computer.*

Even Harry, our garbage collector who cheerfully passes by my office window every Thursday morning, reminds me of this fact as I hunch over my word processor.

"You should get a real computer, Mrs. D. Think of your children."

"We've got to buy a real computer," I announce to my husband at dinner. "We have to think of our children."

"Who informed you of this grievous injustice perpetrated on our children?"

"Harry, our garbage collector. He has the Mac IIsi. Says he couldn't live without it."

The next day we headed over to Computerville. The parking lot was filled to capacity. Hundreds of people were pushing and shoving to get into the store.

"Must be some sale going on!" my husband exclaimed as we worked our way up to the electronics department.

We were handed a number.

"You don't understand," I said in a confidential whisper to a bored, gum-chewing clerk. "We're here to look at computers." This was stated as if I were a major player announcing my presence at the International Monetary Conference.

"Take a number."

We were awed at the scene before us. Otherwise ordinary-looking individuals were engaged in hand-to-hand combat over monitors and keyboards and modums and printers. This was war! And I was not going to be left out of the action.

"Gimme a Mac LC, the 12" RGB color display monitor, a Personal LaserWriter, the Panamac power surge mechanism and the pad. $3423 plus tax and warranty? No prob."

"Are you <u>crazy</u>?" shouted my husband amidst the ensuing pandemonium. "You're talking about what used to be the price of a CAR. Hold on. We have to talk about this."

"We don't have time to talk." I yelled back, wrestling an AppleColor High Resolution Monitor away from a grim-faced middle-aged matron. "This is for our children. How can you stand there? Get your credit card while I protect our CD ROM!"

I grinned bravely as I fought off a pin-striped invader intent on taking my 40-megabyte hard drive. My husband, caught up in the heat of battle at last, charged up to the service desk waving his VISA card like a bazooka.

We marched out of Computerville triumphantly carrying every piece of hardware and software known to man. We arrived home and ceremoniously dumped our spoils of war in front of our children who viewed the mysterious boxes with a certain interest.

"Cool!" Is it a CD player with giant speakers?"

"No way, it's gotta be SuperNintendo!"

"Children," I croaked proudly, "Your father and I have bought you a computer!"

"A computer? Big deal, we have them at school."

"What's wrong with your word processor, Mom? It works fine."

I can't wait until Thursday. That's the day Harry and I are going to have a little talk...

Around the House

Whether you are the proud owners of a charming old Victorian or you are renting a flat in a contemporary new building, we all need a pool of everyday resources to efficiently run a household. When time is of the essence, when quality is a high priority and when you have more important things in your life to think about, consider the recommendations below. I have tried to offer several choices in each category so that you can decide which suits you best.

INTERIOR DESIGNERS

Barbara Scavullo
1796-18th Street
558-8774

Does exclusively residential work. There is an in-house architect as well as a competent team of designers on staff. Every effort is made to work with the individual's style and taste instead of merely dictating to it. A beautiful and balanced design appeal.

Ruth G. Preucell
292-5964

With over ten years of design experience in both the commercial and residential field, Ruth Preucell infuses every project with a special vision.

Design Options
461-3620

This Marin team combines a fresh, easy approach to home design with an affordable price.

Sunrise Interiors
831 B St., San Rafael
456-3939

Definitely worth a trip to Marin. A lovely shop filled with design-quality furniture and accessories. A full staff of on-site complimentary home designers is there to help.

Decorator Previews
3049 Fillmore
563-3977

The people at Decorator Previews call themselves the "decorating psychologists". For $100, you get a two-hour consultation and slide show where you view the work of fifty designers to determine what style you prefer and what is in your price range. You also save yourself the nightmare of hiring the wrong designer. By appointment.

Kensington Interiors
3485 Sacramento
771-1768

"The only game in town", proudly states owner Barbara Hutchings, "to find high-end, design quality home furnishings normally available only to interior designers". Combines an elegant storefront on Sacramento Street filled with lovely furniture and home accessories of quality design. Home consulting also available.

TIPS TO CONSIDER

1. *State your requirements clearly in an initial visit. How positive and responsive is the potential service person?*

2. *How long have they been in business and do they have a particular specialty which you require? For example, a certain painter may specialize in painting the intricate facade of your peeling Edwardian wonder.*

3. *Ask for a reference from one, or even two, previous clients. Go and view the work done.*

ARCHITECTS

Scheiber Design Group
558-8833

Vickie Lateano is the delightful and knowledgeable spokeswoman for this excellent full-service design group. With twenty years experience, there is an emphasis here on high-end residential re-models. Encompasses a full range of design styles as well as an expertise in furniture design to fit the space.

Kurtzman & Associates
900 North Point Suite 430
771-2730

Ken Kurtzman and his talented group specialize in residential architecture. They focus on renovation work and construction of all styles. He also works closely with an interior design group called Group Four, headed up by his wife, noted designer Caryl Kurtzman.

Tom Higley Architect
346-9376

Residential design work. Kitchens and bathrooms a specialty.

Dan Phipps & Associates
1031 Post
776-1606

General residential re-modelling and architectural design. Specialize in kitchens and there is an interior designer in-house. 75% of his work is restoration on all styles of buildings. Custom design furniture is also available.

Gary Millar Building Design
453-6656

This talented architect will work closely with clients to personalize architectural projects to their needs and requirements. Highly capable, reasonably priced.

CONTRACTORS

David Hardman-Reidell
673-9379

Highly recommended general contractor. Easy to work with. Kitchens are a specialty.

John Millar
488-0152

Licensed general contractor with a specialty in woodwork design.

Plath & Co.
751-3631

Specializes in re-modelling Victorians. Custom residential work.

E. Jensen & Son
755-5621

New construction and remodelling are a specialty. Also concentrates on additions, kitchens and baths.

Johnson Chin
753-6632

New construction and re-models.

Forde-Mazzola
885-4900

High-quality work in re-modelling and new construction. Highly recommended from those in the trade.

PLUMBERS

Lipsey Plumbing
621-6030

This plumbing and heating service prides itself on being problem solvers for high-end plumbing fixtures and fittings. They also specialize in repairing tankless water heaters.

Larry Selli Plumbers
362-1968

General plumbing, heating contractors.

Malcomb Plumbers
931-1985

High-quality plumbing and heating service.

PAINTERS

Windy City West
824-5876

This group of extremely competent all-women painters (there are three crews!) work indoors and out. They mainly focus on large residential jobs. They do no advertising. All work is based on personal recommendation. There is an emphasis on "prep" work and the willingness to work closely with the clients for full satisfaction.

Color Quest
921-1121

This group has been in business since 1975 and work on high-end residential properties with an emphasis on Victorians. They also do restoration and have an in-house color consultant. Recommendations can also be made for faux finishing, stenciling, etc. Featured in "Painted Ladies Revisited".

Pat Regan
821-1292

Pat is a recommended, moderately-priced residential painter who employs a crew of six to seven. Also does not advertise and gets most work through the "Pacific Heights hotline" of satisfied customers.

Valasquez Painting
897-7453

Tom Velasquez is very neat, quick and reasonable in price. He is happy to do small jobs as well as painting a whole house.

Dean Hoffman
387-4687

A moderately-priced recommended painter for small jobs.

FOR FABULOUS FAUX!

For a faux-marble look or Provence stenciled detailing, the following firms specialize in painted finishes, glazing and stencilling.

Brushworks
456-0336

Specialists in faux finishes and custom-designed hand-cut stencils. Also paint on walls, fabric and furniture in a wonderful trompe l'oeil effect. Featured in many Decorator Showcase homes.

Chimera
488-4418

Incredible faux and textural finishes as well as stenciling, trompe l'oeil. Also specialize in antique restoration and gilding. Will pick up and deliver.

Day Studio Workshop
1504 Bryant
626-9300

Classes are offered in all different forms of decorative painting.

GARDENERS

Delaney & Cochran
495-5800

San Francisco's hottest landscape design team. Delaney claims that "a home landscape for a client is very personal, so you do a lot of listening". They work on the principle that less is more and select plants or shrubbery that will work.

Dennis Westler
861-5999

Interior and exterior plant maintenance as well as garden design.

Jonathan Plant & Associates
(510) 283-5574

With offices in Lafayette and St. Helena, Jonathan Plant services much of the Bay Area. He is a licensed landscape architect and is an expert in horticulture. Works with high-end residential landscaping design projects.

PLANT CARE RESOURCES
In The Green
731-7812

Owner Gail Lubin works primarily with businesses to install, design and maintain plants in an interior setting.

Indoor Plant Design
363-8768

"Plantscape" design and maintenance for home interiors.

Paxton Gate
1204 Stevenson St.
255-5955

What The Gardener is to Berkeley
and
Smith & Hawken is to Marin,
now Paxton Gate is
The City's answer to the
ultimate garden shop.

Charming, eclectic and reasonably priced, great things are being said about this narrow space on Stevenson Street within eyeshot of the hip Zuni Cafe on Market.

Ornamental Horticulture
Department
City College of San Francisco

This is a wonderful phone referral service for a one-time landscape design job or an on-going project in design, installation, maintenance and seasonal pruning. Fees are moderate and negotiated by each individual landscape designer. For information call 239-3236. Leave a message for a call back.

ALARM COMPANIES

National Guardian
824-5830

Full service security system specializing in business and residential systems. Fire and burglar systems installed and maintained quarterly, as well as regular system monitoring.

ADT
991-3000

With locations all over the Bay Area, ADT offers a full-service fire and burglar system which is set up to indicate any problems areas, therefore eliminating the need for regular checks.

LOCKSMITHS

CSS (California Security Systems)
200 6th Avenue
929-9200

This company offers a wide range of repair services for residents and automobiles. Bonded, insured and registered. Emergency service is a specialty.

Warman Security
1720 Sacramento off Polk
775-8513 (24-hour service available)

For over fifty years, Warman's has provided a variety of security related services including locks and keys changed and installed, auto lock service, safes and custom installations.

"BOYS IN THE HOOD"

If you feel as if you've been ripped off by your auto mechanic, you're probably not alone. Not knowing what's under the hood makes it hard to get a fair deal. Consider the following tips:

CarPro
(800) 222-7776

A toll-free hotline service. For $49 annual membership, you call and discuss your auto problems with qualified and certified experts who will make suggestions, estimates and recommendations.

Cal State Automobile Assoc.
565-2012

For hands-on diagnostic help for your car, try one of three diagnostic clinics including the Answer Van, a mobile unit which will check your mechanical and electrical system.

AAA will also recommend a trustworthy mechanic by referring members to an approved list of over 800 shops which must pass stringent and on-going guidelines for recommendation.

Bay Area Consumer Checkbook
397-8305

This local magazine publishes an excellent report on auto repairs.

Bureau of Auto Repair
(800) 952-5210

A mediation bureau to contact when you can't resolve a complaint or on-going problem with your mechanic.

AUTO SERVICE & REPAIR

Charles Henry Company
1540 Bush
673-7900

High-quality body shop only which services all makes and models.

Melrose
4818 Geary
495-6810

Concentrates on strictly engine work on all makes of cars.

Metropolitan Motors
721 Bryant
495-6810

Basic servicing, excluding body and tire work.

Auto Analysts
256 Turk
673-8686

Full-service shop which provides expertise in electrical, body, mechanical and tire needs.

California Auto Detailing
1776 Green
441-5762

Full-service shop with a specialty in car detailing.

Yamato Auto Repair
1899 Bush at Laguna
346-5116

Mike Dobashi provides a high quality of workmanship in basic auto repair. Also will do smog check and service.

USEFUL AUTOMOTIVE RESOURCES

The Dent Wizard
(510) 283-6890

This eager team does indeed perform magic on small dings and dents, without bodywork, filler or paint. Will travel anywhere in Bay Area and work is often done on site. A valuable resource!

Catering Car Wash
931-5289

Perry Peirano will provide a professional hand-washing, polishing, full shampooing, white wall bleaching and complete interior clean. He can come to your home, office or drop it off at 2001 Union.

A Clean Limousine
921-5377

The ultimate stretch limo.

Enterprise Rent-A-Car
1133 Van Ness
441-3369

With locations all over the Bay Area, this highly-regarded rental car service will deliver a car to your home, office or repair shop.

DRY CLEANERS

Sandy's Cleaners
364 West Portal
564-8020

Laundry, dry-cleaning and alterations. Located on the "Other side of Park".

Century Cleaners
2501 Lake Street
668-7033

Top-notch cleaners in the Sea Cliff area.

New Parisian
2903 Baker Street
931-6697

Highly recommended in the Cow Hollow area.

Ray's French Laundry
1205 Union
885-4171

The only dry-cleaner on Russian Hill.

"Excellent Cleaners"
2nd and California
751-7654

Quality cleaners and laundry with a recommended in-house dressmaker. All work done in-house. Located in the "Avenues".

Peninou French Laundry
3707 Sacramento
751-9200

Super expensive, but a must for your finest apparel. Absolute attention to detail. No laundry. Located in the Presidio Heights area.

Locust Cleaners
3587 Sacramento
346-9271

Located down the street from Peninou, the perfect alternative for ordinary, not so critical, dry-cleaning and laundry.

DRESSMAKERS AND SEAMSTRESSES

Locust Cleaners
3585 Sacramento
346-9271

Fine dressmaker/seamstress on site.

"Excellent Cleaners"
2nd and California
668-3455

Also offers a highly competent dressmaking service on premises.

The Fitting Room
1654 Union
474-5039

Tailoring by Lois
(707) 576-7964

Have dressmaker will travel. Lois will come to you and offers some of the finest dressmaking skills in the Bay Area. By appointment.

DOMESTIC HELP

Aunt Ann's
421-8442

Provides domestic help by day or live-in weekly, monthly or on a permanent basis. All applicants for jobs are carefully screened for full client satisfaction.

Here's Help, Inc.
931-HELP

A full-service, highly recommended, agency which offers full-time and temporary nannies, housekeepers and cleaning persons.

WORK
255-2325

Works with thirty independent contractors to perform both "mundane and unique" household services.

Enterprise For
High School Students
921-6554

A wonderful non-profit organization which provides jobs for willing and able high school students in an array of different areas including babysitting, gardening, cleaning and hauling, party help, envelope stuffing and much much more. Not only are you getting hardworking assistance for those difficult to fill jobs, but you are also helping teens get much-wanted and needed jobs.

WHIM
931-WHIM

Offers one-stop shopping for every household need from window washers to household help. Concentrates in large part on entertainment-related needs such as serving help, caterers, entertainers, etc. Does some household referrals.

USEFUL HOUSEHOLD RESOURCES

TRAVEL AGENTS

Averette Hansson Worldwide
110 Sutter Suite 502
362-7172

Full-service corporate or personal travel agents. Extremely well-organized, knowledgeable and helpful.

ELECTRICIANS

Ike's Electric (Ike Garcia)
861-6417

J. Hill Electric
665-2401

Tom Jarvis
648-0494

Century Electric (Jim Reed)
861-6522

JEWELRY REPAIR

Tigges Jewelers
5848 Geary
221-0804

This modest jewelry store in the Avenues has a wonderful in-house department which will repair all kinds of watches and jewelry.

Downtown Watch Repair
210 Post Street #304
986-1469

Works on all makes watches. Repairs are done in-house. Also works on small clocks.

CRYSTAL REPAIR

Mark Harrington Glassware
3041 Fillmore
931-2157

Repair not only crystal and glass, but also fix porcelain, pottery and just about everything but silver.

SHOE REPAIR

Anthony's Shoe Repair
30 Geary
781-1338

One of the oldest shoe repair shops in the City where everyone goes to have their fine shoes shod. Now located in a handsome storefront in the heart of Union Square. Expensive but worth it.

PICTURE FRAMERS

Walter-Adams
355 Presidio at Sacramento
346-1860

This excellent framers also houses a marvelous crafts and art gallery in its storefront on Presidio.

RUG & UPHOLSTERY CLEANERS

Appleby Cleaners
(510) 351-5230

CHIMNEY CLEANERS

Fireplace Safety Services
381-1550

Joe Rizzo will check and clean your fireplace and troubleshoot any potential problems.

UPHOLSTERERS

Sutter Furniture
621-15447

Excellent City upholsterers, but you must make arrangements for your furniture to be picked up and delivered. See "Delivery Service".

Luque Upholsterer
(510) 521-2100

General upholstery work. Slipcovers are done by outside specialist:
Maria (510) 534-3904

DELIVERY SERVICE

D & P Delivery Service
621-4949

Reasonaby-priced and conscientious delivery service for furniture.

APPLIANCE REPAIR

Bestway Appliance Repair
665-1540

Repairs all brands major appliances.

SECRETARIAL HELP

"Private Secretaries"
2750 Broadway
346-2157

Will provide a full range of secretarial services from computer work to filing and mailings. Will work in or out of your office or home.

HARDWOOD FLOORS

"Tree Lovers"
863-6833

Will do new installation as well as repair and refinish existing hardwood floors.

Comstock Thurman Floor Co.
863-5559

Will perform new installation as well as sanding, staining and refinishing existing floors. Oak hardwood kitchen floors are a specialty.

FURNITURE RESTORATION

Cow Hollow Woodworks
3100 Steiner
929-0218

Excellent reputation for antique restoration, repairs and caning. Pick-up and delivery. Free estimates.

Pet Services

The recommendations below should help address some of the concerns and needs pet owners face when trying to determine where top quality pet services in the City can be found. I strongly urge you to make an appointment with a prospective veterinarian to meet him or her personally and to inspect the facilities before making a choice.

VETERINARIANS

Arguello Pet Hospital
530 Arguello
751-3242

Pets are seen by appointment only on Monday, Wednesday and Friday from 7:30AM to 6PM and on Saturday from 8AM to 1PM. Closed 12 to 2PM daily for lunch. Dogs, cats, rabbits (and guinea pigs!) are treated. Pet boarding as well.

Mission Pet Hospital
720 Valencia at 18th Street
552-1969

Cats, dogs and exotic birds and reptiles. No boarding facility. Open seven days a week.

EMERGENCIES

*Most SF pet hospitals refer off-hour animal emergencies to: **All Animals Emergency Hospital** at 1333 9th Avenue, 566-0531. On call Monday through Friday 6 PM to 8 AM. Open 24 hours on weekends and holidays. This facility is equipped to care for a wide variety of pets.*

Pets Unlimited Veterinary Hospital
2343 Fillmore
563-6700

Cats and dogs only are treated here and cats may be boarded. Regular hours seven days a week as well as a 24-hour emergency service.

Avenue Pet Hospital
2221 Taravel
681-4313

Cats and dogs only are treated here and there is no boarding facility.

Marina Pet Hospital
2024 Lombard
921-0410

A wide range of animals are treated here from dogs to turtles. Open seven days a week. Monday through Friday 7AM-7:30 PM. High-quality pet care is offered.

PET SUPPLIES

Pet Food Express
371 West Portal   1798-19th Avenue
759-1400   **759-7777**

Both locations are worth a trip to this pet supply club. There is a savings for members although you don't have to join. Nominal membership fee entitles you to take advantage of substantial discounts for pet food and supplies.

Nippon Goldfish Co.
3109 Geary
668-2203

This venerable tropical fish store has been around since 1911 selling a complete range of the latest tropical fish, aquarium equipment and supplies. Installation and maintenance are offered.

Dee's
K-9 Korner
3518 Geary
221-0060

Carries a full line of equipment for dogs as well as pet food.

Cal's Discount Pet Store
5950 California at 22nd Ave.
386-1720

Specializes in food for all small pets. Open seven days a week.

Animal Crackers
780 Stanyan
387-3001

No membership fee for purchasing discounted pet food and supplies.

 # GROOMERS

Silvervue Grooming
938 Clement
752-7167

Grooms dogs and cats. However will not do afghans, sheepdogs, standard poodles or chows.

By George
2979 21st Street
648-4846

Will groom any breed of dog or cat. No boarding facility. Open Tues through Saturdays.

BOARDING & PET RESOURCES

Pet Express
1000 Iowa Street
between 23rd and 25th St.
821-7111

This licensed boarding kennel offers each dog an indoor and outdoor run. Floors are heated indoors and animals are not kept in cages. Last day of boarding is free if dog is groomed that day. Cats are also boarded and groomed and there is a choice of indoor/outdoor runs.

Jean Morgan
386-4057

Jean has had twenty years of experience in taking care of birds, cats and small animals (except dogs) in her home. Clients provide food and litter boxes.

Sherlock Bones
1 (800) 942-BONES (6637)

This is an amazing service provided by John Keane who specializes in finding lost pets nation-wide.

Picolo Pet Vacations
776-4422

Jean Marie Campbell has been in the business for eight years of placing dogs only in private homes while you are away. Owners have the opportunity to interview the potential sitter in their home. She will agree to walk, feed, play and care for your dog in a nurturing home environment.

Long Walks and Sweet Talks
824-0188

Ronda Bonati will take wonderful care of your cat and specializes in cat sitting. She will also take care of your house, water the plants and bring in the mail and newspaper and walk the dog.

Club Canine
905-8888

This licensed, bonded insured and highly qualified dog-walking service will specifically design and tailor "playgroups" and walks to your dog's needs. Attractively-priced rates from a highly-qualified staff. Call for a consultation.

Pet-In-Housesitting
552-2593

Roger Rowell cares for your dog and house-sits in your home at the same time. He also takes care of cats with a daily visit to your home. References.

BOARDING vs PET-SITTING

Many boarding kennels enjoy a deserved reputation of providing excellent care for your pet while you are away. But the bottom line is that your pet is safest and happiest at home. Try and look into house-sitters or pet-sitting services who will come into your home and look in on your pet throughout the day. There are too many stories of pets who became ill and died in even the most reputable kennels.

Clubs and Organizations

One of the most important things you can consider doing, when all is said and done, is to "give back to the community". Here in the Bay Area, it is so easy to take- to take advantage of the magnificent natural environment, the many cultural events, the sheer number of activities which are offered free in a city as diverse and multi-faceted as ours. But you can also gain great satisfaction in giving as well- giving of your time and energy in helping to keep San Francisco as liveable a place as it is.

VOLUNTEER ORGANIZATIONS

San Francisco Volunteer Center
1160 Battery Street
Levi Plaza, Suite 70
982-8999

This comprehensive resource center is the "umbrella" for over 700 agencies and holds orientations six days a week to meet with you and review the many options you have for volunteering, based on your interests, time and abilities. Conveniently located in Levi Plaza, this is a great one-stop effort in finding a non-profit agency which interests you and in which you can be involved.

Big Brothers/Big Sisters
414 Mason
434-4860

This well-known organization focuses on fund-raising events throughout the year to help and assist disadvantaged kids from single parent homes. It encourages a mentor/buddy relationship with these children who might not otherwise get this kind of nurturing.

San Francisco Zoological Society
San Francisco Zoo
45 Avenue at Sloat Blvd.
753-7172

The Zoological Society offers a variety of ways you can participate. First and foremost, you can join as a member, which entitles you to discounted tickets, invitations to the annual Christmas Party and a behind-the-scenes tour of the zoo. But there are also many ways you can actively help in this wonderful institution. There are ten different volunteer programs, including the animal resource center, the docent program and the children's zoo. Volunteers are also needed for special events throughout the year which include the Zoo Run, held the third Sunday in January. This fun run features a ten-mile run as well as a three-mile family run throughout the zoo. Major fund-raising efforts will needed in the near future as "ZOO 2000" gets underway, a long-term expansion plan for creating a dynamic new environment for the animals.

ZOO FACTS

*Did you know that the **San Francisco Zoo** was started in Golden Gate Park in 1899 with exactly one animal, an amiable grizzly bear named Monarch? In the 1920's, Herbert Fleischacker acquired the land on which the current zoo now sits.*

Academy of Science
Golden Gate Park
750-7154

Over 900 volunteers work in all areas of this fascinating museum located in "the Park". There are dozens of areas in which you can become involved, from behind the scenes to helping feed and care for marine life to manning the ticket desk. Fund-raising events are held throughout the year, including the popular "Run to the Far Side" race, inspired by cartoonist Gary Larson and held in late November.

The Guardsmen
115 Sansome
781-6785

This non-profit group of 150 young male professionals work hard to raise money to send disadvantaged children to summer camp. Potential members must be sponsored and must commit to raising a certain amount of money throughout the year. A wide variety of social events are scheduled in this fund-raising effort.

San Francisco Junior League
2226 Fillmore
567-8600

The "League" has come a long way from its early image of a purely social organization. Now encompassing every segment of the population, this is an incredibly dedicated, serious and hard-working group of young women who are wholly committed to furthering the spirit of volunteerism and who raise enormous of money for a wide range of worthwhile charities.

NRDC (National Resources Development Council)
90 New Montgomery Street
777-0220

Composed in large part of scientists and lawyers who focus on environmental issues and concerns, this organization also has a huge membership who have joined the council in support of this effort. Yearly events and benefits are offered to members.

CLUBS OF INTEREST

In a city as diverse as San Francisco, there are hundreds of clubs, both public and private, one may choose to join. Here are just a few.

The Commonwealth Club
595 Market
597-6700

If you had to choose one club to join, the Commonwealth is awfully tempting! Many of the 18,000 members meet during the year at its hallmark Friday noon luncheon and lecture series to hear speakers ranging from Shirley Temple Black or Dan Quayle to the Dalai Llama! This non-partisan current affairs organization was established in 1903. With 600 events available throughout the year, the Commonwealth Club is a must-join.

Current Affairs Forum of the
COMMONWEALTH CLUB

Appeals to younger members and is purely social in nature, offering evenings at restaurant, rafting trips, sporting events, and skiing weekends. Also offered are human relationship lectures on most Friday nights.

MORE NON-PROFIT ORGANIZATIONS TO CONSIDER

Friends of the San Francisco Library
558-3770

San Francisco Museum of Modern Art
863-8800

American Conservatory Theatre (ACT)
771-3880

Exploratorium
563-3200

Planned Parenthood
441-5454

Glide Memorial Church
771-4014

Jewish Community Federation
777-0411

OPPORTUNITY KNOCKS!

This is a wonderful resource for all those interested in both paid positions and volunteerism in the social services and non-profit sector. The newspaper is published by Management Center and for more information, call 362-9735.

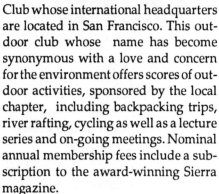

The Sierra Club
National Hdqtrs.
776-2211
Information
923-5660

Predating the Commonwealth Club by a decade, is the Sierra Club whose international headquarters are located in San Francisco. This outdoor club whose name has become synonymous with a love and concern for the environment offers scores of outdoor activities, sponsored by the local chapter, including backpacking trips, river rafting, cycling as well as a lecture series and on-going meetings. Nominal annual membership fees include a subscription to the award-winning Sierra magazine.

The World Trade Club
World Trade Center, Embarcadero
981-1234

This is considered to have one of the best dining room of all the private clubs in the City, not to mention its drop dead views with its bay-side location close to the Financial District. Its member tend to work in international trade and the club has a wonderfully international flavor in the heart of San Francisco.

The City Club
155 Sansome
362-2480

One of the most prestigious private clubs around, the City Club attracts busy professionals who use its five private meeting rooms for business networking, business entertaining, etc. Its 500-1500 members can enjoy associate membership in two hundred resort/athletic and dining clubs around the world, including the San Francisco Tennis Club. There are also social events in which the club prides itself on making it easy to mingle. A breakfast series is also offered twice a month to members & non-members alike.

▶ *Be sure and gaze upon the dramatic Diego Rivera mural as you ascend the beautiful brass stairway leading upstairs to the formal dining room. It had been covered over for decades and was discovered in the rebuilding and refurbishing of the City Club.*

Great Bay Area Getaways

Even after years of living here, I still find myself constantly amazed at the richness and diversity of things to do and places to visit all within a three to four hour range of The Bay Area. It is possible to play tennis on a brisk sunny morning in Marin and be skiing on the slopes of Tahoe that afternoon. Unbelievable. . .

The getaways in this book were generated from an appearance on the KGO Radio program "California Weekend". In researching unique and unusual places to visit, I discovered a world of wonderful getaways, with weather that is remarkably temperate during most of the year. All of the following are within driving distance of the San Francisco Bay Area. Any of the following recommendations would make great day trips such as Napa or Half Moon Bay, weekend getaways such as Mendocino or Carmel or full-scale vacations such as Tahoe. Always try and call ahead for information and reservations and I suggest, whenever possible, to travel off-season. Avoiding crowds, lines and waits is a big plus whenever I want to leave behind the hectic pace of everyday life.

Enjoy. . .

DISTANCE CHART

From San Francisco	Hours (by car)	Miles	Kms.
Sausaltio	20 min.	8	13
Muir Woods	30 min.	15	24
Napa/Sonoma Wine Country	1 hour	44	71
Mendocino	4 hours	156	251
Oakland-Downtown	20 min.	10	16
Berkeley, University of California	25 min.	12	19
Vallejo	45 min.	25	40
Sacramento State Capitol	1-1.5 hrs.	88	143
Lake Tahoe	4 hours	195	314
Reno	4.5 hrs.	230	374
San Francisco International Airport	25 min.	14	23
Half Moon Bay Pillar Point	35 min.	25	40
Stanford University Palo Alto	1 hour	33	53
Santa Cruz	2 hours	74	119
Carmel/Monterey	2.5 hrs.	133	214
Yosemite Nat'l Park	4 hours	210	338
Los Angeles	11 hours	437	coast
	8 hours	389	inland

Getaways North of the Bay

MARIN

Across the Bridge to the North is one of the closest, easiest getaways going. Marin offers a diversity of outdoor activities, especially in the summer.

HOW TO GET THERE:

By car: take 101 North over the Golden Gate Bridge. Toll taken in southbound lane only. Discount books available.

By Ferry: Golden Gate Transit offers ferry service from the City to and from Larkspur and Sausalito. Call 362-6600 for schedules. Tiburon Ferry is run by the Red & White Fleet at 546-2628. Discount books available.

By Bus: Golden Gate Transit operates bus service between San Francisco, Marin and Sonoma Counties. 332-6600

THE BRIDGE

There is only one bridge that counts, of course, and that is the Golden Gate. She is world-renowned, boasts breath-taking views from every angle. There are, however, a few minor drawbacks which the experienced Bridge driver adheres to with all seriousness. Driving on the inside lane of the Golden Gate Bridge is considered the equivalent of playing Russian Roulette. Picture cars and trucks hurtling at each other from opposite directions on a swaying and often fog-shrouded structure, separated only by little plastic markers! It is not hard to understand why the average driver stays as far right as possible.

BEST PLACES TO EAT IN MARIN

Sam's Anchor Cafe
27 Main Street
Tiburon
435-4527

For great views, great burgers and great people-watching, try the back deck at Sam's. On a sunny day, this place is hopping so plan on eating early or relaxing over a cold beer while you wait for a table. **Warning:** The gulls are entirely too familiar for my taste!

Il Fornaio
Corte Madera Town Centre
Corte Madera
927-4400

Il Fornaio enjoys a reputation for fine Italian fare in Marin, as well as in its City locations. Always busy, always good. Sitting in the outside terrace in the summer, overlooking Marin's beloved local mountain, Mt. Tamalpais, is a pleasant way to pass the time.

The Lark Creek Inn
234 Magnolia
Larkspur
924-7766

One of the Bay Area's most famous eating spots, The Lark Creek puts out some pretty spectacular food on a regular basis. Try the Sunday Brunch, lunch out on the terrace or dinner in this elegant Victorian set in a redwood grove.

▷ *We love to grab a hamburger at the bar and catch all the action at the front of the restaurant, where there are no reservations and you can order off the bar or regular menu.*

Half Day Cafe
848 College Avenue
Kentfield
459-0291

Where Magnolia ends at College Avenue is one of the most popular breakfast and lunch spots in Marin (with a charming little bookstore called First Street Books next door). The Half Day is always crowded and for good reason. The ambience is sparkling and fresh, with french doors opening onto a garden setting. The food is bountiful and delicious and the lattes are perfect to linger over on a wet winter morning.

Remillard's
125 E. Sir Francis Drake
Larkspur
461-3700

Elegant dining in the dramatic setting of a historic brick kiln. There is also patio dining for lunch.

WHY NOT TOUR LARKSPUR'S GOURMET GHETTO!

Look out, Berkeley. Here comes Larkspur! Larkspur? That's right. This charming, quaint little Marin town is flexing its culinary muscle these days. And if Larkspur is the new Berkeley, than Magnolia Avenue is its Shattuck Avenue, as the following shops will prove:

Pasticceria Rulli
464 Magnolia
924-7478
One of the premier Italian pastry shops and coffee houses in the Bay Area, routinely baking creative culinary gems.

Bread and Chocolate
1139 Magnolia
461-9154
Less glamorous than its neighbors, nevertheless, this little bakery turns out the best fresh Challah on Fridays. Perfect for weekend french toast!

Divine Delights
1125 Magnolia
461-2999
This delightful bakery in Marin is aptly named. Walk in and fall in love with the truffles or order a specially designed cake for a wedding or event. My personal favorite is the chocolate hazlenut torte. Divine!

MEANDERING IN MILL VALLEY

Do plan on a visit to Mill Valley. You'll find you will want to return again and again to this delightful picture postcard small town in Marin. To get there: Take the East Blithedale exit off 101 North.

Be sure and eat at: Jenny Low's, for Chinese fare, at 36 Miller 388-8868.

Or stop by bustling De Angelos at 22 Miller 388-2000 for great pasta.

Do visit: Smith and Hawken, at 35 Corte Madera Avenue 381-1800, the original location for the last word in upscale garden supplies.

Browse through the paintings, mixed media, sculpture and fine jewelry to be found at the Susan Cummings Gallery at 12 Miller Avenue 383-1512.

Check out the exciting new Summer House Gallery for eclectic gifts, furniture and jewelry. The main store is at 21 Throckmorton, 383-6695, and the smaller kids store is at 14 Miller, 383-6690.

And lastly, pick up your groceries at the fabulous new Living Foods, 159 Throckmorton, 383-7121 all organic, free-range meat and produce. There is a Gourmet Natural Deli and expert nutritional counselling is available.

The Buckeye Roadhouse
17 Shoreline Hwy.
Mill Valley
331-2600

The Buckeye has been brought to you by the same folks who created the Fog City Diner in the City and Mustards in Napa. Located in a wonderful wood-paneled old roadhouse, The Buckeye is a happening place; relaxed, lots of good food and a busy bar scene.

Casa Madrona
801 Bridgeway
Sausalito
332-0502

Contemporary American cuisine served in the lovely dining room of a charming inn. Views at sunset are breathtaking.

Guaymas
5 Main Street
Tiburon
435-6300

Located on Tiburon's Main Street, is this bustling Mexican restaurant with drop-dead views of San Francisco. It's fun to sip a Margarita on a summer night and gaze upon the fog-shrouded cityscape in the distance.

TIBURON TIPS

The Tiburon ferry from the City drops you right off at Guaymas for a quick dinner with time enough for the return ferry ride home. Or drive over the Golden Gate on a weekend afternoon, park your car in Blackie's Pasture, the Greenfield Beach Drive exit off Tiburon Blvd., and bike along the scenic bike path into Tiburon for drinks or dinner.

WALKS, TREKS, JOGS & HIKES IN MARIN

A **walk** around **San Rafael Avenue** in **Belvedere** at sunset is always something special. Challenge yourself to keep going and you can continue on up **Corinthian Island**, home of the rich and super-rich in a magical setting. One of the most popular walks in Marin is the 20 minute scenic **Verna Dunshea Trail** around the peak of Mt. Tamalpais, ranking with some of the most beautiful walks in the world!

For **hiking** enthusiasts, **Muir Woods** and **Mt. Tamalpais** are all-round Bay Area favorites with glorious natural scenery. Getting there is half the fun. Mt. Tamalpais has one of the most magnificent drives going, with vistas at every turn. Suggested hikes would be **Steep Ravine Trail** at the Pantoll Station on the Panoramic Hwy.

▶ *Lunch at The Mountain Home Inn, sublime views, good food, great resting spot.*

Mt. Tamalpais State Park
801 Panoramic Highway
Ranger Station
388-2070

Mountain Home Inn
810 Panoramic Highway
Mill Valley
381-9000

BEST BEACHES

Marin's beaches provide an idyllic setting for just about anything you might want to do, except swim! The waters everywhere tend to be remarkably cold and often have strong undertows. But that doesn't mean people don't flock to them year-round, as the beaches along the coast are magnificent, unspoiled and perfect for a variety of things to do- in the sand! Here's just a sampling:

MOST POPULAR BEACH

Stinson Beach is the clear favorite with its weekend crowds, lifeguards, beautiful views, great sand and safe swimming area.

▶ *All kids, big and small, love the **Parkside hot dog and burger stand** at Stinson. A landmark since 1949, it serves up some pretty great dogs and shakes! Check out the world's most delicious breakfasts in its restaurant next door!*

MOUNTAIN BIKING

*Did you know that mountain-biking was born in Marin County? A particular favorite of bikers is **Paradise Drive** in Tiburon and **Camino Alto** in Mill Valley, but these curving roads can be dangerous to all but the most seasoned and brave-hearted of cyclists. **Lake Lagunitas** is considered an excellent introduction to mountain biking.*

BEST TIDE-POOLING

- **McClures Beach** in Pt. Reyes. A steep trail leads you down to abundant tide-pools and elks may greet you on your return to the parking area!

- **Agate Beach**, at the end of Elm Road in Bolinas, also offers some great tide-pooling.

BEST BIRD-WATCHING

- **Kehoe Beach.** "Birders" love the half-mile trail to this long sandy beach, flanked by cliffs, because it has a marsh that attracts year-round birds and migratory waterfowl.

- **Rodeo Beach** in the Marin Headlands is a good bird-watching spot thanks to a nearby lagoon. Parking and hiking is also very good here.

MOST DRAMATIC VISTAS

- **Palomarin Beach** offers stunning views of the coastline in the half-mile hike to this beach five miles north of Bolinas.

- **Point Reyes** is a clear winner with its turbulent windswept landscape and spectacular meeting of sand and sea.

WHALE WATCHING

At Point Reyes from December to April is the best time to witness this amazing odyssey, especially when the weather is clear and sunny. Early in the morning is best. There are tremendous views and you may even catch glimpses of those amazing creatures.

BEST SANDY BEACH

Limantour Beach is a favorite and a good jumping-off point for long walks and hikes around Pt. Reyes. Also great "birding" nearby.

BEST WEATHER

Heart's Desire Beach makes this claim. Located in Tomales Bay State Park. A nearby trail leads to Indian Beach complete with tepees!

BEST FAMILY BEACH

- **McNear's Beach** is a public beach at the tip of Marin which is run like a resort. It offers a large pool, tennis courts, snack bar, and, oh yes, a sandy beach. Very popular family spot in the summer.

- **Paradise Beach**, in Tiburon, is a 19-acre open space area with a sandy beach facing the Bay. It can be cold and windy, but families love its close proximity to the City.

BEST OVERNIGHT CAMPING

Steep Ravine Beach
(800) 444-PARK

Ten rustic cabins and six campsites make for a great overnight experience. Reservations are required.

Final Thought

You may want to pick up a copy of "California Coastal Access Guide" (University of California $15.95) for details and information on Beaches along the coast.

FOR BUDDING NATURALISTS

Did you know the fastest growing spectator sport is "birding" as in bird-watching? One of the premier spots in the Bay Area is **Richardson Bay**, home of the **Audubon Center** and the bird-watcher's equivalent of Candlestick Park, where eighty-nine species of water birds set up housekeeping.

Richardson Bay
Audubon Center and Sanctuary
376 Greenwood Beach Road
Tiburon
388-2524

THE WILDS OF WEST MARIN

If any part of Marin could be said to be natural and untamed, West Marin fits this description. One of its most well-known getaways is **Manka's Inverness Lodge,** nestled in the tree-lined hills overlooking Tomales Bay. Featuring a wonderfully rustic dining room which regularly turns out grilled quail and game, Manka's also offers rooms with log-style canopy beds. The perfect retreat from urban life.

Manka's Inverness Lodge
Argyle & Callender
Inverness
669-1034

SHOPPING AREAS IN MARIN

Town Center
Tamalpais Drive (off Hwy 101)
and Madera Blvd.
50 specialty shops, with open-air courtyards and fountains create a feeling of a Mediterranean-style square.

Village at Corte Madera
Hwy 101 at Redwood Hwy
Upscale shopping. Includes Macy's, Nordstrom and 95 specialty shops. The place to shop.

Larkspur Landing
2257 Larkspur Landing Circle
at Sir Francis Drake Blvd.
An open-air, New England-style village center conveniently located next to the SF/Larkspur ferry landing. Features 55 small specialty shops, restaurants and four movie theaters.

Marin City Flea Market
Donahue and Drake Ave., Marin City
You can find just about anything at this flea market held weekends year round. Arrive early! Admission free.

Downtown Sausalito
Bridgeway at El Portal Lane
A National Historical Landmark located on the waterfront featuring ferry service to SF. Renowned tourist and artist's colony known for the fine shops, restaurants, and galleries.

Downtown Tiburon
Main Street and Ark Row
Unique gifts, antiques and specialty shops. A favorite with locals and tourists alike. Accessible from SF by ferry.

SONOMA

Sonoma is content to lie in the shadow of her flashier, glitzier neighbor, Napa. Nevertheless, Sonoma has just as many wineries and great places to eat as well as having some of the most beautiful natural scenery going.

BEST PLACES TO STAY

The Beltane Ranch
11775 Sonoma Hwy.
(707) 996-6501

A delightful B&B with a colorful history all its own. Also has a tennis court and lovely views out over the hills.

Kenwood Inn & Restaurant
10400 Sonoma Hwy.
Kenwood
(707) 833-1293

A sophisticated, Italian-style pensione. Great restaurant as well.

Madrona Manor
1001 Westside Rd.
Healdsburg
(707) 433-4231

The Madrona Manor gets rave reviews for luxury, great food and beautiful surroundings.

The Sonoma Mission Inn & Spa
18140 Hwy 12
Boyes Hot Springs
(707) 938-9000

One of the most well-known and highly-regarded inns in California, it was at one time the site of the old Sonoma Mission. Spend some time in the Spa or enjoy playing on one of its several tennis courts. A lovely pool area in a garden setting.

Applewood, an Estate Inn
13555 Highway 116
Pocket Canyon
(707) 869-9093

Nestled up on a hill, amidst a redwood grove, is an upscale auberge called Applewood. Housed in a 1920's Mission-style mansion, there are ten guest suites, several beautiful common rooms and one of the best up-and-coming dining rooms in Sonoma. Not your standard B&B and well worth a visit.

BEST PLACES TO EAT

Kenwood Restaurant
9900 Hwy. 12
Kenwood
(707) 833-6326

Regina's Sonoma
Sonoma Hotel
110 West Spain St.
(707) 938-0254

Eastside Oyster Bar & Grill
133 E. Napa St.
(707) 939-1266

Piatti
El Dorado Hotel
405 First Street West
(707) 996-2351

BIKING IN SONOMA

Biking the scenic and sometime challenging trails of Sonoma County is the hottest thing going these days. One of my favorite trails is the following. There is little traffic and you can stop off at the many wineries that dot West Dry Creek.

Start your adventure in Healdsburg at Lambert Bridge Road to West Dry Creek to Westside Drive to Eastside Drive back to Healdsburg.

Ready for a break? A great place to stop along the way for a picnic is the beautiful setting of **Lambert Bridge Winery** at 4085 West Dry Creek Road, Healdsburg (707) 431-9600. Pick up picnic supplies beforehand at the **Dry Creek General Store** on 3495 Dry Creek Road, Healdsburg (707) 433-4171. Another spot to eat well is **Jakes** at 405 Warm Springs Road, Kenwood, (707) 833-1350. Jakes is a great deli with delicious take-out sandwiches and salads.

Time: A half day Bike tour. Challenging but exciting!

DAY EXCURSIONS

There's apple picking at Walker Farm, pumpkin picking at Frank's Corner and a favorite among locals is **The Little Hills Xmas Tree Farm** in Petaluma to cut your own tree. Don't forget to stock up on the world's freshest and most delicious oysters at **Johnson's Oyster & Seafood Company.**

Walker Apples
Upp Road
Graton
(707) 823-4310

Frank's Corner
1794 Gravenstein Highway
Sebastopol

Little Hills Xmas Farm
Chapman La.
Petaluma
(707) 763-4678

Johnson's Oyster and Seafood
253 McDowell Blvd.
Petaluma
(707) 763-4161

BEST BETS IN SONOMA

Jack London State Park in Glen Ellen. The museum and grounds containing the ruins of Jack London's dream castle, Wolf House, is one of my favorite spots in Sonoma.

Jack London Museum
2400 London Ranch Rd.
Glen Ellen
(707) 938-5216

The Sonoma Cattle Company
Jack London State Park
(707) 996-8566

This well-known company offers some wonderful trail rides through the park.

Air Flambuoyant
250 Pleasant Ave.
Santa Rosa
(800) 456-4711

Enjoy a hot air balloon ride over the valley, ending with a champagne brunch!

NAPA

Napa needs no introduction. It is one of the loveliest spots on earth any time of the year and is so close to the City you can return over and over and over again ... Of the two main roads which traverse the Napa Valley, Hwy. 29 and The Silverado Trail, it is the latter which is the more scenic and meandering.

HOW TO GET THERE:

101 N to Hwy 37 (Vallejo-Napa exit). Follow 37 to Hwy 121 (follow signs to Napa). Take 121 to Hwy 29.

THE PERFECT FIRST VISIT

A perfect day in Napa would include an early morning Hot Air Balloon Ride, a luncheon ride on The Napa Valley Wine Train (a thirty-six mile adventure), a mud bath in Calistoga and a casual dinner at Mustards Grill.

Once In A Lifetime Hot Air Balloon Rides
Lincoln Ave. at the airstrip
(707) 942-6541

The Napa Valley Wine Train
For reservations, call
(707) 253-2111

Mustards Grill
7399 Hwy. 25
Yountville
(707) 944-2424

BEST PLACES TO VISIT

Graystone Winery
2555 Main St.
St. Helena
(707) 963-0763

Housed in one of the most spectacular buildings in the wine country in the charming town of St. Helena, Graystone is also a must-visit. Have lunch or dinner at nearby Terra, located in an old stone winery, or outside on the terrace at Tra Vigne, a personal favorite.

The Hess Collection
4411 Redwood Road
(707) 255-1144

Combines great wines with some pretty interesting modern art. Worth a visit to linger through the galleries.

Franciscan Winery
1178 Galleron Road
(707) 963-1111

Offers one of the finest wine-tastings in Napa on a daily basis. One of the oldest wineries in the valley.

Clos Pegase
1060 Dunaweal Lane
Calistoga
(707) 942-4981

Consider a trip out to this visually stunning winery, an architectural masterpiece designed by Michael Graves. Combine it with a visit to one of the many spas located in Calistoga, and experience first-hand a famous mud bath!

The Jessel Gallery
1019 Atlas Peak Road
(707) 257-2350

Try and visit this charming gallery located in an old stone winery near Silverado Country Club. It has become a haven for Northern Californian artists and crafts people. I have never walked out of there without purchasing something I simply couldn't live without!

Donna Karan Company Store
Village Outlets of Napa
3111 N. St Helena Hwy.
St Helena
(707)963-8755

What the heck. So you go outlet shopping in one of the most scenically-beautiful areas of the world. If this wasn't Donna Karan, I wouldn't mention the word "shopping" in connection with Napa, but you will find great deals in this new outlet center, tucked away in St. Helena, including Go Silk, Coach Leather goods, Brooks Brothers, and Joan & David.

BEST PLACES TO STAY IN NAPA

Meadowood Resort
900 Meadowood Lane
St. Helena
(707) 963-3646 or (800) 458-8080

An extravagant and enchanting getaway which includes a formal croquet field, tennis courts, a brand-new full-service spa, hiking and biking in its miles of wooded paths and a first-class restaurant. There's not much Meadowood misses on, including excellent service.

Oak Knoll Inn
2200 East Oak Knoll Ave.
(707)255-2200

A tranquil retreat with suites of rooms grouped around a sparkling pool. It is a quiet, private and tranquil setting.

BEST PICNIC SPOTS

Vichon Winery
1595 Oakville Grade
(707) 944-2811

Rutherford Hill Winery
200 Rutherford Hill Road,
Rutherford
(707) 963-1871

PICNIC SUPPLIES

Oakville Grocery
Hwy 29
Oakville
(707) 944-8802
The Oakville Grocery is the premier place to stock up on picnic supplies for the Ultimate Picnic.

Auberge du Soleil
180 Rutherford Hill Road
Rutherford
(707) 963-1211 or (800) 348-5406

The ultimate in elegant hotel accommodations, world-class restaurant (be sure to lunch on the deck overlooking the valley) and an exceptional spa.

**Silverado Golf
and Country Club**
1600 Atlas Peak Rd.
(707) 257-0200 or (800) 532-0500

The ultimate golfer's dream vacation. Silverado offers condominium resort accommodations, all-star golf, a large tennis facility and several choices of restaurants. A perfect family getaway, especially on 4th of July weekend, with its old-fashioned barbecue and dramatic fireworks. It's expensive,but extremely popular.

Timberhill Ranch
35755 Hausec Bridge Road
Cazadero
(707) 847-3258

A country getaway with everything a sophisticated traveler needs – great food, great comfort, great service. Set on eighty acres of rambling grounds.

BEST RESTAURANTS IN NAPA

Auberge du Soleil
180 Rutherford Hill Road
Rutherford
(707) 963-1211

Brava Terrace
3010 N. St Helena Hwy.
St. Helena
(707) 963-9300

Domaine Chandon
California Dr.
Yountville
(707) 944-2892

French Laundry
Washington at Creek Street
Yountville
(707) 944-2380

Piatti Ristorante
6480 Washington Street
Yountville
(707) 944-2070

Restaurant Terra
1345 Railroad Ave.
St. Helena
(707) 963-8931

The Restaurant at Meadowood Resort
900 Meadowood La.
St. Helena
(707) 963-3646

Tra Vigne
1050 Charter Oak Road
St. Helena
(707) 963-4444

BEST PLACES TO GO FOR MUD

When you speak of Mud, Calistoga immediately comes to mind. The entire town is devoted to the rejuvenation of your body and spirit. There is a wide range of mud treatments in many spas.

International Spa
1300 Washington St.
Calistoga
(707)942-6122

Treatments done on site for both men and women. Accommodations are offered as well.

Dr. Wilkinson's Hot Springs
1507 Lincoln Ave.
Calistoga
(707) 942-4102

Sounds like a name right out of the Old West! Comfortable & rustic.

Silver Rose Inn
351 Rosedale Rd.
Calistoga
(707) 942-6122 or (800) 995-9381

This is a great bed and breakfast inn with beautiful rock gardens, waterfalls and a "natural" outdoor jacuzzi. A good place to stay while you are taking the baths.

"The whole neighborhood of Mount Saint Helena is full of sulphur and of boiling springs ... and Calistoga itself seems to repose on a mere film above a boiling subterranean lake."
–Robert Louis Stevenson in The Silverado Squatters

The North Coast

There are two well known routes to get to Mendocino. The Coast route which is magnificent, tortuous and long, and the route which I prefer, which is the Shoreline Rd. including stopovers in Sea Ranch and Gualala.

GUALALA

Gualala is a lovely old coastal town which has a number of delightful places to stay.

St. Orres Inn & Restaurant
36601 S. Hwy 1
(707) 884-3303

A fascinating, Russian-style chalet of hand-carved wood and stained glass. There are eight rooms in the main house and eleven cabins up the road. Elegant dining is another plus to this unique inn.

GRAY WHALE WEEKEND

*Travel to Gualala in the months of December, January and February to visit this delightful structure originally built in 1870 and destroyed in the '06 Quake. Stay in simple cliffside cottages, adjacent to **Point Arena Lighthouse**. Observe the extraordinary gray whales, hike Manchester Beach and just explore. A bargain weekend for the whole family. Very rustic.*

Point Arena Lighthouse
2 miles off Hwy. 1
(707) 882-2777

Old Milano Hotel
38300 Hwy 1
(707) 884-3256

An irresistible turn of the century bed and breakfast spot.

Whale Watch Inn
35100 Hwy 1
(707) 884-3667 or **(800) 942-5342**

A small retreat of only eighteen charming suites overlooking the rugged coastline. A perfect vista for whale-watching.

SEA RANCH

Sea Ranch is a private community of architecturally award-winning homes scattered along the seashore. There are stupendous views, great hiking, and an incredibly private peaceful environment. Available for weekend rental.

Sea Ranch Rentals
(707) 785-2579 or **(800) 643-8899**

Sea Ranch Escape
(707) 785-2426 or **(800) 842-3270**

MENDOCINO

For a rejuvenating, peaceful escape from everyday life, pack up all your cares and woes and head for Mendocino. I think the best time of year to go is in the fall or in the spring. Summer is hectic and crowded. Off-season can be idyllic.

BEST PLACES TO STAY

Agate Cove
11201 N. Lansing St.
(707) 937-0551 or (800) 529-3111
Cozy comfortable ocean-front accommodations with great views.

McCallum House
45020 Albion St.
(707) 937-0289

A rustic and romantic spot. Home of the well-known Gray Whale Restaurant and Bar.

Heritage House
5200 N. Hwy.
(707) 937-5885 or (800) 235-5885

Many people know this as the setting for the movie, "Same Time Next Year". This is a scenic lodge with majestic views. In recent years, it has also become a well-known dining spot. Breakfast and dinner are included in the room rate.

Rachel's Inn
P.O. Box 134
(707) 937-0088

There are only nine rooms in this charming renovated 1860's farmhouse run by a delightful painter/caterer named Rachel. A bountiful breakfast is included in the room rate.

MUST DO'S

Picnics

*There are great picnic spots along the way to Mendocino on Hwy. 128 including **Indian Creek City Park** in Booneville. Hike the **Headlands** and **Big River State Park**, but dress warmly!*

Fort Bragg

*Fort Bragg is located fifteen miles North of Mendocino, and hosts several interesting events throughout the year. The annual **World's Largest Salmon Barbecue** is in July. Proceeds benefit re-stocking Northern California salmon runs. Fort Bragg is the home of the renowned **Skunk Train**, a year-round attraction, which travels through forty miles of redwood forest between Fort Bragg and Willets.*

Getaways East of the Bay

BROWSING IN BERKELEY

The free-wheeling spirit under which this whole town operates obviously attracts some of the best and brightest creative talent in the Bay Area. If you had to pick one spot in the East Bay to linger, Berkeley would be the perfect day's outing.

HOW TO GET THERE:

By car: Take I-80 East over the Oakland Bay Bridge to Alameda County. Toll in westbound lane.

By bus: AC Transit operates buses daily from San Francisco to Alameda and Contra Costa Counties. (510) 839-2882.

By BART: Bay Area Rapid Transit is a wonderful, usually-hassle-free, way of going to the East Bay. Operates rail lines and express buses from the City to Alameda and Contra Costa Counties. 788-BART.

A DAY IN BERKELEY

9 AM.

Park yourself at Cafe Fanny's (another Alice Waters production) for a latte and a bowl of her famous homemade granola with fresh strawberries on top.

Cafe Fanny
603 San Pablo
Avenue
(510) 524-5447

10 AM-12 AM

Plan the perfect "Foodie's" morning. Wander next door to **Acme Bread** and stock up on the best bread in the West (it freezes extremely well, by the way). Next door, and sharing the same address, is **Kermit Lynch Wines**. This unique wine shop handles imported French and Italian handcrafted wines only. They are considered The source for European wines in the Bay Area. Work your way over to **Monterey Market**, the standard by which other markets measure themselves in terms of freshness, taste and, above all, quality. Don't leave without a visit to the **Monterey Fish Market**.

Acme Bread
1605 San Pablo Ave.
(510) 524-1327

Kermit Lynch Wines
1605 San Pablo Ave.
(510) 524-1524

Monterey Market
1550 Hopkins
(510) 526- 6042

Monterey Fish Market
1582 Hopkins
(510) 525-5600

12:30 PM

Stop in for a quick lunch at wonderful **Panini's** for mouth-watering Italian sandwiches and light salads.

Panini's
2115 Allston Way
(510) 849-0405

1:30 PM-4:00 PM

Now for an afternoon of real shopping! Head directly to Fourth and Hearst, do not pass Go, where you will find some amazing stores all within one block of each other. Don't' miss the following:

The Gardener
1836 Fourth
(510) 548-4545

The ultimate upscale gardening mecca.

Hearthsong
1812 Fourth
(510) 849-3956

For wonderful old-fashioned toys.

Crate & Barrel Outlet
1785 Fourth
(510) 528-5500

For discount household gems.

The Nature Company
Fourth & Hearst
(510) 524-9052

The original flagship store.

4:30-5:30 PM

C'mon! You can handle a quick run over to the University Art Museum to view the permanent collection or catch the latest travelling show.

 Museum is closed on Tuesdays.

University Art Museum
2626 Bancroft Way
General Information: **(510) 642-0808**

6-7:30 PM

Dinner at **Chez Panisse** of course! It's time to squander both your wallet and your waistline. If you want to go easier on both, book a table upstairs at the Grill instead–just as popular and delicious! Or you may want to consider something completely different! Berkeley's best-kept dining secret is **O Chame**, an extraordinary blend of Japanese and Western cuisine.

Chez Panisse
1517 Shattuck Ave.
(510) 548-5525

O Chame
1830 Fourth St.
(510) 841-8783

8 PM

Collapse in your chair and prepare for first-class theatre at the renowned Berkeley Repertory Theatre, one of the best in the country. "The Rep" is a beloved favorite of all Berkeley-ites.

Berkeley Repertory Theatre
2025 Addison Way
(510) 845-4700

Getaways South of the Bay

There are some fascinating excursions south of San Francisco, whether you travel the dramatic coast route of Hwy 1, or you take the rolling hills of Hwy 280.

HALF MOON BAY

FILOLI
Canada Road, Woodside
(take the Edgewood Rd. exit off 280)
364-2880

This is <u>the</u> place to visit in the spring. Open to the public from Feb-mid-November, guided tours are by reservation only. Fridays are self-guided tour days, and reservations are not required. Filoli itself is an Old World Manor House and was the site for the filming of the movie, "Heaven Can Wait" and "Dying Young". It is set in 650 acres, seventeen of them magnificent formal gardens, which are open to the public.

Año Nuevo State Reserve
Located 30 miles south of
Half Moon Bay on Hwy 1
879-2025

This is the gathering place for the elephant seals in their natural habitat. There is a three-mile hike into the reserve by permit only. Permits are issued free at the State Reserve office, and naturalists are on duty throughout the reserve. Every effort is made to preserve the beauty and delicate ecological balance. Dress warmly, the weather tends to be windy and cool. Open April 1-Nov. 30.

Don't miss the Art and Pumpkin Festival in October, including the Great Pumpkin Parade through Half Moon Bay. The sight of hundreds of acres of rolling pumpkin fields on a crisp autumn day is something to savor. The pumpkin picking is the best anywhere, but it's no secret, so go early in the day.

HOW TO GET THERE:

Take Hwy 1, about 25 miles south of the City.

BEST BETS IN HALF MOON BAY

The Old Thyme Inn
779 Main Street
726-1616

Cute, cozy and moderately-priced.

Sea Horse Ranch
726-2362
and
Friendly Acres
726-9871

Both places offer wonderful trail rides on horseback. Hayrides are also available. Call for directions and info.

BEST WHALE WATCHING

Whale-watching expeditions leave from nearby Princeton By the Sea. They are sponsored by the Oceanic Society and reservations are necessary. **474-3385**

Try and stay at the Pillar Point Inn, an eleven room charmer on the harbor, if you're planning to linger overnight.
Pillar Point Inn
380 Capistrano Rd.
728-7377

PESCADERO

Be sure and experience a stay at Pigeon Point Lighthouse Hostel for families or couples. Built in 1871, this scenic lighthouse and adjacent bungalows are simple, rustic and extremely reasonably priced. Great tide-pooling as well.

Pigeon Point Lighthouse Hostel
Pigeon Point Rd.
879-0633

SANTA CRUZ

This seaside college town has long been a popular summer beach resort close enough to San Francisco to visit for a day. Hard-hit by the Great Quake of '89, Santa Cruz has stubbornly and determinedly come back to life and is as popular a getaway spot as ever.

HOW TO GET THERE:

Take Hwy. 1 South all the way. Signs indicate approach to Santa Cruz.

BEST BETS IN SANTA CRUZ

Babbling Brooks
Bed & Breakfast
1025 Laurel St.
(408) 427-2437

A secluded hillside inn built in 1909, surrounded by beautiful grounds. A short walk from the beach.

Shadowbrook Restaurant
1750 Wharf Rd.
Capitola
(408) 475-1511

Although this restaurant is in nearby Capitola, an artsy craftsy beach town, this is undoubtedly one of the most romantic restaurants around.

Seal Rock
Lighthouse Point
West Cliff Drive

This is a great spot for observing herds of sea lions who make their home here. Steamer's Lane, nearby, is the place to watch the surfers in action.

Natural Bridges State Park
2531 West Cliff Drive
(408) 423-4609

One of the finest places to view the monarch butterflies that flock there every winter. There are also good beaches, tide pools and birding. Call for schedule of guided walks.

Santa Cruz Boardwalk
400 Beach Road
(408) 426-7433

I would be remiss not to mention the last remaining boardwalk on the West Coast! Built in 1907, but renovated several years ago, it is still deliciously tacky, noisy and crowded. This ofcourse translates as every child's delight! Thrills and chills include the Giant Dipper, a rickety, scary old monster rated by *The New York Times* as one of the ten best roller coasters in the country.

PACIFIC GROVE & MONTEREY PENINSULA

The Monterey Peninsula summons forth the image of spectacular coastlines, seaside communities, rolling hills and cypress forests. There is no off-season here, so be sure and make reservations well in advance.

MONARCH BUTTERFLIES

Viewing in Pacific Grove

This major event in the area, aka Butterfly Town USA, occurs between October and March and is reason enough to plan a visit during these months. The mystery is how these amazing creatures find their way back each year when the life span of a Monarch is only nine months . . . Sunny days between 10 am and 4 pm are the best viewing times. On cold foggy days they huddle together, rather like us humans.

BEST PLACES TO STAY

Monterey Bay Inn
242 Cannery Row
Monterey
(408) 373-6242

A perfect place to stay right on Cannery Row. This elegant inn has views of the bay and in close proximity to Fisherman's Wharf and the Aquarium.

Gosby House
643 Lighthouse Ave.
Pacific Grove
(408) 375-1287

A delightful Victorian bed and breakfast which does not offer ocean views but is more reasonable in price.

Seven Gables Inn
555 Ocean View Blvd.
Pacific Grove
(408) 372-4341

A multi-gabled Queen Anne-styled mansion with dramatic views looking out over the ocean.

▶ *Do try and dine at Old Bath House, just down the street from the Seven Gables at 620 Ocean View Blvd., for great view and excellent food. Call (408) 375-5195 for dinner reservations.*

BEST BETS IN MONTEREY

Point Pinos Lighthouse
Assilomar Blvd.

The oldest continuously operating lighthouse on the Pacific coast. There is great picnicking, tidepooling and otter watching to be done.

Monterey Bay Aquarium
886 Cannery Row
(408) 648-4888

An impressive forty million dollar structure which provides a close-up view of the Monterey Bay and its spectacular marine life. It is considered the world's largest seawater aquarium! This is a must-see for young and old alike.

Kitty Hawks Kites
1 Reservation Rd./Marina
(408) 384-2622

Hang gliders soar like seagulls over a six-mile stretch of Monterey Bay beaches and sand dunes. This is *the* place to learn to hang glide on the dunes east of Monterey.

Western Hang Gliders
(408) 384-2622

Operates off scenic Marina Beach, 10 minutes north of Monterey, on Hwy. 1. Three-hour beginner courses offered.

Monterey Bay Kayaks
693 Del Monte Ave.
(408) 373-KELP (5357)

A delightful way to observe sea lions and otters at close range. Tour includes a half hour of safety instruction.

▶ *Kayakers can also discover the wonders of Elkorn Slough Reserve. Located north of Monterey near Moss Landing, there is a winding seven-mile river channel that comprises 2,500 acres of homeland and feeding grounds for thousands of shorebirds, fish, seals, otters, foxes and falcons. For information, call the Elkorn Reserve at (408) 728-2822.*

Adventures By The Sea
(408) 372-1807

Bay Bike Rentals
(408) 646-9090

Leisurely cyclists and in-line skaters will delight in the paved Shoreline Bike Path that runs along the Monterey waterfront. Rentals available at these shops.

Final Thought

Take a drive on the "Poor Man's 17-Mile Drive"! Free to the public, unlike its more illustrious neighbor in Carmel, it is a delightful four-and-a-half mile drive which passes along rugged coastal seascapes and charming Victorian homes.

CARMEL

Quaint, charming and sought-after, Carmel is an understandably popular spot for tourists. It is a town which boasts no billboards, no electric signs, no tall buildings, and absolutely no high heels on sidewalks!

HOW TO GET THERE:

Take 19th Avenue to 280. Exit at Hwy 17 and follow signs for Carmel. The more dramatic tour is, of course, Hwy 1.

BEST PLACES TO STAY:

When $$$ Is No Object

John Gardiner's Tennis Ranch
Carmel Valley Road
(408) 659-2207

This is the consummate tennis resort, where "whites" are required on court, and evening clothes are "suggested" for the sumptuous dinners you will enjoy. Located in the heart of the Carmel Valley, there are fourteen courts and fourteen beautifully-appointed guest cottages.

Quail Lodge
8205 Valley Greens Drive
Carmel Valley
(408) 624-1581

Also located in the Carmel Valley, where the weather tends to be more temperate than the resorts along the coast, Quail Lodge is a beautiful resort with tennis, an eighteen-hole golf course and fine dining in an elegant restaurant setting.

The Lodge at Pebble Beach
17 Mile Drive
Pebble Beach
(408) 624-3811

Another legendary retreat of the rich and famous located on the fabulous 17-Mile Drive. This getaway is a golfer's paradise, but you pay handsomely for the privilege of playing on this world-class course.

Stonepine Estate Resort
150 East Carmel Valley Road
(408) 659-2245

Located on over three hundred acres of forests and meadows. There are only eleven lavishly-appointed suites, decorated with the finest of antiques.

A Moderate Alternative $

Vagabond's House Inn
4th & Dolores
(408) 624-7738

A cozy, English Tudor-style inn which opens onto a charming courtyard.

RESERVATIONS

Book accommodations well in advance and try to go off-season. Carmel's weather is similar to San Francisco's, so summers will not necessarily be hot and sunny. However, reservations are suggested regardless of the time of year.

BEST BETS IN CARMEL

Carmel Beach
The foot of Ocean Avenue

A wonderful beach for strolling, especially at sunset. But watch out, the water is usually too frigid for more than walking along!

17-Mile Drive
Pebble Beach Drive off Hwy 1
(408) 649-8500

There isn't much that hasn't been written about this world-famous drive, and every word is true. Each trip we take to Carmel usually culminates in driving this famous stretch of stunning seascapes, showplace estates and long stretches of Pebble Beach Golf Course. There's always something different that catches our eye. There is a nominal charge for every vehicle entering the Drive. Bicycles are permitted on 17-Mile Drive during daylight hours only.

Point Lobos State Park
3 miles south of Hwy 1
(408) 824-4909

This point has been called the greatest meeting of land and water in the world. It provides an excellent opportunity to study the rustic, undeveloped beauty of the Peninsula. Guided walks are scheduled in the summer, or you can follow self-guided tours.

▶ *Dress warmly and bring binoculars to view more than 250 species of birds and animals, including the popular sea otters!*

BEST PLACES TO EAT

Hog's Breath Inn
San Carlos at 5th
(408) 625-1044

Clint Eastwood owns this prominent eating place. A relaxed, unpretentious spot with great food. A favorite with locals and tourists alike.

La Boheme
Dolores & 7th
(408) 624-7500

A small European-style cafe with a prixe fixe menu that changes daily.

Pacific's Edge
Highlands Inn
Hwy 1
(408) 624-0471

BEST NEW DISCOVERY

Post Ranch Inn
Hwy 1, Box 219
Big Sur
(800) 527-2200

Exclusive and private, the ranch was carefully constructed to fit into Big Sur's rugged wilderness. There are nature walks, horseback riding or just relaxing in the basking pool overlooking the Pacific. Julia Child referred the chef & Barbra Streisand suggested massage tables in every room. I can handle that...

BIG SUR

The drive alone from Carmel along Hwy. 1 is worth it. It is beyond doubt the most stupendous drive in the world! Take it slow. There is no "there" there, but instead a series of spots stretching along Hwy. 1 for about six miles. Big Sur is almost a state of mind more than an actual place. It is no wonder that this tiny piece of paradise was a long-time retreat of literary giant Henry Miller.

BEST BETS IN BIG SUR

Nepenthe
Hwy 1
(408) 667-2345

If you want to linger over a glass of wine while gazing upon vistas of unimagined beauty, this is the spot! Designed by a student of Frank Lloyd Wright, Nepenthe was the honeymoon locale of Orson Welles and Rita Hayworth.

Ventana Inn
Hwy 1
(408) 667-2331 or **(800) 628-6500**

Located on the jagged outcroppings of Big Sur, the Ventana Inn offers a ringside view of the pounding, endless surf. Every guest room has a private balcony that faces the sea or mountains.

▶ *Bathing suits are optional attire around the hot tub!*

HIKING

*Be sure and hike **Julia Pfeiffer Burns State Park** and **Pfeiffer Beach** which offer two thousand acres of prime hiking territory and are more private and less developed than the popular Pfeiffer Big Sur State Park.*

SAN SIMEON ADVENTURE

This small town, located seventy-five miles south of Big Sur, is the setting for the fabulous Hearst Castle.

Hearst Castle
San Simeon
(805) 927-2000
Hearst Castle was the fabulous estate of William Randolph Hearst and is filled with art treasures and antiques from all over the world. It contains thirty-eight bedrooms, thirty-one bathrooms and a private zoo. Yet it was never completed. Now an Historical Monument, maintained by the State of California. Reservations are a must. Four different tours are available. Wear comfortable shoes!

Key Holiday Tours
1510 Parkside Drive, Walnut Creek
(510) 945-8687
This tour service offers a wonderful and relaxing way to travel to Hearst Castle. Get a taste of the whole area in a leisurely manner, including stops in San Luis Obispo and Morrow Bay, a fishing village, bird sanctuary and site of a huge prehistoric volcanic rock.

Getaways Beyond the Bay

YOSEMITE

*To catch a glimpse of the Yosemite described by John Muir and photographed by Ansel Adams, consider a visit off-season. In fall, the autumn foliage is breathtaking, in winter, the dusting of snow is exquisite and in spring, the waterfalls are extraordinary. I still haven't figured out why anyone even goes in the summer. . . The park is overwhelming, so be sure and visit **El Capitan**, the largest mass of exposed granite in the world and **Yosemite Falls**, the highest in the Northern Hemisphere.*

HOW TO GET THERE:

Take 580 East to I-5 South. Exit at 132 East to Hwy 120. Follow signs.

All concessions and accommodations are run by the Yosemite Park Company. Call the following numbers for overall information.

Accommodations: (209) 252-4848

Visitor's Info.: (209) 372-0200

Campground: (800) 365-CAMP

BEST PLACES TO STAY

Actually, there are only a few places to stay in Yosemite, not including camp grounds. Call the "Accommodations" number listed above.

Curry Village

This is the most reasonable level of accommodations. You can even reserve "tent cabins" which have minimal heating. Somewhat rustic, but perfect for summer weather.

Yosemite Lodge

Also offers reasonable accommodations. You can rent bicycles to tour the area. Maps and information are provided for your convenience.

Ahwanee Lodge
Dinner Reservations:
(209) 372-1488

The premier place to stay in Yosemite. Luxurious, elegant, world-famous and worth a stay, if you can afford it. There is a dress code in the dining room at night.

Wawona Hotel

A wonderful old hotel, with a wrap-around porch, and surrounded by several out buildings. Some rooms have private baths. There is also a nine-hole golf course, two tennis courts and a pool with rolling grounds. There is even a Western village next door, with stage coach rides and horse rentals. The Wawona is not so crowded, reasonably-priced and great for families. Reserve far in advance.

BEST BETS IN YOSEMITE

Yosemite Mountineering School
Curry Village
(209) 372-1244

This is considered one of the finest mountaineering schools in the world. Classes in rock and mountain climbing are held year-round.

Valley Stables
(209) 372-1200

You can enjoy guided horseback trips through the park.

Curry Village Ice Rink
Curry Village
(209) 372-1442

Consider ice skating in a breathtaking setting beneath Glacier Point and Half Dome at this scenic outdoor rink.

Badger Pass Ski Resort
Off Hwy 41, on Glacier Point Road
(209) 372-1330

Skiing in Yosemite is always a delight. One of the oldest and most popular skiing areas is Badger Pass, a perfect place for beginners, intermediates and cross-country enthusiasts. Ask about the bargain mid-week ski package.

ANNUAL EVENT

*Bracebridge Dinner
at the Ahwanee Lodge*

Since the lodge opened in 1927, this has been an annual event held on December 22nd, 24th and 25th only. Spend Christmas at the Ahwanee, enjoying a seven-course feast, complete with pageantry, carolers and jesters. This event is so popular that reservations are applied for a year in advance, and guests are chosen by lottery!

THINK "MISTIX"

Management Information Systems Ticketing, a private company which handles reservations for 82 of California's most popular State Parks.
(800) 444-7275

Also consider "California Camping" a complete guide to California's recreational areas by author Tom Sienstra.

THE GOLD COUNTRY

This renowned area, often called The Mother Lode, stretches one hundred thirty-five miles east of San Francisco, along the entire route of Hwy 49, south of Mariposa and north through Nevada City. Stakes are still being claimed today by optimistic gold diggers! Some things never change.

JAMESTOWN & COLUMBIA

Ralph Stock's Gold Prospecting Expeditions
18170 Main St.
Jamestown
(209) 984-GOLD (4653)

In the southern-most gold town of Jamestown is this wonderful store, and one of the best places around for learning how to pan for gold. Operating out of an old stable, Ralph also organizes prospecting trips geared towards families, with a motto of "finders keepers"!

Railtown 1897
Jamestown

Look for this real-life working railroad and the site of countless westerns, including "High Noon". It is that authentic. From Feb. to November, one-hour rides are offered on the historic steam train known as the Mother Lode Cannon ball.

"A gold mine is a hole in the ground with a liar at the entrance."
–Mark Twain

Sonka's Apple Ranch
19200 Cherokee Road
Tuolomne
(209) 928-4689

Be sure and buy a mile-high apple pie. They are so good, you should buy a dozen and freeze them as the natives do.

GOLD COUNTRY

*Try and concentrate on one of three general areas: the **Southern Mines**, centered around Columbia and Jamestown, the **Central Mother Lode**, centered around Jackson or the **Northern Mines**, centered around Nevada City. Each has its own unique flavor and spirit and is chock full of history, adventure and scenic beauty.*

Try and plan a visit in the fall to take advantage of the stunning fall colors along Hwy. 108. Call for general information about visiting the Gold Country.

Placer County
Visitors Information
(916) 887-2111

Gunn House Motel
286 S. Washington St.
Sonora
(209) 532-3421

Looking for a place to bed down? Try this circa 1850 antique-filled adobe house turned inn.

Stagecoach Ride
Main Street
Columbia
(209) 532-0663

Start off your visit to Columbia with an authentic, fifteen-minute visit back into time.

State Park Information
Columbia
(209) 532-4301 or 532-0150

This was the richest mining town in the world in the 1850's. Today, it has retained much of its original flavor through loving restoration. No cars allowed!

Columbia Candy Kitchen
Main Street
Columbia
(209) 532-7886

An old-fashioned, four-generation family affair filled with mouth-watering homemade candies. Wave hello to Phineas outside, a local character and self-proclaimed original prospector.

Mark Twain's Cabin
Jackass Hill
Columbia

Any native can direct you to the famous abode where Twain is said to have written "The Celebrated Jumping Frog of Calavaras County". Frog-jumping is an event still celebrated each spring at the Calavaras County Fairgrounds.

BEST PLACES TO STAY IN COLUMBIA

City Hotel
Main Street
(209) 532-1479

Fallon Hotel
Washington St.
(209) 532-1470

Both hotels are run by the State of California and are beautifully restored and authentically re-created Victorian structures. Guests cheerfully trek down the hall from their rooms to use the bathrooms, armed with slippers, bathrobe, soap or shampoo loaned by the hotels, when necessary. Don't miss dinner at the City Hotel. Its dining room is renowned and the cuisine is lovingly and elegantly prepared.

Fallon House Theatre
Washington St.
(209) 532-4644

The Fallon House was another lovely old Victorian inn. During the summer, you may want to inquire about tickets for performances at the Fallon House Theatre, continuously in operation since the 1880's.

GOLD DISCOVERY

James Marshall
Gold Discovery Site
State Historic Park
Coloma
(916) 622-3470

Stop by this historic site in Coloma where gold was officially struck.

NEVADA CITY & SUTTER CREEK

Nevada City is a picturesque, scenic and extremely well-preserved mining town. The fall colors are renowned in this area. Sutter Creek has great antiquing and is in close proximity to Daffodil Hill, a must-see in the spring when over three hundred thousand daffodils are in riotous bloom.

BEST PLACES TO STAY

Grandmere's Inn
449 Broad St.
Nevada City
(916) 265-4660

A beautifully-decorated Colonial Revival home built in 1861 and now a lovely and welcoming inn.

National Hotel
211 Broad St.
Nevada City
(916) 265-4551

This hotel, built in 1856, is considered to be the state's oldest, continuously-operating hotel.

Red Castle Inn
109 Prospect
Nevada City
(916) 265-5135

A Gothic Revival gingerbread-trimmed home-turned-inn located up on a hilltop with wonderful views. There are dramatic furnishings and impressive art. All seven guest suites have private baths and are decorated in vivid colors.

▶ *Book a reservation well in advance for the Victorian Christmas Celebration Feast.*

Sutter Creek Inn
75 Main Street
Sutter Creek
(209) 267-5606

A charming inn and a perfect place to relax as you explore the surrounding area.

BEST PLACES TO EAT

Peter Salaya's California Restaurant
320 Broad St.
Nevada City
(916) 265-5697

Country Rose Cafe
300 Commercial
Nevada City
(916) 265-6248

Creek Side Cafe
101 Broad St.
Nevada City
(916) 265-3445

Getaways to Lake Tahoe

So much has been written about The Lake, that it is difficult not to be redundant. I think Tahoe's most extraordinary feature is that it is a year-round resort of unbelievable beauty. It is the second-deepest lake in the world with an average summer temperature of sixty-eight degrees, dropping to only fifty degrees in the dead of winter. So swimmers be prepared, the water is brisk and invigorating!

THE SOUTH SHORE

Much of the action in Tahoe is focused on the South Shore (or the Nevada side), with its legalized gambling. Unending flocks of tourists, and those who love the glitzy Vegas-style shows, can be found here year round.

HOW TO GET THERE:

From the Bay Area, take Hwy 80 East to get to the North Shore. To connect to the South Shore, pick up Hwy 50.

THE LAKE

Drive around the Lake, at least once, in its entirety. In the fall it is particularly lovely, when the leaves are turning, the air is crisp and the roads are empty. However, be forewarned, road crews are hard at work after the Labor Day crush, frantically preparing the roads for the impending skiers who descend upon Tahoe in the winter. Stopped traffic and closed roads can be the norm in the fall. Ordinarily, this seventy-two mile meandering drive should take around three hours to complete.

BEST BETS IN SOUTH SHORE

Lake Tahoe Cruises
970 Ski Run Blvd.
(916) 541-3364

Take a Lake cruise to Emerald Bay on the Tahoe Queen paddlewheeler. Be sure and check out the sunset dinner dance cruise.

▶ *Speaking of Emerald Bay, be sure and allow enough time to hike down to Vikingsholm Castle. The hike is an easy trek on paved road and it has beautiful vistas of the lake. You will enjoy touring the magnificent thirty-nine room Swedish castle facing Lake Tahoe.*

Camp Richardson
Corral Pack Station
Hwy 89 North, Camp Richardson
(916) 541-3113

Try a horseback ride on forest trails around the lake!

Heavenly Valley Tram
Top of Ski Run Blvd.
(916) 544-6263

For unsurpassed views of the Lake and the Tahoe Basin, take a ride up in the tram. Have lunch on top of the world.

BEST PLACES TO STAY ON THE SOUTH SHORE

Inn by the Lake
3300 Lake Tahoe Blvd.
(800) 535-0330

This quiet inn has attractive, modern, comfortable rooms and offers free shuttle service to the casinos.

Glenbrook
(702) 749-5663

Summer and winter accommodations are available in the elegant Glenbrook condominium complex which includes a sunny, sandy beach, tennis, golf and hiking and biking trails. Three-night minimum stay in the winter and one week minimum in the summer.

Accommodation Station
(916) 541-2355

This is an excellent service which will assist you in finding the appropriate condo, cabin or home on the South Shore.

Harrah's Hotel & Casino
(800) 648-3773

This is considered the grand dame of the South Shore and offers exciting live shows, a bustling casino scene and some of the best dining in the area with views that don't end. Call for room rates and information.

EASTERN SIERRAS

Bodi State Historic Park
(619) 647-6445

Bodi is the least-known, Best Little Ghost Town in the West. Just getting to this decaying relic of the past is an adventure along "washboard" dirt roads. Upon arriving, it is truly as though you are frozen in time as you gaze at over a hundred and twenty abandoned buildings. These still contain the personal effects, tools, and clothes of its inhabitants who seemed to have left in the middle of the night. What's left is only 5% of this once-thriving town, now in a state of arrested decay. In its heyday, Bodi was known as the "baddest bad town in the West", with its legions of saloons and houses of ill repute. Today, Bodi is no sanitized, commercialized tourist town. Its eerie quality haunts you long after you've left.

How to get there: Take Hwy. 395 to Bodi exit (Hwy 270) east for thirteen miles.

BEST PLACES TO SKI ON THE SOUTH SHORE

Heavenly Valley
For reservations: **(800) 2-HEAVEN**
For information: **(702) 586-7000**

How To Get There: Take Hwy I-80 E. to Hwy 50. Exit at Stateline.

Time: 3.5 hours from the Bay Area

Heavenly is aptly named. Extending over two states with stunning views of the Lake, Heavenly offers 4,800 skiable acres with 25 lifts, including a high speed quad, from gentle cruisers to double black diamonds. There are six strategically-placed day lodges, with full restaurant facilities. 175 trained staffers teach kids from age 3 through adults. Private and group lessons available for all levels. Call for info. on ski packages.

Sugar Bowl
Information: **(916) 426-3651**
Snow Phone: **(916) 426-3847**

How To Get There: Hwy I-80 East. Exit at Soda Springs/Norden

Time: 2.5 hours from the Bay Area

Sugar Bowl is the closest major ski resort for Northern California skiers approximately one-hour less drive time than other resorts. Located on a breathtaking three mountain complex on Donner Summit, Sugar Bowl has 1000 acres of skiable terrain and boasts the deepest annual snowfall in North America. Spring skiing is popular due to its north-facing slopes. Classes and private lessons available for all ages and ability levels. Childcare for youngsters age 3-6.

▶ *Consider a stay at the historic Sugar Bowl Lodge, built in 1939.*

BEST PLACES TO EAT IN THE SOUTH SHORE

The Summit Restaurant
Harrah's Hotel & Casino
(702) 588-6611

Elegant and expensive with drop-dead views out over Tahoe Basin.

▶ *Most of the casino hotels offer first class dining rooms.*

Swiss Chalet Restaurant
2540 Lake Tahoe Blvd.
(916) 544-3304

European continental cuisine is served for dinner only. Specialties are veal dishes at this Swiss-style eatery.

Carlos Murphy's
3678 Lake Tahoe Blvd.
(916) 542-1741

There are parties nightly at Carlos Murphy's—one of the best Mexican restaurants around. You'll find the Balloon Lady, Trivia Network games, taped music, lots of children running around, and a crowded bar scene. Lunch and dinner daily, with Brunch on Sundays.

> *"I thought it must surely be the fairest picture the whole Earth affords."*
>
> *–Mark Twain*

THE NORTH SHORE

Most people in the Bay Area head for the quieter, more scenically-beautiful North Shore. They are delighted to leave the casinos and noise far behind, searching instead for great skiing in the winter and hiking, biking and relaxing in the summer.

BEST SKI RESORTS

Alpine Meadows
Hwy 89 off I-80, six miles
from Lake Tahoe
(916) 583-6914 or (800) 441-4423

From its summit of 8000 feet and extending over 2000 acres, Alpine is a perfect family resort which offers more than 100 runs on majestic mountains. Alpine offers one of Tahoe's longest skiing seasons. There is a Snow School for kids age 4-6 as well as a complete range of ski instruction for all ability levels.

Squaw Valley
Hwy 89 off I-80
196 miles from San Francisco
Central reservations: **(800) 545-4350**

A challenging ski resort with a world-class reputation, Squaw is spread out over six separate Sierra peaks and offers 4000 acres of terrain for skiers of all ability levels. There is an impressive network of 33 lifts, including a Super Gondola. 30% of the mountain will satisfy the desires of the most avid and daring of skiers. Most runs are quite challenging, even at the intermediate level. Although Squaw maintains that 25% of the runs are gentle, novice skiers might want to consider other resorts

with a less challenging terrain and more options. There is an excellent ski school and a children's supervised ski playground facility called Papoose.

▷ *Check out the High Camp Bath & Tennis Club which offers a variety of recreational activities, including an outdoor Olympic-sized ice rink, tennis courts heated for winter play and five restaurants.*

WHERE TO STAY IN SQUAW VALLEY

- **Squaw Valley Lodge**
  201 Squaw Peak Rd.
  (916) 583-5500 or (800) 545-4350

  Located conveniently at the foot of the lifts, with ski-in, ski-out features, this is a comfortable and well-run year-round hotel.

- **The Resort at Squaw Creek**
  P.O. Box 3333
  Olympic Valley
  (916) 583-6300 or (800) 545-4350

  A premier luxury resort with ski-in, ski-out features, this full-service resort offers over-sized suites, fitness center, ice rink, three restaurants and a variety of shops.

Diamond Peak

(formerly Ski Incline)
Incline Village, Nevada
Skier's Information **(702) 831-3249**
Snow Phone **(702) 831-3211**

While not technically on the North Shore, Diamond Peak has long been recognized as one of the most popular resorts in the Tahoe area. It has the largest percentage of snowmaking coverage of any mountain in Tahoe, so you can always count on good snow. Not as large and overwhelming as some of the other ski areas, it offers a smaller, but challenging, series of runs. The resort offers great mid-week ski bargains, including a First Time Beginner's Special. There is a wonderful ski school for kids and adults. Free shuttle service is available throughout Incline Village.

WHERE TO STAY IN INCLINE VILLAGE

Hyatt Lake Tahoe

Incline Village, Nevada
(702) 831-1111 or **(800) 553-3288**

Accommodations at the recently remodeled Hyatt near Diamond Peak make this the most convenient place to stay. There are some fine restaurants, an indoor health club and a sparkling casino. There is also a shuttle bus which will take you to the slopes. Look into the midweek ski packages or the beginner's Ski Package.

▶ *In the summer, you can enjoy swimming and tennis as well. You'll find the Hyatt has one of the nicest sandy beaches on the Lake.*

Northstar at Tahoe

Hwy 267 off I-80
(800) 533-6787

Just outside the charming old mining town of Truckee is one of the best all-round family ski resorts. For sheer convenience this can't be beat. It has less wind and more crowd control than many of the other resorts around. The slopes are well groomed and there is a wide variety of intermediate runs. Advanced skiers may scoff at Northstar, but intermediate skiers find it ideal!

WHERE TO STAY IN NORTHSTAR

Northstar is a self-contained resort, and accommodations are ideal. There are condos in convenient locations throughout the resort, with shuttle buses constantly circling to pick up and drop off skiers. Within the village is the Lodge, a variety of shops including a grocery store and deli, and a choice of restaurants. There is also a recreation center with an outdoor hot tub, pool and a well-stocked game room.

▶ *Both **Northstar** and **Squaw Valley** are also great summer vacation spots. Though neither is located directly on the lake, they still offer full resort amenities and lower prices than some of the lakeside resorts.*

Royal Gorge
Cross Country Ski Resort
P.O. Box 1100 Soda Springs, Ca.
(800) 634-3086

While most resorts offer cross country skiing as part of their facility, Royal Gorge personifies this increasingly popular sport. There is a Ski School, open daily for all ability levels. There are also a wide variety of trails, with three ideally located surface lifts, to help negotiate the steeper inclines and to practice downhill techniques. You can ski all the way to Rainbow Lodge from the Summit Station, a 22km trail of breathtaking descents and vistas! Adventurous skiers can even ski to Sugar Bowl Resort, 17km away, and take a shuttle back in the afternoon. There are endless trails to enjoy in this world-class cross country skiing resort.

WHERE TO STAY AT ROYAL GORGE

Wilderness Lodge
(916) 426-3871

Located in the heart of Royal Gorge and featuring 35 private rooms, French country cuisine, sauna and hot tub. Your stay begins with a sleigh ride, wrapped in fur robes, from Summit Station to the Lodge.

Rainbow Lodge
(916) 426-3871

A beautiful old mountain bed and breakfast hotel built in the 20's, with 32 guest rooms and the elegant Engadine Cafe. Check out the Rainbow Midweek Skier's Special.

BEST PLACES TO EAT ON THE NORTH SHORE

Christy Hill
115 Grove St., Tahoe City
(916) 583-8551

Fabulous California-style cuisine in an elegant setting.

Wolfdale's
640 N. Lake Blvd., Tahoe City
(916) 583-5700

A rare blend of California goes Far Eastern. Delicious fare.

Captain Jon's
7220 N. Lake Blvd., Tahoe City
(916) 546-4819

One of the oldest and most popular eateries on the North Shore.

BEST PLACES TO STAY IN THE SUMMER

Rocky Ridge
1877 N. Lake Tahoe Blvd.
Tahoe City
(916) 583-3723

A cluster of contemporary condominiums, located on a ridge above the lake, offer stunning views of the surrounding area. A great summertime resort, complete with tennis courts and pool.

Chinquapin
3600 N. Lake Tahoe Blvd.
Carnelian Bay
(916) 583-6991

Located on the lake with full amenities, this is an elegantly-appointed series of townhouses and condos. Beautiful grounds.

Tahoe Taverns
300 W. Lake Tahoe Blvd.
(916) 583-7528

Just outside Tahoe City is this popular summer resort. Generous grounds and landscaping make it a tranquil getaway on the lake. Book early in the year. This place fills up quickly with City families yearning for a cool, sunny mountain retreat.

ACCOMMODATIONS

Taking a chance in the classifieds is always dicey (my family still hasn't forgiven me for going that route one summer!). However, one of your best bets in getting quality accommodations can be found in the vacation rental section of Focus Magazine or The Junior League's monthly newsletter, The Fogcutter.

You may also want to book accommodations at the North Shore through two well-known real estate companies in the area who book vacation rentals:

Martis Valley Realty
(916) 587-8100

Miller & Associates/
Better Homes & Gardens
(916) 583-1566

BEST SUMMER BETS ON THE NORTH SHORE

You will love "whitewater" rafting on the Truckee River in the summer. It's not exactly a class IV river, but it is great fun for young and old alike. Begin your adventure in Tahoe City and end it some three hours later at the River Ranch Restaurant.

Truckee River Rafting
205 River Road
Hwy. 89
Tahoe City
(916) 583-7238

North Tahoe Visitor's Bureau
(916) 583-3494

Hiking trails and campsites are open year-round at Sugar Pine Point State Park. For camp information call the North Tahoe Visitor's Bureau.

Ponderosa Ranch
Tahoe Blvd.
Incline Village
(702) 831- 0691

There is a whole new generation who do not immediately recognize the Ponderosa or names like Hoss, Pa and Little Joe! But this site for the long-running TV western, "Bonanza", is still fun to visit. Closed during the winter, open from May-October.

Community Services

Throughout San Francisco, there is a network of community services to draw upon, whether in an emergency situation or just for a useful referral. Keep the handy resources listed below in mind.

SOCIAL SERVICES

Catholic Charities of SF County
1049 Market St.
864-7400

There is a wide range of services this organization offers including adoption, aging, AIDS-ARC, counselling, family resource center, grief care, homeless, pregnancy, child abuse and much more.

Jewish Family & Children's Services
1600 Scott at Divisadero
567-8860

This wonderful agency offers a plethora of support services created to fit the needs of the community. Groups for families, seniors, people with AIDS, prospective adoptive parents, troubled teens, emigre resettlement and individual counselling are just a few of the programs available by agency professionals.

Childcare Switchboard
1435 Market, 3rd floor
864-1234

Provides a free referral
service for in-home care,
family day care homes, shared care, day
care centers and playgroups.

▶ *There is a also a library of child-related books and services as well as a toy lending library.*

Lawyer Referral Service
764-1616

Sponsored by the SF Bar Association, this service will provide a half-hour consultation with an attorney in an area of law relating to the prospective client's needs. The Service also acts as a referral service which will direct people to other legal resources available.

TAXES

Federal (IRS)
(510) 839-1040

State
(800) 852-5711

CITY INFORMATION
Mayor's Office
554-6141

City Hall General Information
554-4000

Board of Supervisors
554-5184

BAY AREA INFORMATION

Highway Patrol
(Non-Emergency)- (707) 648-5550

Volunteer Center of SF
982-8999

Time
767-8900 (POPCORN)

Weather
936-1212

Highway Road Conditions
557-3755

US CONGRESSIONAL REPRESENTATIVES

Nancy Pelosi (8th District)
450 Golden Gate Ave.
556-4862

Tom Lantos (12th District)
400 El Camino Real Suite 850
San Mateo
342-0300

US SENATORS

Barbara Boxer
1390 Market
556-8440

Dianne Feinstein
211 Main St.
905-1666

STATE ASSEMBLY

Willie Brown (17th District)
1388 Sutter
557-0784

John Burton (16th District)
350 McAllister
557-2253

Jackie Speier (19th District)
220 S. Spruce, SSF
871-4100

GOVERNMENT AGENCIES

SPCA
554-3000

Animal Care Control
Shelter
554-6364

Lost Pet Service
567-8738

Department of Motor Vehicles
Drivers Licenses/
Vehicle Registration
557-1179

Neighborhood residential parking stickers
554-4466

Registrar of Voters
Register to Vote
554-4398

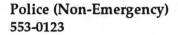

Absentee Ballot
554-4399

Police (Non-Emergency)
553-0123

Fire (Non-Emergency)
861-8000

SF Library
General Information **557-4400**

UTILITIES

PG&E
974-1555

Water Department
Customer Service- **923-2400**

Pacific Bell
(800) 773-2355

Cable Television
VIACAM Cable
863-6000

Garbage & Sanitation
Golden Gate Disposal
626-4000
Sunset Scavengers
330-1300

Recycling and Environmental Information
Recycling program hotline
554-6193

Hazardous Waste hotline (24-hour)
1-800-258-6942

San Francisco League of Urban Gardeners (SLUG)
468-0110

ADULT EDUCATION

SF Community College District
Adult Education Department
241-2221

SF City College
Adult Extension
50 Phelan Ave.
239-3000

UC San Francisco
513 Parnassus
476-9000

University of San Francisco
Golden Gate Avenue
666-6886

UC Berkeley
Extension Center
(510) 642-4111

SF State University Extension
338-1373

ART SMARTS

SF Art Institute
800 Chestnut
771-7020

Established in 1871, the Art Institute is the "art heart" of the City and has been turning out internationally-acclaimed artists since its inception. These include the artists of the "Bay Area Figurative School" of the fifties and sixties. Richard Diebenkorn, David Park, Paul Wonner, Elmer Bischoff, Manuel Neri and Nathan Oliviera, were just a few luminaries who worked and taught at this extraordinary institution.

NEWSPAPERS

San Francisco Chronicle
(Morning Daily)
Circulation-**777-7000**

San Francisco Examiner
(Afternoon Daily)
Circulation-**777-7800**

EMERGENCY INFORMATION

American Red Cross
202-0600

Poison Control
(24-hour service)
(800) 523-2222

SF Office of Emergency Services
554-6556

Irwin Memorial Blood Bank
270 Masonic
567-6400

Cancer Information Center of California
(800) 422-6237

San Francisco Health Department
554-9000

AIDS & Cancer Research Foundation hotline
(800) 373-4572

UNITED WAY Helpline
772-4357

City Parking & Transportation

Whenever possible, try and walk it, bike it, Muni it, carpool it, cable car it or even taxi it to where you are going. Cabs often work out to be less money and less aggravation than trying to find an affordable parking garage or a coveted space on the street.

HELPFUL PARKING TIPS

A tip for a surefire parking place on the street is to book your appointment five to ten minutes after street cleaning on any given street. See posted signs indicating days and times to successfully implement this strategy. You'll find the street magically devoid of cars for a few brief moments.

Remember, it is also easy to park anywhere on the street in the Financial District or the Union Square area between 5:45 and 6 PM, because "No Parking" generally ends at 6 PM on most signs posted.

"On the prowl for a parking space, the City driver is like a tigress stalking a snack for her young. Deaf to the threatening honks behind him, he inches down the street, shoulders hunched, his knuckles showing white on the wheel, his eyes narrowed and menacing. And when he spots a space, he is ready to fight to the death for it..."

–Herb Caen

PARKING GARAGES

There is no such thing as a reasonable place to park in San Francisco. There are only parking garages that are prohibitive, less prohibitive and least prohibitive. There are two kinds of garages operating in San Francisco, city-owned garages, which tend to be less expensive, and privately-owned garages. Here are a few of my recommendations for coping with The High Cost of Parking in The City.

UNION SQUARE AREA

Sutter & Stockton
444 Stockton/330 Sutter

This City-owned garage is one of the least expensive places to park in the City, although you sometimes have to wind your way up seven-plus flights to find a spot. The good news is that you can choose to exit on the fourth floor, as I always do.

Union Square Garage
333 Post

This privately-owned garage is located in the heart of Union Square with an entrance on Geary. It's more expensive than most, but convenience is a factor.

Ellis O'Farrell Garage
123 O'Farrell

This city-owned garage located behind Macy's is one of the best deals going. Inexpensive and little-used, and each floor has valet parking. Keep your head up and eyes open when you exit on Ellis, but for a quick run into Macy's or Magnin's, it can't be beat.

FINANCIAL DISTRICT

Portsmouth Square Garage
733 Kearny
Between Washington and Clay

Park here if you must go to Chinatown. There are problems getting a space at this popular city-owned garage during peak hours and on weekends.

St. Mary's Square
433 Kearny

Located across from the Bank of America, between Pine and California, is this privately owned garage within easy walking distance of Chinatown and the Financial District. One of the most expensive due to its convenient locale.

Embarcadero 1,2,3,4

Privately-owned garages beneath this mighty complex can be quite expensive during the day, but some restaurants in the Embarcadero do validate parking. Also, parking is often complimentary on the weekends to stimulate shopping in this otherwise quiet time.

SOUTH OF MARKET

Fifth & Mission
833 Mission

This large city-owned garage offers easy access to big hotels in the area as well as Moscone Center and the renowned San Francisco Center with its flagship store, Nordstrom. Big and inexpensive, there are a number of exits, so be sure and ask directions if you are uncertain.

Moscone Center Garage
255 Third Street
between Howard & Folsom

This is the place to park if you're visiting or exhibiting at the Center (located at 255 Third Street). However, traffic can really pile up during exhibition hours.

THE PARKING ZONE

One final piece of advice when parking the streets of San Francisco. CURB your wheels on hills and commit to memory the color codings on the curbs.

Yellow: Truck loading and unloading. Commercial plates only. Violators will be towed plus a fine.

Blue: Parking for vehicles with special disabled person plates or placards only. A hefty fine of $103.

White: Passenger loading and unloading only. Nominal fine.

Green: parking for a limited time, usually indicated on curb.

Red: No parking at any time. Vehicles in bus stops will be towed.

Gray: Yesssssssssssssssssssss!

CIVIC CENTER

Civic Center Plaza
Polk and McAllister

This underground parking facility is inexpensive, always has room and is located only a couple of blocks from City Hall and the Civic Center. The drawback? The area attracts a large number of panhandlers.

Performing Arts Garage
360 Grove

This is one of the newer garages around and is a great place to park on days and nights of performances. Clean, easy to get into and out of. Only problem is that it closes at midnight.

OTHER GARAGES

Japan Center

With entrances on Geary and Fillmore, this garage provides easy access to the shops and restaurants in Japan Center.

▶ *This is the perfect place to park to catch a movie at the best movie house in the City- The Kabuki 8! Check out the Bargain Matinee until 6 PM, the validated parking, the complimentary second box of popcorn and special awards coupons!*

2055 Lombard

Located between Fillmore and Webster, this is a good spot to know about when you need a place to park in the bustling Union Street area. Only 205 spaces.

766 Vallejo

Located between Stockton and Powell, this offers one of the few good places to park in the busy North Beach area.

USEFUL RESOURCES

RIDES for Bay Area Commuters
(800) 755-7665

Provides commuters throughout the Bay Area with information about carpools and vanpools.

KGO Radio
(81 AM on your dial)

Gives current road conditions on a regular basis.

Highway Road Conditions
(24-hour dispatcher) in San Francisco
553-0123

For recorded information on road and driving conditions throughout the State:
(800) 427-7623

Golden Gate Bridge District
921-5858

For information on conditions on the Bridge.

TAXI CAB SERVICES
Radio Dispatched

Veterans	**552-1300**
Yellow Cab	**626-2345**
Luxor	**282-4141**
De Soto	**673-1505**

CAR RENTALS

National	**(800) 227-7368**
Avis	**(800) 331-1212**
Budget	**(800) 527-0700**
Hertz	**(800) 654-3131**

PUBLIC TRANSPORTATION

Public transportation is a viable alternative to the hassles of City parking or maneuvering by car on crowded streets.

SAN FRANCISCO

BART
Bay Area Rapid Transit
788-BART

Operates rail lines and express buses throughout San Francisco, also to Daly City, Alameda and Contra Costa Counties. Fast, clean, safe and mindless!

MUNI
S.F. Municipal Railway
673-MUNI

Operates buses throughout San Francisco and to northern portions of Daily City. Special monthly rate applicable on Cable cars and Bart within S.F. Discount passes available for youths and seniors.

NORTH BAY

Golden Gate Transit
332-6600

Operates buses and ferries from San Francisco north to Marin and Sonoma County. Includes Larkspur and Sausalito ferries only.

▶ *Beware the human stampede out of the Larkspur Ferry during peak commute hours in the evening. It's a cross between the running of the bulls at Pamplona and the Bay to Breakers, as otherwise ordinary-looking business executives charge off the ferry in a frenzied race to their cars!*

Red & White Fleet
546-2815

One of the most scenic commutes going can be found on these ferries which operate between Sausalito and Tiburon in Marin and San Francisco.

▶ *Two wonderful excursions on the Red and White Fleet:*

- *Alcatraz: Scheduled tours from San Francisco to Alcatraz. Book in advance, especially in the summer.*

- *Angel Island: Tours (self-guided) from Tiburon to Angel Island. Plan a day of picnicking, riding bikes and exploring. The island has anything but an "angelic history" for it was the site in which thousands of Japanese-Americans and their families were interned during the anti-Japanese hysteria of World War II.*

Marin Airporter
461-4222

Leaves every half hour from Larkspur and other designated stops in Marin County to SFO, with return shuttles.

EAST BAY

AC Transit
(510) 839-2882

Operates daily bus service from San Francisco to Alameda and Contra Costa counties.

BART (Bay Area Rapid Transit)
788-BART

Operates rail lines and express buses from San Francisco to Daly City, Alameda and Contra Costa counties.

Alameda-Oakland Ferry
(510) 522-3300

Offers daily commuter and excursion service between Alameda, Oakland and San Francisco.

SOUTH BAY

Sam Trans
(800) 660-4287

Operates buses to Daly City and Hayward BART stations, SF International Airport, Southern Pacific Cal train stations, SF Grayhound Depot, Stonestown and Santa Clara County Transit. Also connects with AC Transit and Golden Gate Transit.

BART
788-BART

Operates rail lines and express buses from San Francisco to Daly City.

Cal Train
(800) 558-8661

Operates trains from San Francisco and San Jose, with stops in many cities on the Peninsula.

AIRPORT TRANSPORTATION

SuperShuttle
558-8500

Convenient and inexpensive door to door airport service

SFO Airporter
673-2432

Limousine service from downtown San Francisco to SFO.

AIRPORTS

San Francisco International Airport (SFO)
761-0800

Oakland International Airport
(510) 839-7488

San Jose International Airport
(408) 277-4759

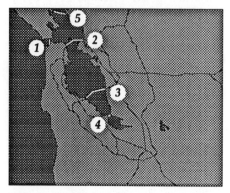

Refer to side bar for information on bridges.

BRIDGING THE BAY

1 - Golden Gate Bridge
Opened May 27, 1937. Location Hwy 101 between San Francisco and Marin Counties. Toll Southbound. Length 1.7 miles. Average daily traffic 120,500. Structure Suspension.

2 - San Francisco-Oakland
*   Bay Bridge*
Opened November 12, 1936. Location I-80 between San Francisco and Alameda Counties. Toll Westbound. Length 8.4 miles. Average daily traffic 250,000. Structure Suspension, tunnel and cantilever.

3 - San Mateo-Hayward Bridge
Opened October 31, 1967. Location Hwy. 92 between San Mateo and Alameda Counties. Toll Westbound. Length 6.9 miles. Average daily traffic 64,000. Structure Steel plate girder and concrete trestle.

4 - Dumbarton Bridge
Opened December, 1984. Location Hwy. 84 between San Mateo and Alameda Counties. Toll Westbound. Length 1.6 miles. Average daily traffic 41,500. Structure Steel box girder and pre-stressed concrete approach spans.

5 - Richmond-San Rafael Bridge
Opened September 1, 1956. Location Hwy. 17 between Contra Costa and Marin Counties. Toll Westbound. Length 5.5 miles. Average daily traffic 44,000. Structure Cantilever truss.

How to Survive the Great Quake

Californians are in a constant state of earthquake awareness and clearly understand the potential for damage and dangerous conditions. When an earthquake hits, experts say personal safety should be the number one priority. The bottom line is to be prepared, be aware and be knowledgeable. Nothing can stop an earthquake, but the following ideas and suggestions may help you and your family to survive it more safely.

4 BASICS TO DO DURING AN EARTHQUAKE

1. STAY CALM

2. **Inside:** Stand in a doorway, but be careful not to put you fingers in the door jamb. Doors can start swinging wildly during a quake. Crouch under a heavy table or desk. Stay away from windows, glass dividers, bookshelves or heavy, unsecured objects.

3. **Outside:** Stand away from buildings, trees, telephone and electrical lines. Find as open a space as possible to wait it out.

4. **On the road:** Drive away from underpasses or overpasses; stop in a safe area as soon as you can. Stay in your vehicle.

▶ *You may want to keep a "survival bag" in your trunk, in the event that you are forced to leave your car some distance from your home. It should contain a pair of sneakers or running shoes, a warm sweater, a flashlight, a packet of dried food, such as trail mix or a power bar, and packaged water. You should also get in the habit of keeping a full tank of gas in your car. In an emergency, this can make a big difference.*

PARENT'S NIGHTMARE

My son happened to be on a fifth-grade outdoor education trip in Santa Cruz, at the very epicenter of the Loma Prieta Quake in '89. Because he was outside, on an open grassy field, it felt like a giant roller coaster ride. He loved every minute of it and was incredibly annoyed to have to return home early to his hysterical parents!

5 BASICS TO DO AFTER A QUAKE

1. Check for injuries. Provide first aid.

2. Check for safety. Check for gas, water, sewage breaks, downed electrical lines and shorts. Turn off appropriate utilities; check for building damage and potential safety problems during the aftershocks, such as a cracked chimney or foundation.

3. Carefully clean up dangerous spills. Wear heavy shoes and gloves. There could be broken glass, nails and sharp fragments everywhere.

4. Turn on radio and listen for instructions from emergency agencies.

5. Don't use the telephone except for emergency use.

"The single most effective thing you can do to prepare for an earthquake is to get to know your neighbors and find out how you can respond to each other's needs."
–Earthquake Preparedness Booklet

PREPARING FOR THE BIG ONE

What you need in your home to get through the first 72 hours:

THE BASICS

1. One gallon of water per person per day.

2. Canned, freeze-dried or dehydrated food, including foods for pets, infants and persons with special dietary needs. Food should be sufficient for a week. Purchase a manual can opener.

▶ *A good way to remember to change your bottled water and check out all earthquake supplies is do it when Daylight Savings Time goes into effect in the spring and check again when it ends in the fall. Keep in mind that canned goods have a normal shelf life of one year.*

3. A good first aid kit and instructions.

▶ *At least one member in the family should have basic first aid and CPR skills.*

4. Critical medications, extra eyeglasses, contacts, etc.

5. A top-quality battery-operated radio and extra batteries, flashlights, battery-operated lanterns, extra dry cell batteries, candles, matches dipped in wax and kept in waterproof container.

SAFETY SUPPLIES

1. Heavy shoes and gloves, blankets, change of clothing, including sweaters and foul weather gear.

2. Sharp knife or razor blades, garden hose for fighting fires.

3. Fire extinguisher (dry chemical type). Smoke detector properly installed. Portable fire escape ladder for homes/apartments with multiple floors.

4. Adjustable wrench to be kept near the shut-off valve to turn on/off your gas. Every family member who is old enough should be taught where this is and how to shut it off. This also applies to the water.

▶ *You may want to invest in an automatic gas shut-off valve called the Sismo (made by Vespro in San Rafael, $180). In the event that you are not at home during the next quake, this handy valve will automatically turn off your gas in at least a 5.3 Richter scale quake. For more information, call 459-7311.*

SANITATION SUPPLIES

1. Large plastic trash cans, extra plastic trash bags and ground cloth.

2. Liquid detergent, personal hygiene needs, toilet paper, etc.

3. Powdered chlorinated lime (for sanitation) and extra newspapers to wrap garbage and waste.

▶ *These same trash cans can serve as a storage container for many of your emergency supplies. Mark the cans clearly and put in a cool, dry and accessible spot.*

COOKING SUPPLIES

1. Barbecue items including charcoal, lighter, Sterno stove with fuel.

▶ *Use of such stove should not take place until it is determined that there is no gas leak in the area. Charcoal should be burned only out of doors.*

2. Sealable plastic bags, paper plates, utensils and cups.

3. Three pots with lids, serving utensils, heavy-duty aluminum foil.

TOOLS AND MISCELLANEOUS

1. Pencils, paper and tape for leaving notes.

2. Screwdriver, pliers, wire cutters, hammer, axe, shovel, crowbar, rope, duct tape, broom and dust pan. These are everyday tools which are found in most homes. However, just after an earthquake, you want to be able to get to these essential items quickly and easily.

3. You might want to keep a special "grab bag" in a closet near the front door, filled with the following objects, in case you must leave the house suddenly:
   • An envelope with sufficient cash, including change.

   • A list of important phone numbers.

   • Family photos, to track down missing family members who have become separated during the quake.

EARTHQUAKE SUPPLIES

I.O.R (Immediate Organized Rescue), Inc.
(510) 528-3051

Earthquake Preparedness Supply
(510)839-0617

Marin Outdoors
49 Simms Street
San Rafael
453-3400

For the last ten years, this store has proven to be a reliable source for emergency supplies and information throughout the Bay Area.

Earthquake Preparedness & Survival Center
(510) 770-1906

EARTHQUAKE SERVICES

New toll-free earthquake Safety Hotline
(800) 286-7233

American Red Cross
202-0600

San Francisco Earthquake Preparedness Coalition
731-NEPC

Federal Emergency Management Agency (FEMA)
923-7250

Pacific Gas & Electric
972-2559

EARTHQUAKE CONSULTANTS

Earthquake Preparedness Consultants
924-8181

Provides an excellent referral service for information, leads, tips and sources for earthquake preparedness.

Earthquake Protection Systems
1045 Sansome
956-0550

This structural engineering company specializes in seismic strengthening of residential and commercial buildings.

**Tom Young
Earthquake Consulting**
663-9422

Tom Young is available as a consultant for homes, businesses, schools and neighborhood planning groups to personally advise on earthquake preparedness. He is also an excellent resource on where to go for supplies in your area.

The Big One

My husband is famous for going out of town whenever disaster strikes. It doesn't even have to be a natural disaster. He'll settle for man-made.

"Honey," he mentioned casually one January as he glanced at the headlines of the Chronicle. "I'm leaving for Hong Kong on Tuesday. Big deal pending."

"WHAT?" I said in astonishment. "What are you talking about? President Bush is going to invade Iraq next Tuesday. You can't leave us undefended."

"I really think you're overreacting a little. Bush is bluffing. You and the children will be perfectly safe. It doesn't look like the Iraquis have included Kentfield as an oil-rich depository worth sending troops to..."

"Very funny. I insist you stay home and protect us."

He left for Hong Kong on Tuesday morning. On Tuesday evening at 8 PM, the United States invaded Iraq. I knew it. The American Congress knew it. General Schwarzkopf knew it.

Only Saddam Hussein and my husband didn't know it.

Another time it was a trip to Mexico City.

"The upcoming Free Trade Agreement should have interesting tax consequences," he said with a gleam in his eye. I ignored him as I studied the sky.

"Don't you think the sky is an awfully odd color?"

He barely looked looked up as he packed his suitcase. "Looks like a brush fire to me. Easily contained."

"But why is it that murky orangey-grayish color? Maybe we should call the radio station and find out..."

"Honey! It's nothing to worry about." That afternoon was the infamous Firestorm of Oakland.

Considering his track record, why should I have been surprised that he was in New York in October of '89? Throughout the Bay Area, people can still remember exactly where they were when the Big One hit. My husband, the Disaster Dodger, was in the middle of negotiations on Wall Street.

Last winter, we woke up to emergency broadcast warnings of flash floods, mudslides, hurricane-force winds and unrelenting rain. The creek surrounding our house was rising at a dangerous level. All reports in the news indicated this was only the beginning of a major natural disaster of biblical proportions.

"What time is your flight, dear?"

"What flight?" my husband responded pleasantly. "I have no plans to go anywhere. I will be right here to pile up the sandbags, batten the hatches and lead you, the children, the dog and the iguana to safety, if need be."

That night the rains tapered off, the winds died down, the creek receded and embarrassed newscasters all over the Bay Area recanted their previous dire prophecies. By morning, the sun was shining brilliantly.

"See?" my husband grinned. "Nothing to worry about..."

Restaurant Guide

$ *Inexpensive . . Entrees under $10*
$$ *Moderate . . . . Entrees under $20*
$$$ *Expensive. . . . Entrees under $40*
$$$$ *Out of sight . . Entrees over $40*

A

Aqua 252 California St. 956-9662 $$$

Auberge du Soleil $$$
180 Rutherford Hill Rd., Rutherford
(707) 963-1211

B

Balboa Cafe 3199 Fillmore 921-3944 $$

Bill's Place 2315 Clement St. 221-5262 $

Bix 56 Gold Street 433-6300 $$$

Blue Fox 659 Merchant St. 981-1177 $$$

Boathouse $
1 Harding Road 681-2727

Bohemian Cigar Store $
566 Columbus 362-0536

Brava Terrace $$$
3010 N. St. Helena Hwy., St. Helena
(707) 963-9300

Buckeye Roadhouse $$
17 Shoreline Hwy., Mill Valley 331-2600

Bus Stop 1901 Union 567-6905 $

C

Cafe Bastille 22 Belden 986-5673 $$

Cafe Claude 7 Claude Lane 392-3505 $$

Cafe Du Nord 2170 Market 861-5016 $$

Cafe Jacqueline 1454 Grant 981-5565 $$$

Cafe Laundry 570 Green St. 989-6745 $

Cafe Tiramisu 28 Belden 421-7044 $$

Caffe Roma   526 Columbus 296-7662 $

Caffe Trinity $
1145 Market at Grove 864-3333

Caffe Greco 423 Columbus 397-6261 $

Caffe Puccini 411 Columbus 989-7033 $

Caffe Sport 574 Green 981-1251 $$

California Pizza Kitchen $
438 Geary 563-8911

Campton Place Restaurant $$$$
340 Stockton 781-5155

Canton 655 Folsom 495-3064 $

Captain Jons $$$
7220 N. Lake Tahoe Blvd., Tahoe City
(916) 546-4819

Caribbean Zone 55 Natoma 541-9465 $$

Casa Madrona $$$
801 Bridgeway, Sausalito 332-0502

Cava 555 555 Second Street 543-2282 $$

Chestnut Street Grill $
2231 Chestnut 922-5558

Chevy's (Several locations) $$
2 Embarcadero Center 391-2323

Chez Panisse $$$$
1517 Shattuck, Berkeley (510) 548-5525

China Moon Cafe 639 Post 775-4789 $$

Christy Hill $$$
115 Grove, Tahoe City (916) 583-8551

Ciao 230 Jackson 982-9500 $$

Country Rose $$
300 Commercial, Nevada City
(916) 265-3445

Cypress Club $$
500 Jackson Street 296-8533

D

Des Alpes 732 Broadway 391-4249 $

Doidge's Kitchen $
2217 Union St. 921-2149

Domaine Chandon $$$$
California Drive, Yountville
(707) 944-2892

Double Rainbow (several locations) $
407 Castro 621-2350

E

Eastside Grill $$
133 E. Napa St., Sonoma (707) 939-1266

Eddie Rickenbackers $$
133 Second Street 543-3498

Elka 1611 Post Street 922-7788 $$$

Ella's 500 Presidio 441-5669 $

Embarko 100 Brannan St. 495-2021 $$

Emporio Armani Express Restaurant $$
1 Grant Avenue 677-9010

Ernie's 847 Montgomery St. 397-5969 $$$

Etrusca $$$
101 Spear St. 777-0330

F

Fleur De Lys 777 Sutter 673-7779 $$$$

Flower Lounge 5322 Geary 692-6666 $$

Fog City Diner 1300 Battery 982-2000 $$

Freed Teller & Freed's $
Embarcadero Cte. West 986-8851

French Laundry $$$
Washington at Creek St., Yountville
(707) 944-2380

Fringale 570 Fourth Street 543-0573 $$

G

Garibaldi 347 Presidio 563-8841 $$

Geordy's One Tillman Place 362-3175 $$$

Gira Polli 659 Union 434-4472 $

Golden Dragon $
816 Washington 398-3920

Golden Gate Grill $
3200 Fillmore 931-4600

Gordon Biersch Brewery $$
2 Harrison Street 243-8246

Greens Restaurant $$
Fort Mason 771-6222

Grill at Chez Panisse $$
1517 Shattuck, Berkeley (510) 548-5525

Guaymas 5 Main St., Tiburon 435-6300 $$

H

Hamburger Mary's $
1582 Folsom 626-5767

Half Day Cafe $$
848 College, Kentfield 459-0291

Harbor Village $$
4 Embarcadero Center 398-8883

Hard Rock Cafe $$
1699 Van Ness 885-1699

Harris' Restaurant $$$
2100 Van Ness 673-1888

Harry Denton's $$
161 Steuart Street 882-1333

Has Beans $
2411 California at Fillmore 563-0226

Hayes Street Grill 324 Hayes 863-5545 $$

Hog's Breath Inn $$
San Carlos at 5th, Carmel (408) 625-1044

Holey Bagel 1206 Masonic 626-9111 $

Holey Bagel 3218 Fillmore 922-1955 $

I

Il Fornaio 1265 Battery 986-0100 $$

Il Fornaio $$
Corte Madera Town Center,
Corte Madera 927-4400

Il Pollaio 555 Columbus 362-7727 $

J

Jack's 615 Sacramento 986-9854 $$

Jackson Fillmore Trattoria $$
2506 Fillmore 346-5288

Jazz at Pearls 256 Columbus 291-8255 $$

Johnny Love's $$
1500 Broadway 931-6053

Julie's Supper Club $$
1123 Folsom 861-0707

Just Desserts 3735 Buchanan 922-8675 $

K

Kelly's on Trinity 333 Bush 362-4454 $

Kenwood Restaurant $$$
9900 Hwy. 12, Kenwood (707) 833-6326

Kimball's $$
300 Grove Street at Franklin 861-5555

Kimball's East $$
5800 Shellmound Emryvi. (510) 658-2555

L

L'Avenue 3854 Geary 386-1555 $$

La Boheme $$$
Dolores at 7th, Carmel (408) 624-7500

La Fiammetta 1701 Octavia 474-5077 $$

La Pergola 2060 Chestnut 563-4500 $$

Lascaux 248 Sutter 391-1555 $$

M

MacArthur Park $$
607 Front Street 398-5700

Mandalay 4344 California 386-3895 $

Masa's 648 Bush 989-7154 $$$$

Max's Opera Deli $
601 Van Ness 771-7300

Mel's Drive In 2165 Lombard 921-3039 $

Mel's Drive In 3355 Geary 387-2244 $

Miss Pearl's Jam House $$
601 Eddy at Larkin 775-5267

Mo's 1322 Grant Avenue 788-3779 $

Moose's 1652 Stockton 989-7800 $$$

N

North Beach Restaurant $$
1512 Stockton 392-1700

O

O Chame $$$
1830 Fourth St., Berkeley (510) 841-8783

Olive's Pizza $
3249 Scott at Lombard 567-4488

One Market $$$
Market and Steuart St 777-5577

P

Pacific's Edge Highland's Inn $$$
Hwy. 1, Carmel (408) 624-0471

Paragon 3251 Scott 922-2456 $$

Pasqua   388 Market   329-9491 $

Pat O'Shea's Mad Hatter $
3848 Geary   752-3148

Pearl City 641 Jackson   398-8383 $

Peets Coffee   2156 Chestnut 931-8302 $

Peter Salaya's $$
320 Broad St., Nevada City (916) 265-5697

Piatti Ristoranti $$$
405 First Street, Sonoma   (707) 996-2351

Piatti Ristoranti 6480 Washington St. $$$
Yountville   (707) 944-2070

Pizzeria Uno (several locations) $$
2200 Lombard   563-3144

Postrio 545 Post 776-7825 $$$

R

Regina's Sonoma - Sonoma Hotel $$
110 W. Spain St., Sonoma   (707) 938-0254

Remillard's   125 E. Sir Francis Drake $$$
Larkspur   461-3700

Ritz Carlton Hotel   High Tea $$
600 Stockton   296-7465

Rory's Twisted Scoop $
2015 Fillmore   346-3692

Roti 155 Steuart St.   495-6500 $$

Rustico $
300 De Haro Street at 16th   252-0180

S

Sam's Anchor Cafe $$
27 Main St., Tiburon   435-4527

Sam's Grill 374 Bush   421-0594 $$

Sears Fine Foods 439 Powell 986-1160 $

Shadowbrook $$$
1750 Wharf Road, Capitola (408) 475-1511

Sheraton Palace Hotel High Tea $$
2 New Montgomery St. 392-8600

Sherman House $$$$
2160 Green Street   563-3600

Slow Club 2501 Miraposa 241-9390 $

South Park Cafe $$
108 South Park 495-7275

Spinelli's Coffee 2455 Fillmore 929-8808 $

Square One 190 Pacific 788-1110 $$$

Starbucks Coffee Company $
1899 Union at Laguna 921-4049

Stars Cafe 555 Golden Gate 861-4344 $$

Stars Restaurant $$$
150 Redwood Alley 861-7827

Suppers 1800 Fillmore 474-3773 $$

Swan Oyster Bar $$
1517 Polk Street   673-1101

T

Tadich Grill 240 California 391-2373 $$

Tommaso's 1042 Kearny 398-9696 $$

Tommy Toys Cuisine Chinois $$$
655 Montgomery 397-4888

Tosca 242 Columbus 391-1244 $$

Trader Vic's 20 Cosmo Place 776-2232 $$

Tra Vigne $$$
1050 Charter Oak Rd., St. Helena
(707) 963-4444

U

Up & Down Club $$
1151 Folsom   626-2388

W

Washington Square Bar & Grill $$
1707 Powell (in Washington Square)
982-8123

Wolfdale's $$$
640 N. Lake Tahoe Blvd., Tahoe City
(916) 583-5700

Wu Kong   Rincon Center $$
101 Spear Street 957-9300

Y

Yank Sing 427 Battery 781-1111 $$

Yoshi's 6030 Claremont Avenue $$
Oakland (510) 652-9200

Z

Zuni Cafe 1658 Market St. 552-2522 $$$

Index

Index

Index

Notes

Notes

"In this work, when it shall be found that much is omitted, let it not be forgotten that much likewise is performed."
—Dr. Samuel Johnson
upon completion of
his dictionary, 1755

How to Order

To purchase a copy of **The San Francisco Survival Guide**, complete and return this order form to:

CrossRoads
314 Woodland Road, Kentfield, CA 94904
or call **(415) 461-8422**

I would like _____ copies at $11.95 a copy

plus $2.00 which includes tax, shipping and handling per book.

Enclosed is my check for $_____ made payable to CrossRoads.

Name _____

Address _____

City _____ State ____ Zip _____

Phone _____